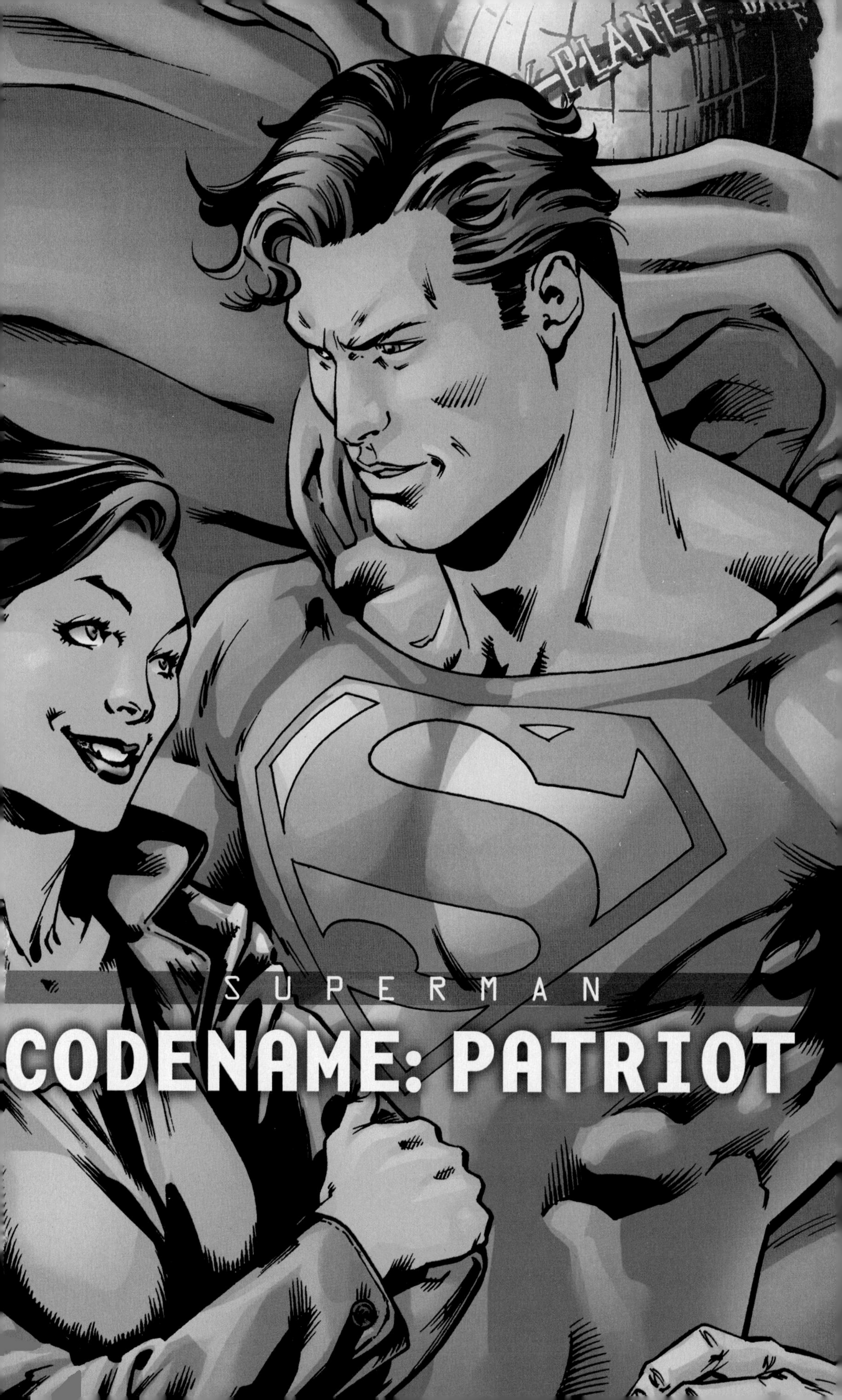
PLANET

SUPERMAN

CODENAME: PATRIOT

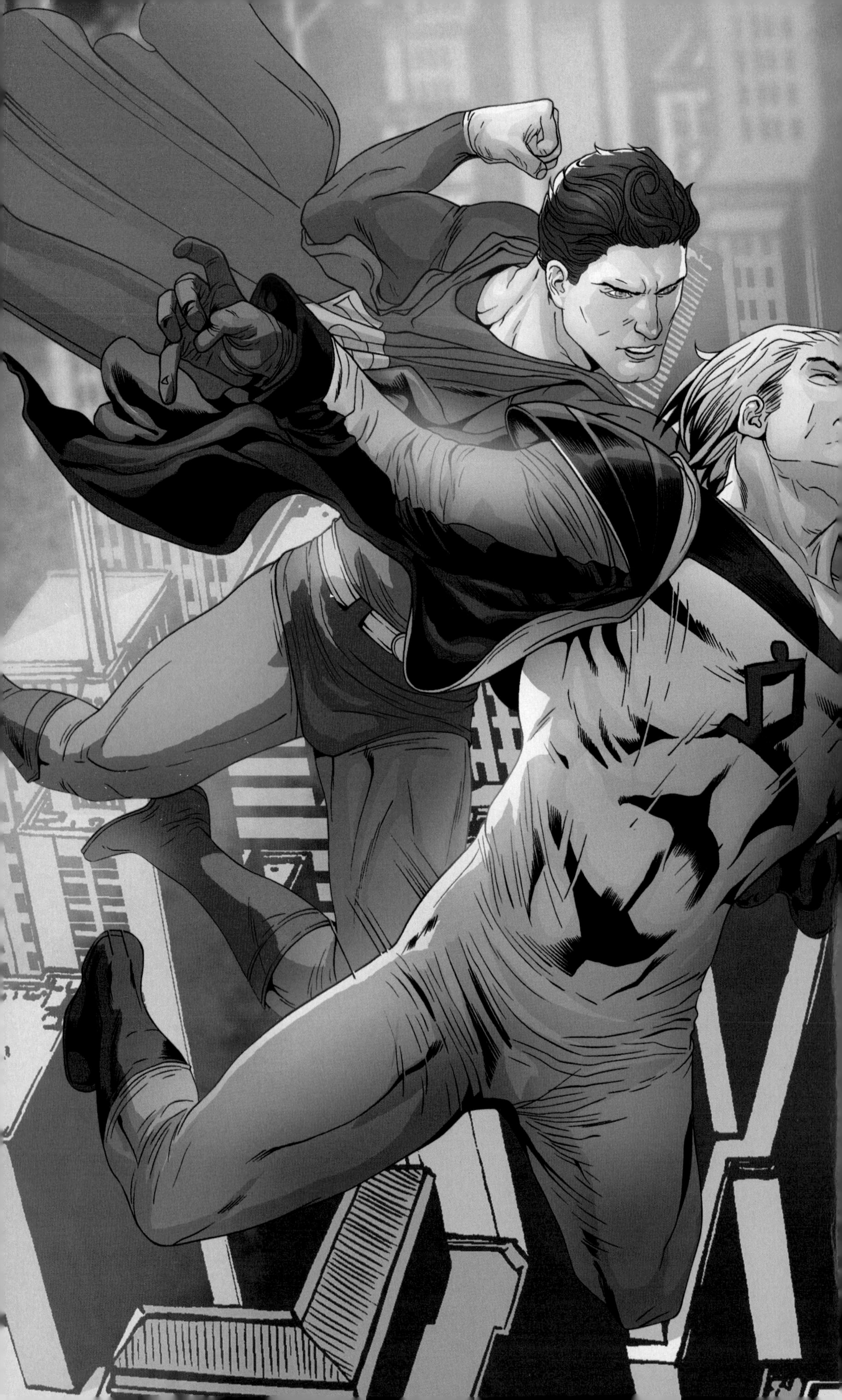

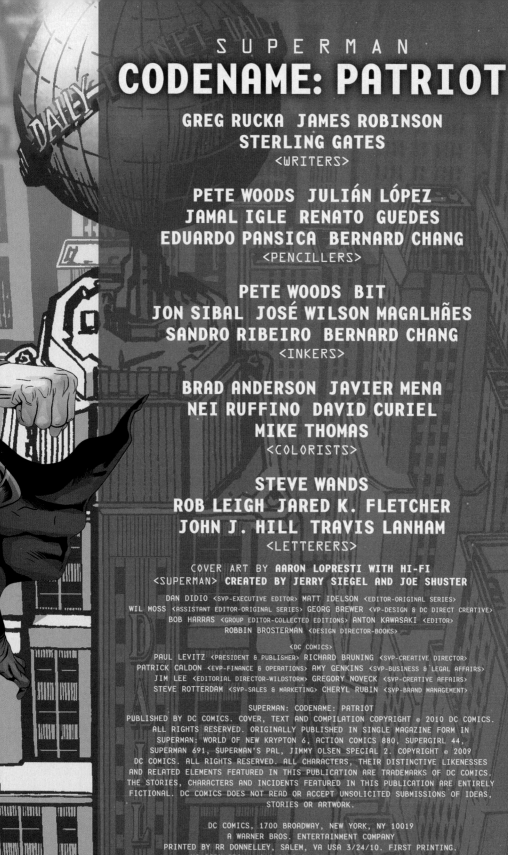

SUPERMAN

CODENAME: PATRIOT

GREG RUCKA JAMES ROBINSON
STERLING GATES
<WRITERS>

PETE WOODS JULIÁN LÓPEZ
JAMAL IGLE RENATO GUEDES
EDUARDO PANSICA BERNARD CHANG
<PENCILLERS>

PETE WOODS BIT
JON SIBAL JOSÉ WILSON MAGALHÃES
SANDRO RIBEIRO BERNARD CHANG
<INKERS>

BRAD ANDERSON JAVIER MENA
NEI RUFFINO DAVID CURIEL
MIKE THOMAS
<COLORISTS>

STEVE WANDS
ROB LEIGH JARED K. FLETCHER
JOHN J. HILL TRAVIS LANHAM
<LETTERERS>

COVER ART BY AARON LOPRESTI WITH HI-FI
<SUPERMAN> CREATED BY JERRY SIEGEL AND JOE SHUSTER

DAN DIDIO <SVP-EXECUTIVE EDITOR> MATT IDELSON <EDITOR-ORIGINAL SERIES>
WIL MOSS <ASSISTANT EDITOR-ORIGINAL SERIES> GEORG BREWER <VP-DESIGN & DC DIRECT CREATIVE>
BOB HARRAS <GROUP EDITOR-COLLECTED EDITIONS> ANTON KAWASAKI <EDITOR>
ROBBIN BROSTERMAN <DESIGN DIRECTOR-BOOKS>

<DC COMICS>
PAUL LEVITZ <PRESIDENT & PUBLISHER> RICHARD BRUNING <SVP-CREATIVE DIRECTOR>
PATRICK CALDON <EVP-FINANCE & OPERATIONS> AMY GENKINS <SVP-BUSINESS & LEGAL AFFAIRS>
JIM LEE <EDITORIAL DIRECTOR-WILDSTORM> GREGORY NOVECK <SVP-CREATIVE AFFAIRS>
STEVE ROTTERDAM <SVP-SALES & MARKETING> CHERYL RUBIN <SVP-BRAND MANAGEMENT>

DC COMICS, 1700 BROADWAY, NEW YORK, NY 10019
A WARNER BROS. ENTERTAINMENT COMPANY
PRINTED BY RR DONNELLEY, SALEM, VA USA 3/24/10. FIRST PRINTING.
HC ISBN:978-1-4012-2658-9 SC ISBN:978-1-4012-2657-2

SUSTAINABLE FORESTRY INITIATIVE
Certified Fiber Sourcing
www.sfiprogram.org

Fiber used in this product line meets the sourcing requirements of the SFI program.
www.sfiprogram.org PWC-SFICOC-260

IT BEGAN WITH AN EPIC BATTLE

BETWEEN EARTH'S GREATEST HERO, SUPERMAN, AND THE EVIL ALIEN BRAINIAC. DURING THAT CLASH, SUPERMAN DISCOVERED THE LOST CITY OF KANDOR TRAPPED IN THE DEPTHS OF THE ALIEN'S SHIP, 100,000 KRYPTONIAN INHABITANTS INSIDE. SUPERMAN WAS REUNITED WITH HIS PEOPLE, BUT AT A HUGE PERSONAL COST: HE WAS UNABLE TO SAVE THE LIFE OF HIS ADOPTIVE FATHER, JONATHAN KENT.

KANDOR WAS FREED AND RELOCATED TO EARTH, BUT THE UNEASY ALLIANCE BETWEEN HUMANS AND KRYPTONIANS QUICKLY DEGENERATED INTO VIOLENCE AND TRAGEDY. A SECRET GOVERNMENT ORGANIZATION, PROJECT 7734, HELPED ORCHESTRATE THE AGGRESSION BETWEEN THE TWO RACES. 7734'S LEADER IS GENERAL SAM LANE, A MAN THOUGHT LONG DEAD, AND HE GAVE THE ORDER TO ASSASSINATE ZOR-EL, SUPERGIRL'S FATHER AND THE LEADER OF THE KRYPTONIANS. MEANWHILE, A TEAM OF KRYPTONIANS BRUTALLY MURDERED SEVERAL OF METROPOLIS'S SCIENCE POLICE ON AMERICAN SOIL.

IN AN EFFORT TO RESOLVE THE GROWING CONFLICT, ZOR-EL'S WIDOW, ALURA, TOOK CHARGE OF THE KRYPTONIANS AND COMBINED BRAINIAC'S TECHNOLOGY WITH KANDOR'S TO CREATE A NEW PLANET — NEW KRYPTON. THE PLANET ESTABLISHED AN ORBIT OPPOSITE EARTH'S OWN. IT APPEARED THAT THE CONFLICT HAD ENDED…BUT LOOKS CAN BE DECEIVING.

WHEN ALURA RELEASED GENERAL ZOD FROM THE PHANTOM ZONE AND GAVE HIM COMMAND OF NEW KRYPTON'S ARMY, SUPERMAN WAS FORCED TO MAKE THE HARDEST DECISION OF HIS LIFE: HE WOULD MOVE TO NEW KRYPTON TO KEEP ZOD IN CHECK.

AMID THE ESCALATING TENSIONS AND SUPERMAN'S ABSENCE, NEW AND OLD HEROES ALIKE HAVE RISEN TO PROTECT THE EARTH. NOW THEY MUST UNITE FOR THE FIRST TIME TO KEEP THE FRAGILE PEACE BETWEEN EARTH AND NEW KRYPTON…

<SUPERMAN: WORLD OF NEW KRYPTON 6>
COVER ART BY **FERNANDO DAGNINO** & **RAÚL FERNANDEZ** WITH **MAZI**

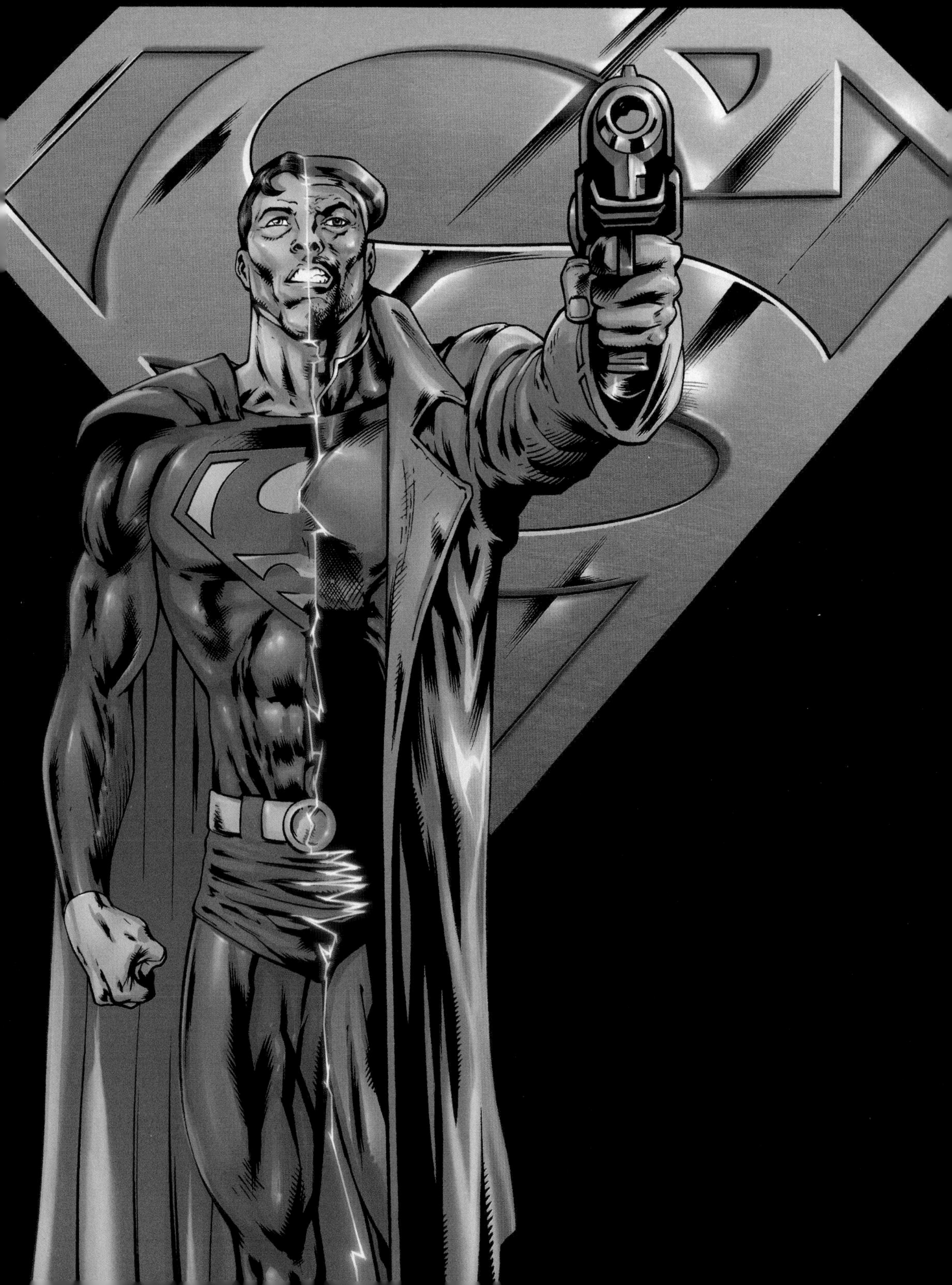

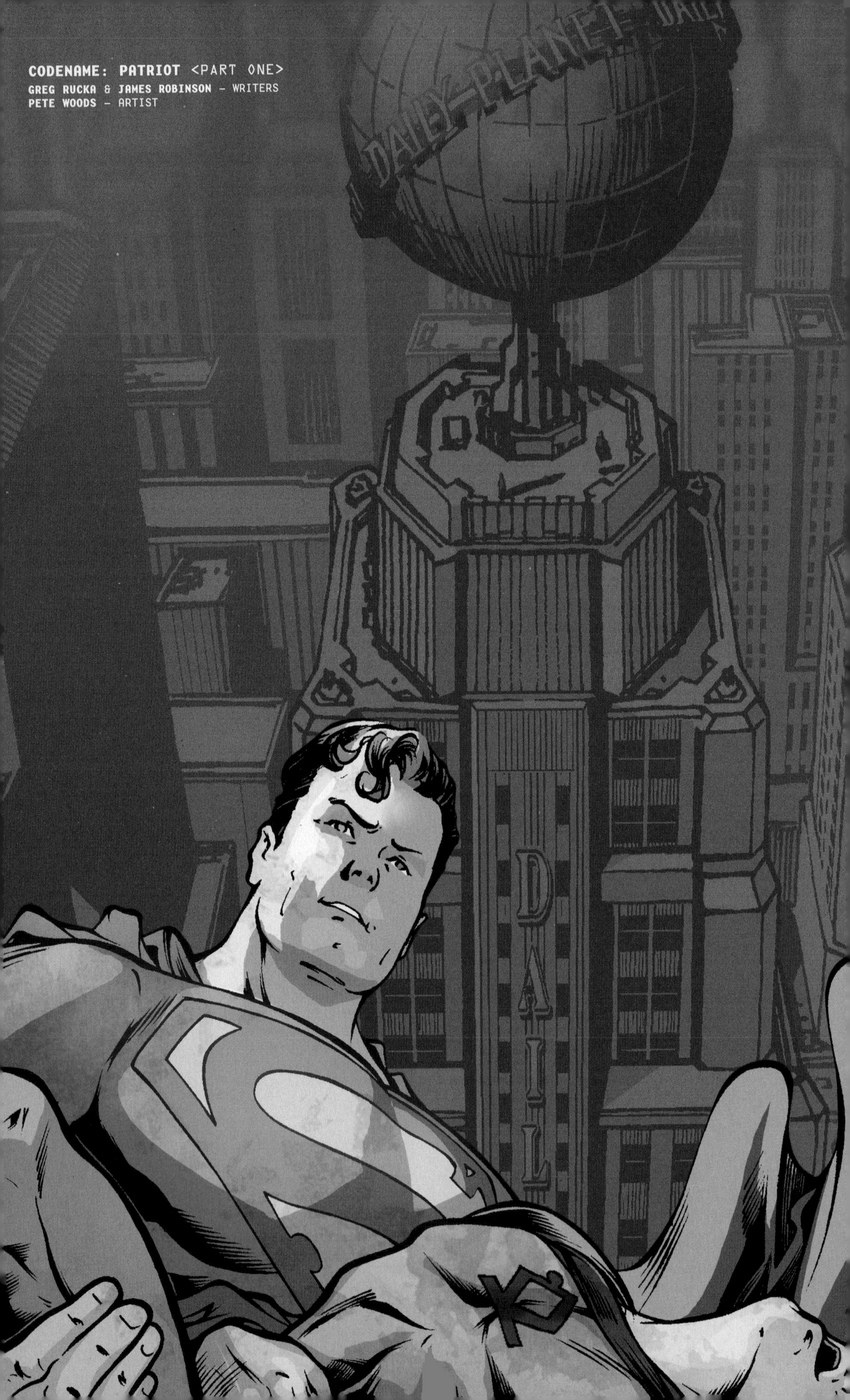
CODENAME: PATRIOT <PART ONE>
GREG RUCKA & JAMES ROBINSON – WRITERS
PETE WOODS – ARTIST
DAILY PLANET
DAILY

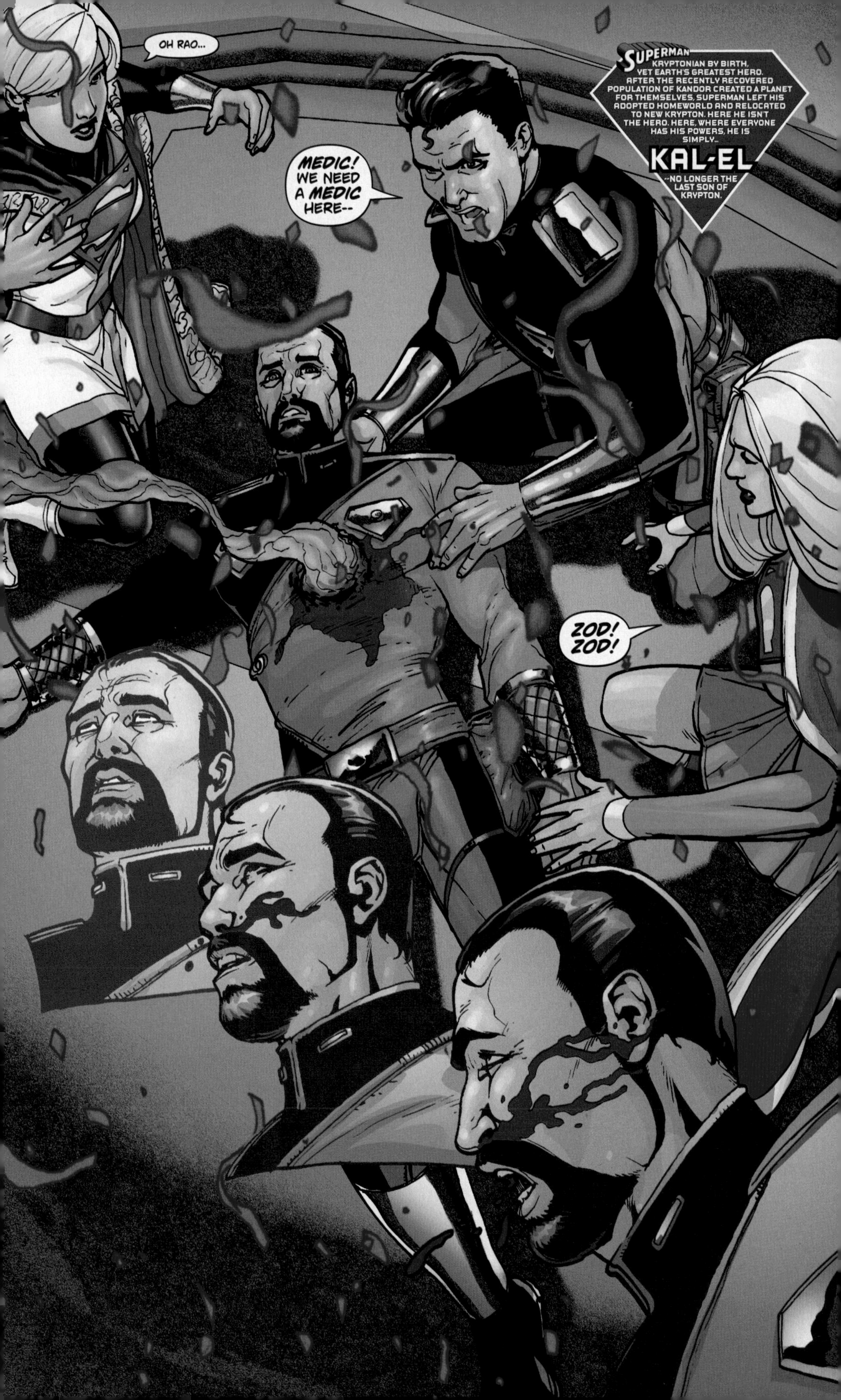
OH RAO...
SUPERMAN
KRYPTONIAN BY BIRTH, YET EARTH'S GREATEST HERO. AFTER THE RECENTLY RECOVERED POPULATION OF KANDOR CREATED A PLANET FOR THEMSELVES, SUPERMAN LEFT HIS ADOPTED HOMEWORLD AND RELOCATED TO NEW KRYPTON. HERE HE ISN'T THE HERO. HERE, WHERE EVERYONE HAS HIS POWERS, HE IS SIMPLY...
KAL-EL
--NO LONGER THE LAST SON OF KRYPTON.
MEDIC! WE NEED A MEDIC HERE--
ZOD! ZOD!

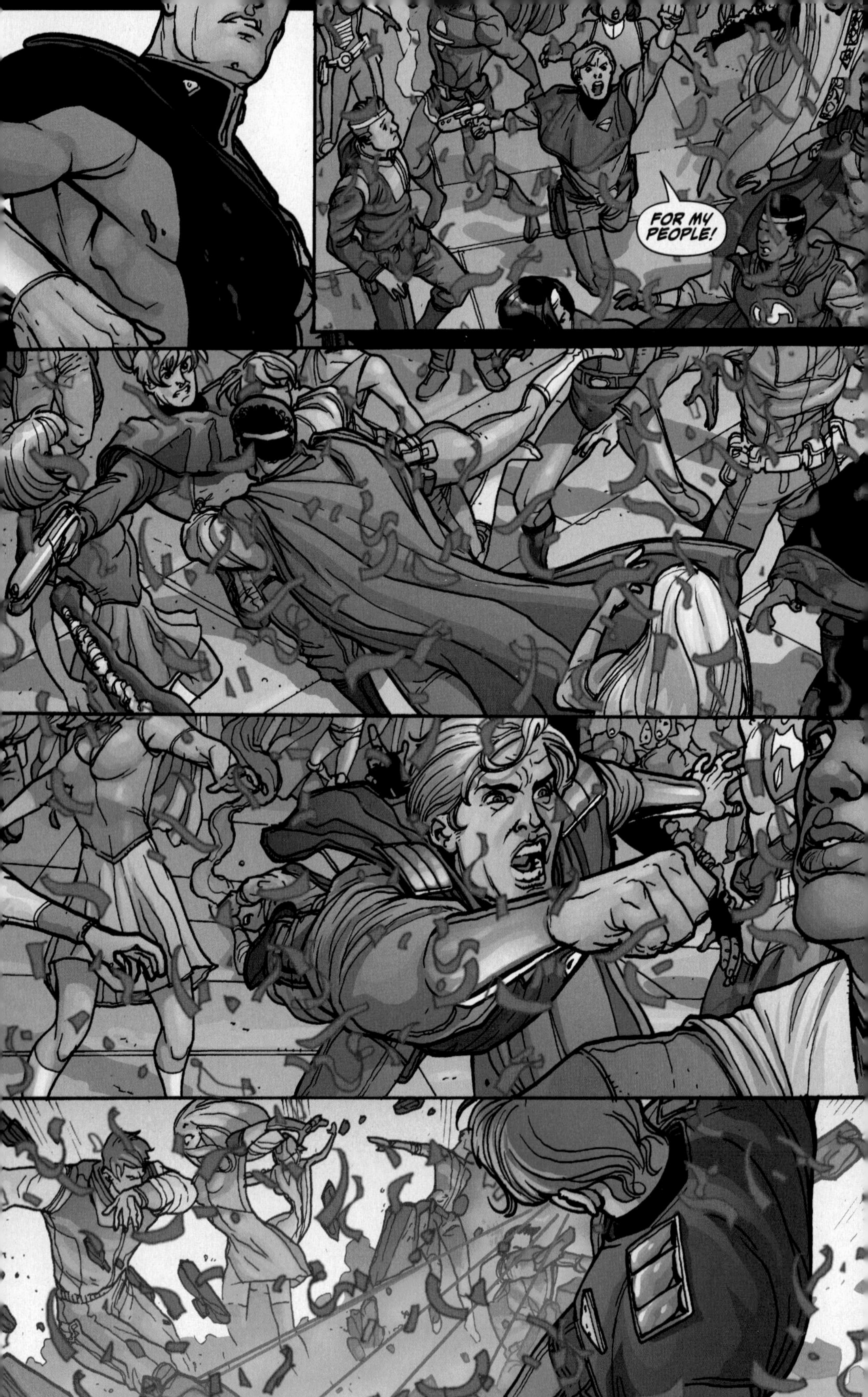
FOR MY PEOPLE!

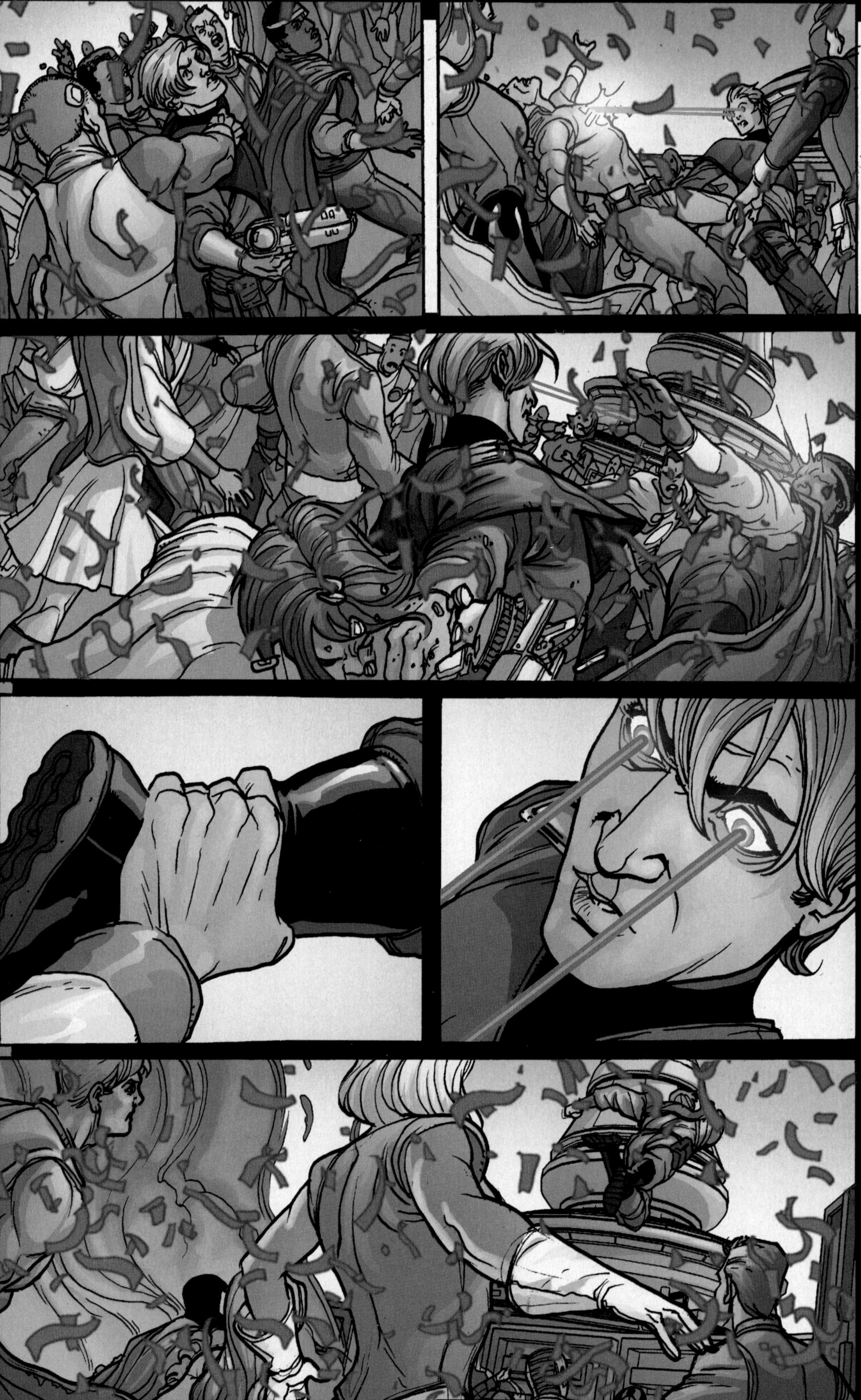

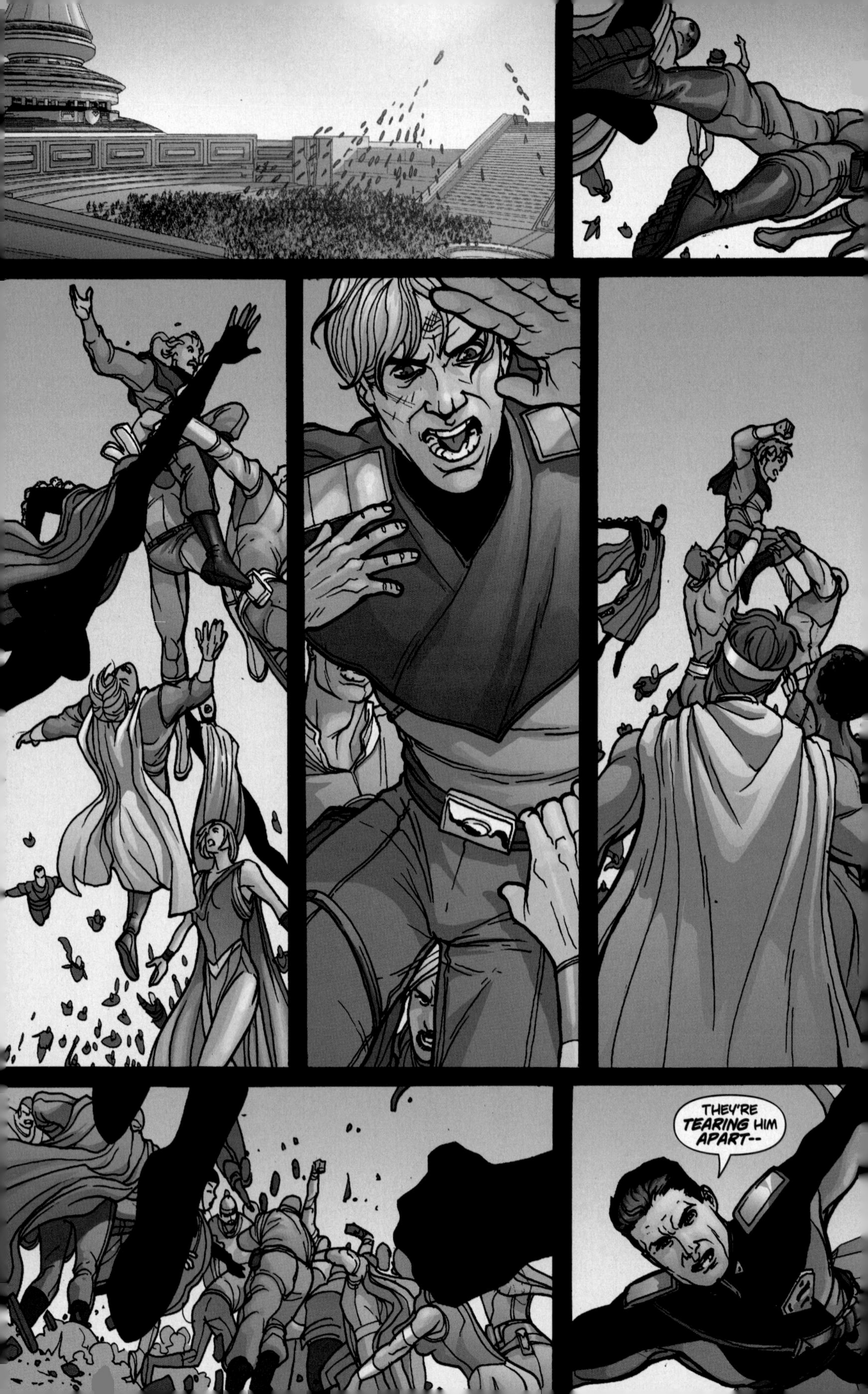
THEY'RE TEARING HIM APART--

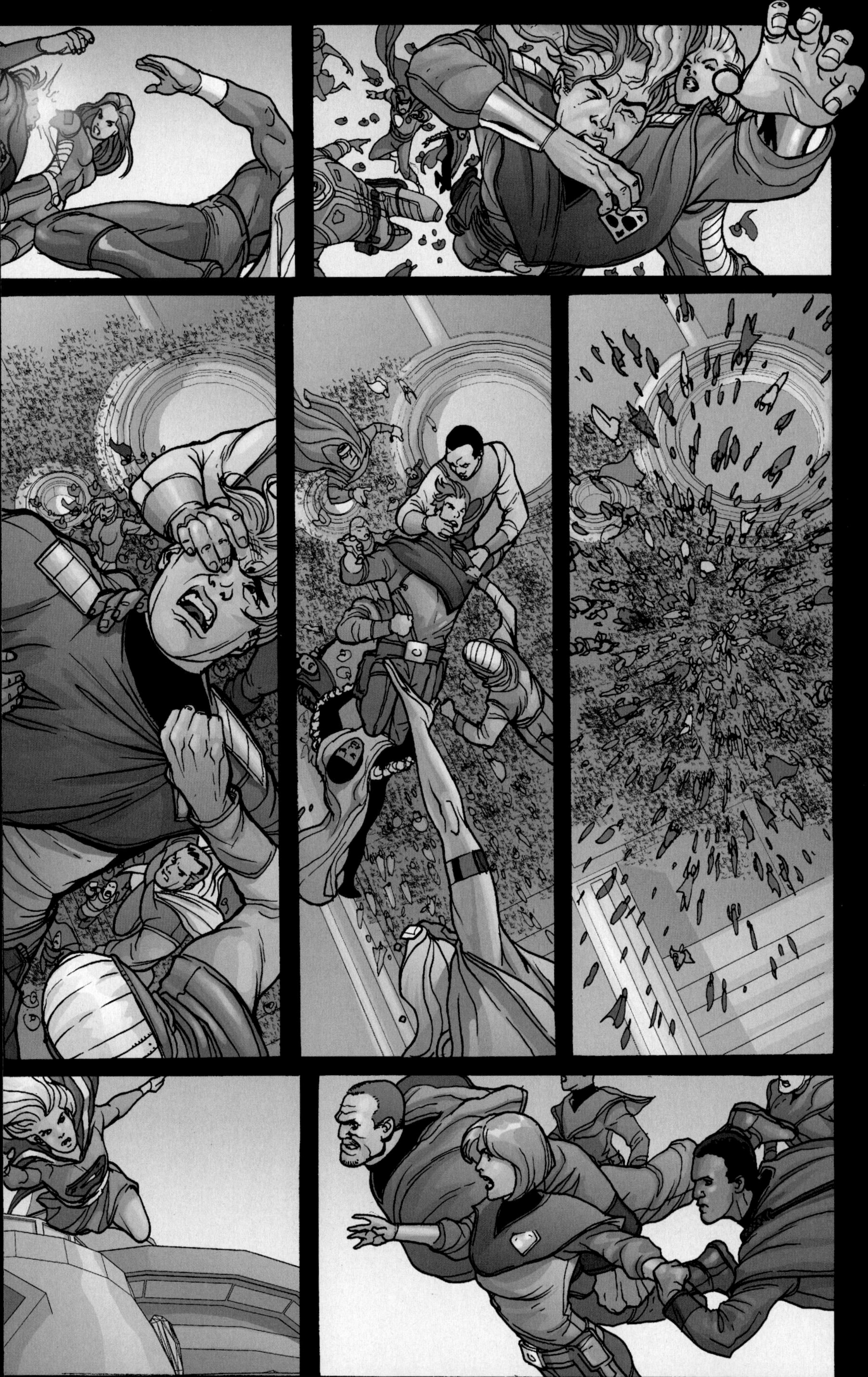

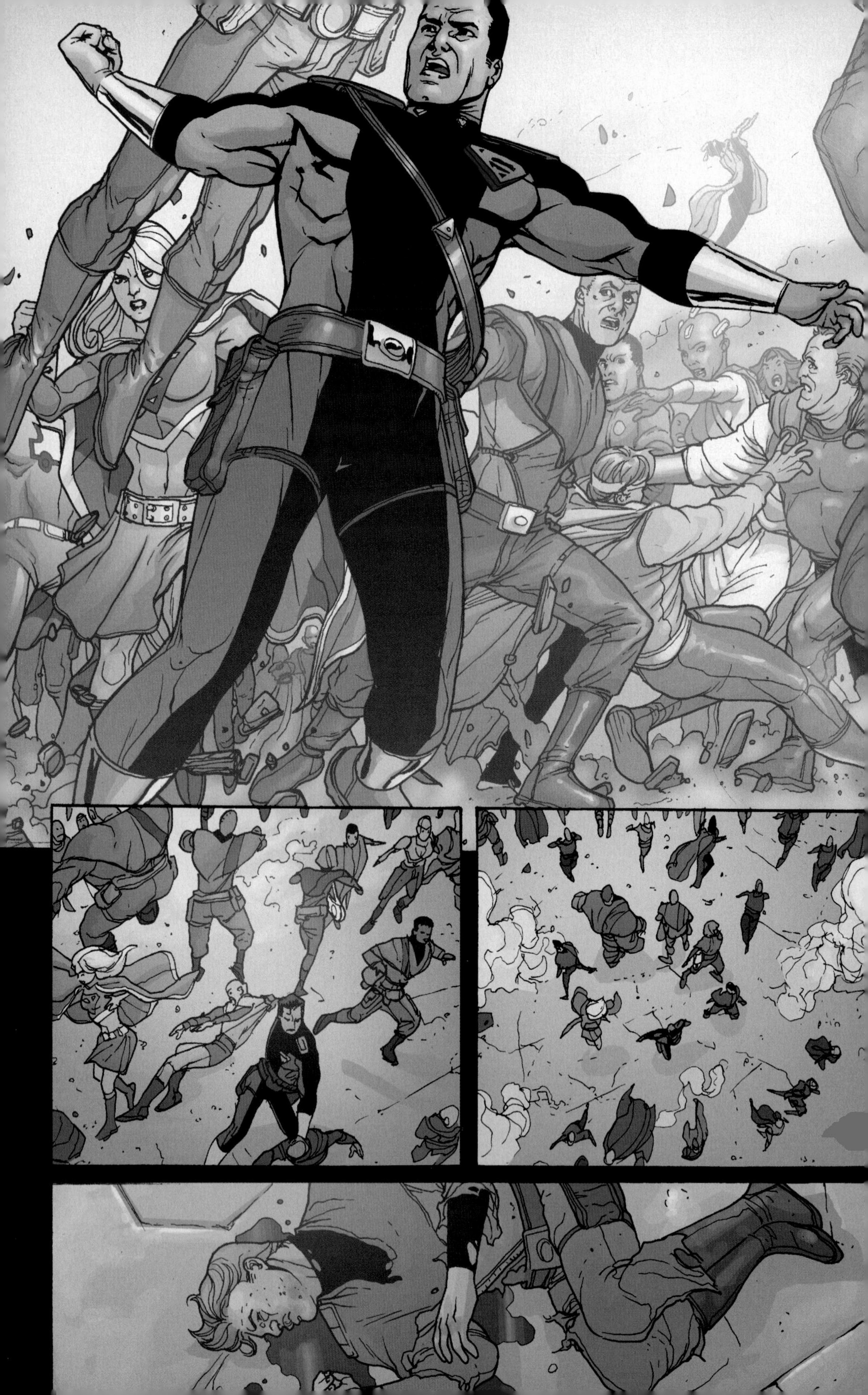

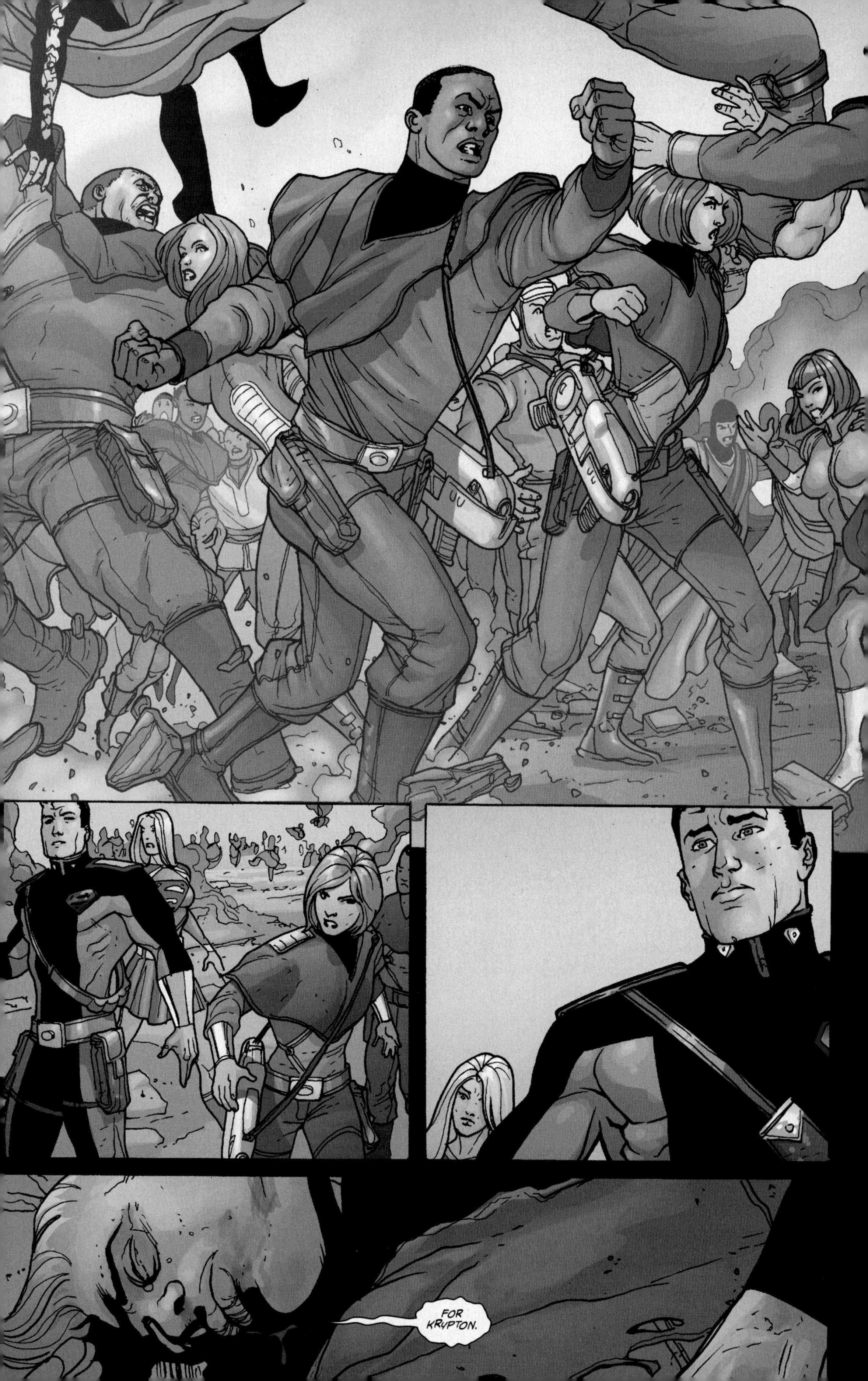
FOR KRYPTON.

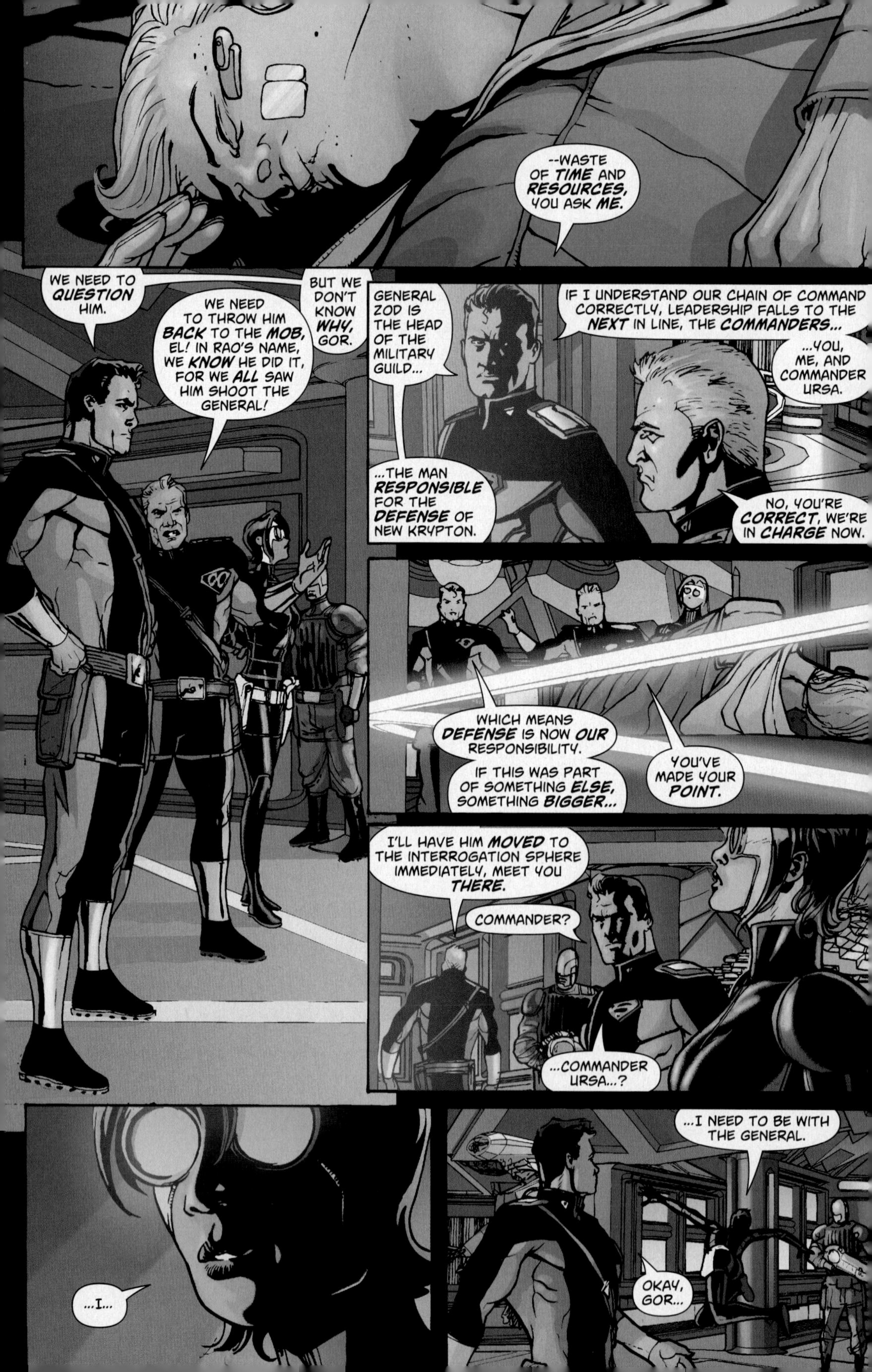
--WASTE OF TIME AND RESOURCES, YOU ASK ME.
WE NEED TO QUESTION HIM.
BUT WE DON'T KNOW WHY, GOR.
WE NEED TO THROW HIM BACK TO THE MOB, EL! IN RAO'S NAME, WE KNOW HE DID IT, FOR WE ALL SAW HIM SHOOT THE GENERAL!
GENERAL ZOD IS THE HEAD OF THE MILITARY GUILD...
...THE MAN RESPONSIBLE FOR THE DEFENSE OF NEW KRYPTON.
IF I UNDERSTAND OUR CHAIN OF COMMAND CORRECTLY, LEADERSHIP FALLS TO THE NEXT IN LINE, THE COMMANDERS...
...YOU, ME, AND COMMANDER URSA.
NO, YOU'RE CORRECT, WE'RE IN CHARGE NOW.
WHICH MEANS DEFENSE IS NOW OUR RESPONSIBILITY.
IF THIS WAS PART OF SOMETHING ELSE, SOMETHING BIGGER...
YOU'VE MADE YOUR POINT.
I'LL HAVE HIM MOVED TO THE INTERROGATION SPHERE IMMEDIATELY, MEET YOU THERE.
COMMANDER?
...COMMANDER URSA...?
...I...
...I NEED TO BE WITH THE GENERAL.
OKAY, GOR...

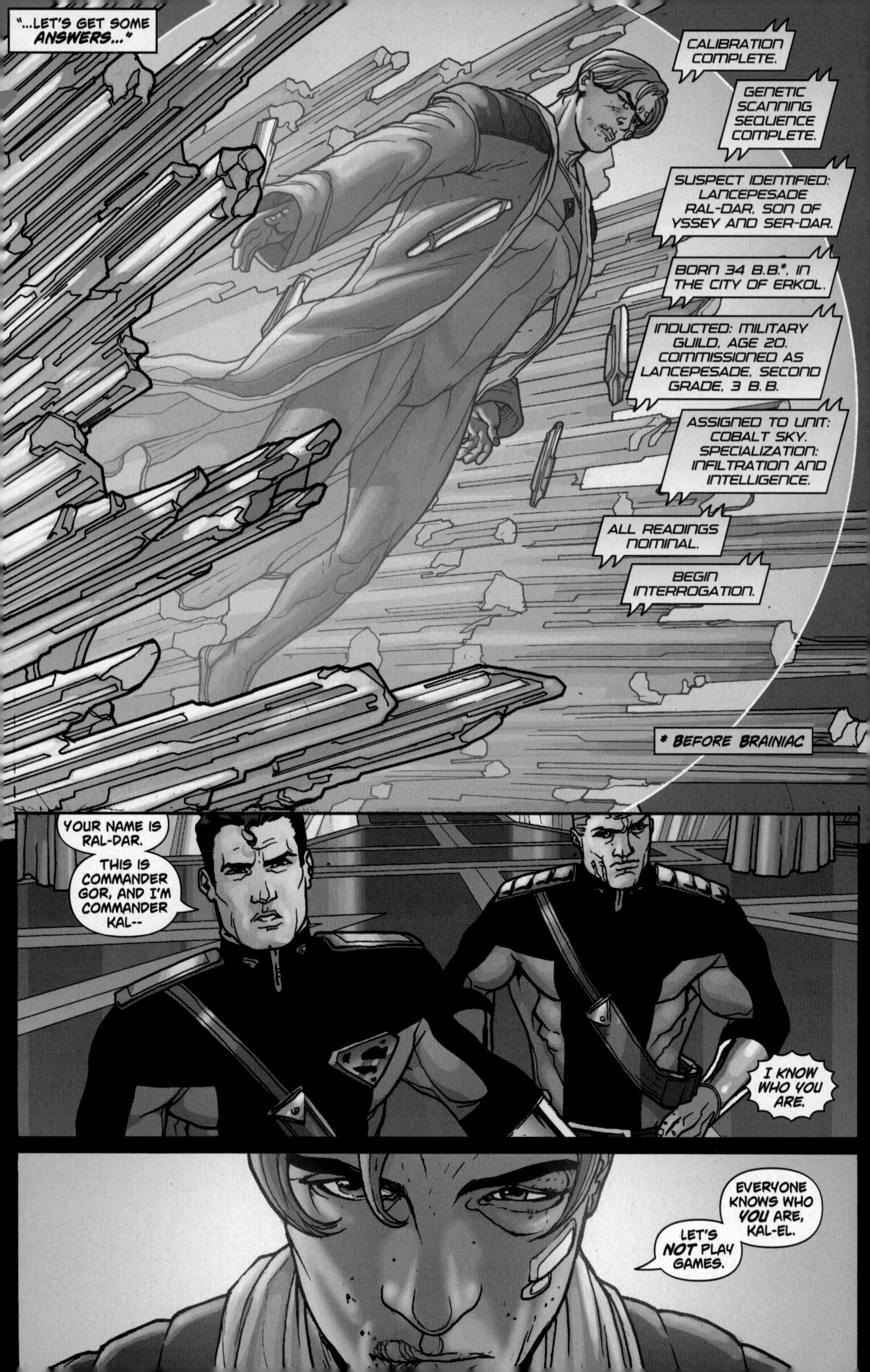
"...LET'S GET SOME ANSWERS..."
CALIBRATION COMPLETE.
GENETIC SCANNING SEQUENCE COMPLETE.
SUSPECT IDENTIFIED: LANCEPESADE RAL-DAR, SON OF YSSEY AND SER-DAR.
BORN 34 B.B.*, IN THE CITY OF ERKOL.
INDUCTED: MILITARY GUILD, AGE 20. COMMISSIONED AS LANCEPESADE, SECOND GRADE, 3 B.B.
ASSIGNED TO UNIT: COBALT SKY. SPECIALIZATION: INFILTRATION AND INTELLIGENCE.
ALL READINGS NOMINAL.
BEGIN INTERROGATION.
* BEFORE BRAINIAC
YOUR NAME IS RAL-DAR.
THIS IS COMMANDER GOR, AND I'M COMMANDER KAL--
I KNOW WHO YOU ARE.
EVERYONE KNOWS WHO YOU ARE, KAL-EL.
LET'S NOT PLAY GAMES.

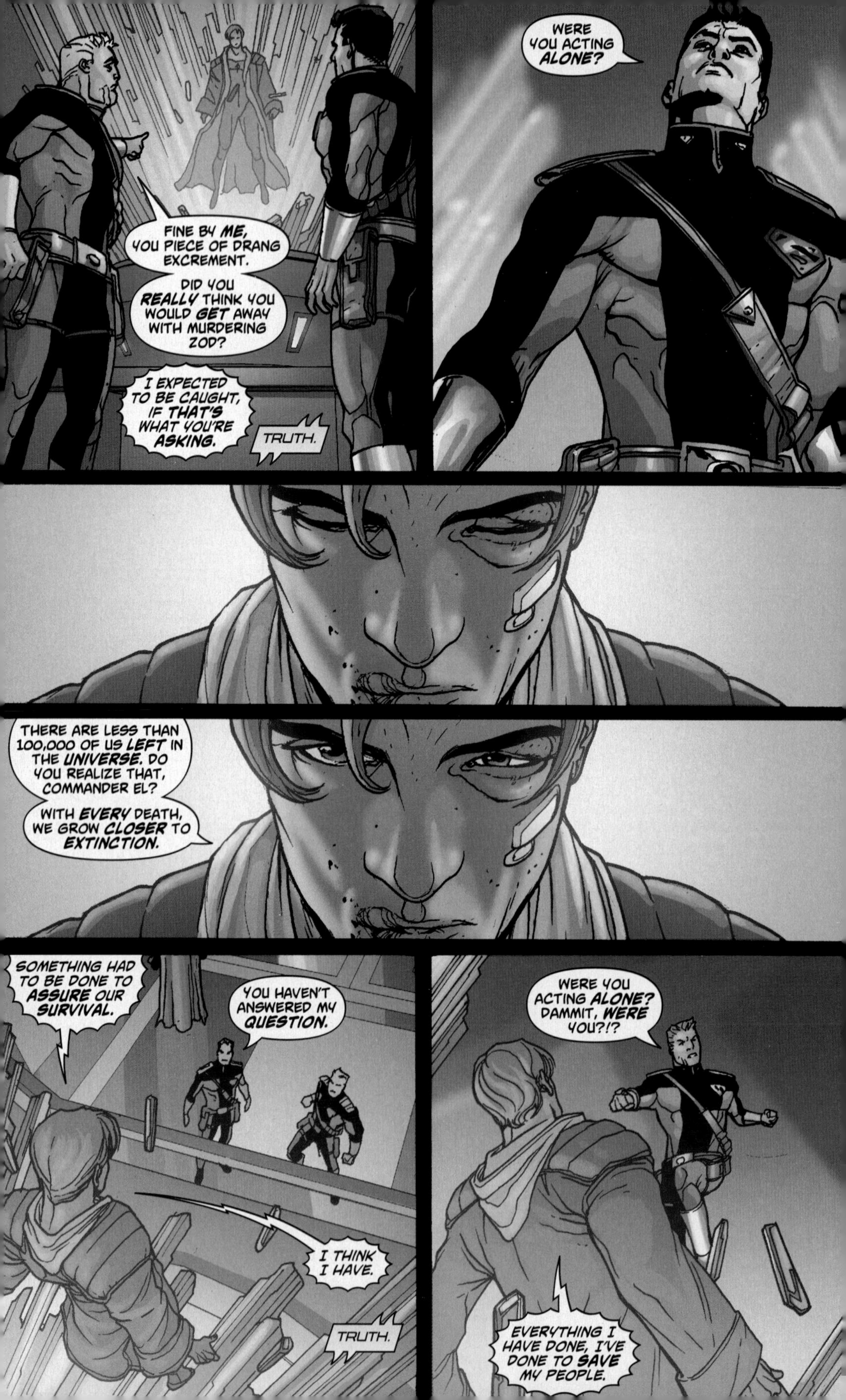
FINE BY ME, YOU PIECE OF DRANG EXCREMENT.
DID YOU REALLY THINK YOU WOULD GET AWAY WITH MURDERING ZOD?
I EXPECTED TO BE CAUGHT, IF THAT'S WHAT YOU'RE ASKING.
TRUTH.
WERE YOU ACTING ALONE?
THERE ARE LESS THAN 100,000 OF US LEFT IN THE UNIVERSE. DO YOU REALIZE THAT, COMMANDER EL?
WITH EVERY DEATH, WE GROW CLOSER TO EXTINCTION.
SOMETHING HAD TO BE DONE TO ASSURE OUR SURVIVAL.
YOU HAVEN'T ANSWERED MY QUESTION.
I THINK I HAVE.
TRUTH.
WERE YOU ACTING ALONE? DAMMIT, WERE YOU?!?
EVERYTHING I HAVE DONE, I'VE DONE TO SAVE MY PEOPLE.

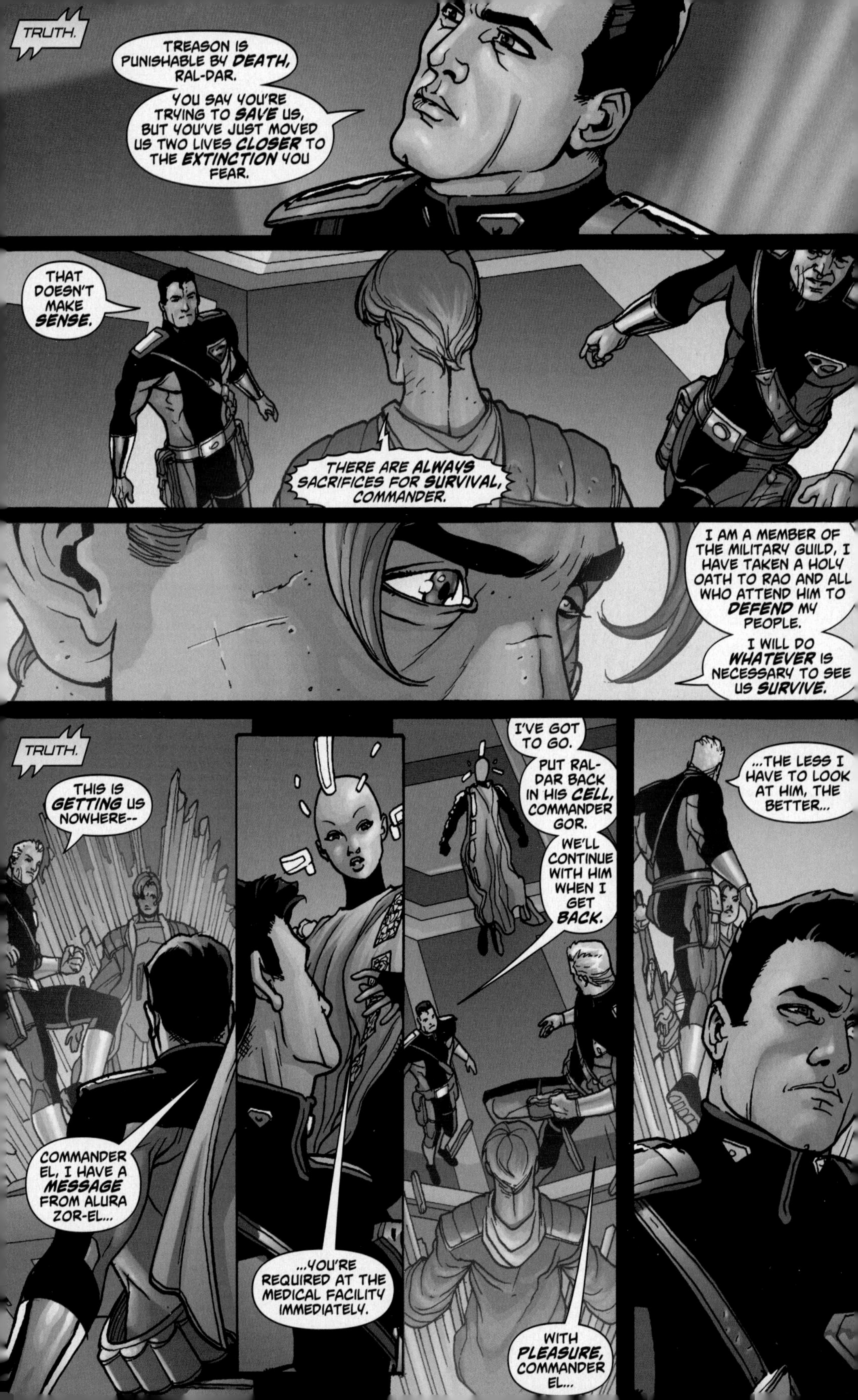
TRUTH.
TREASON IS PUNISHABLE BY DEATH, RAL-DAR.
YOU SAY YOU'RE TRYING TO SAVE US, BUT YOU'VE JUST MOVED US TWO LIVES CLOSER TO THE EXTINCTION YOU FEAR.
THAT DOESN'T MAKE SENSE.
THERE ARE ALWAYS SACRIFICES FOR SURVIVAL, COMMANDER.
I AM A MEMBER OF THE MILITARY GUILD, I HAVE TAKEN A HOLY OATH TO RAO AND ALL WHO ATTEND HIM TO DEFEND MY PEOPLE.
I WILL DO WHATEVER IS NECESSARY TO SEE US SURVIVE.
TRUTH.
THIS IS GETTING US NOWHERE--
COMMANDER EL, I HAVE A MESSAGE FROM ALURA ZOR-EL...
...YOU'RE REQUIRED AT THE MEDICAL FACILITY IMMEDIATELY.
I'VE GOT TO GO.
PUT RAL-DAR BACK IN HIS CELL, COMMANDER GOR.
WE'LL CONTINUE WITH HIM WHEN I GET BACK.
WITH PLEASURE, COMMANDER EL...
...THE LESS I HAVE TO LOOK AT HIM, THE BETTER...

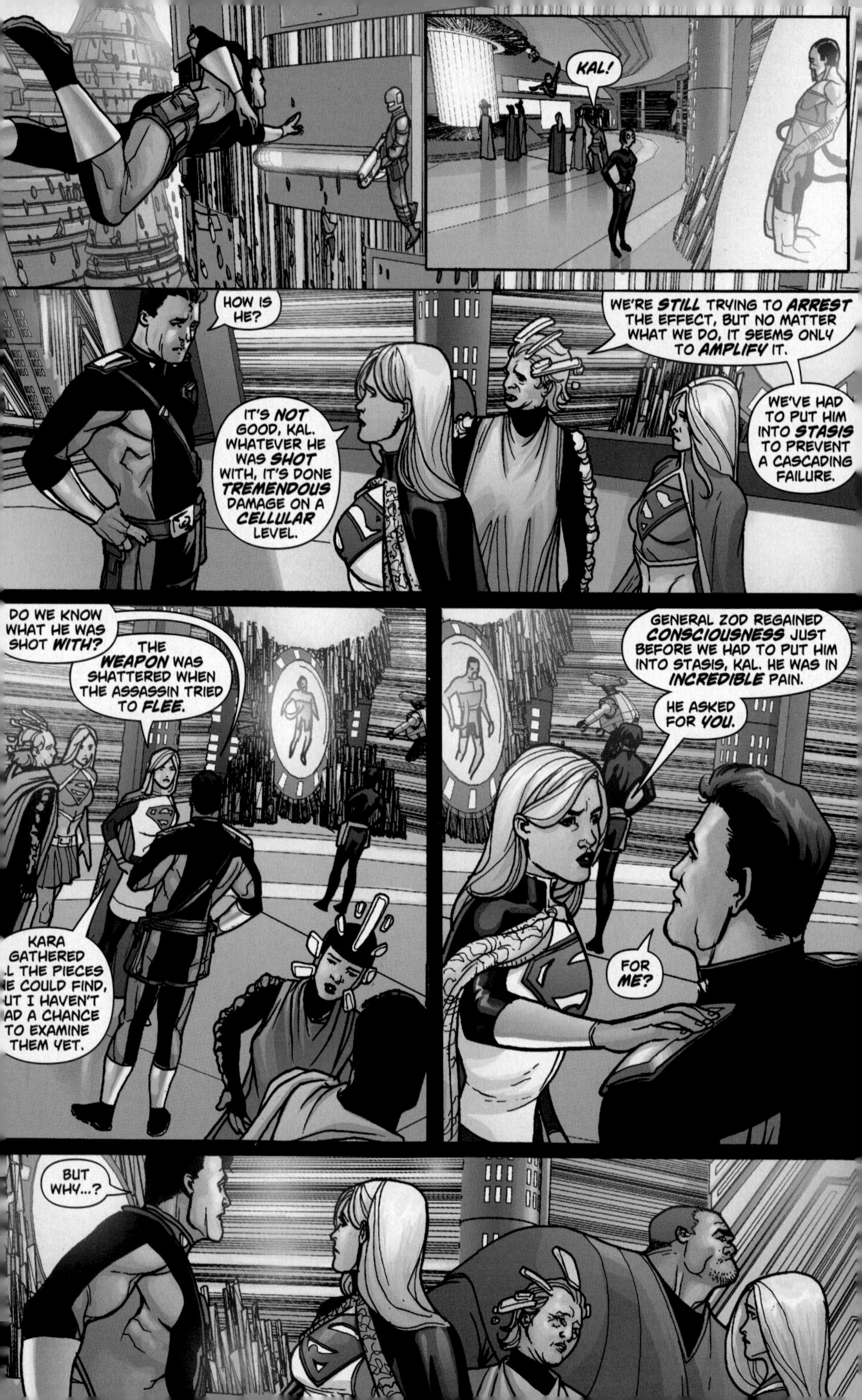
KAL!
HOW IS HE?
IT'S NOT GOOD, KAL. WHATEVER HE WAS SHOT WITH, IT'S DONE TREMENDOUS DAMAGE ON A CELLULAR LEVEL.
WE'RE STILL TRYING TO ARREST THE EFFECT, BUT NO MATTER WHAT WE DO, IT SEEMS ONLY TO AMPLIFY IT.
WE'VE HAD TO PUT HIM INTO STASIS TO PREVENT A CASCADING FAILURE.
DO WE KNOW WHAT HE WAS SHOT WITH?
THE WEAPON WAS SHATTERED WHEN THE ASSASSIN TRIED TO FLEE.
KARA GATHERED
.L THE PIECES
IE COULD FIND,
UT I HAVEN'T
AD A CHANCE
TO EXAMINE THEM YET.
GENERAL ZOD REGAINED CONSCIOUSNESS JUST BEFORE WE HAD TO PUT HIM INTO STASIS, KAL. HE WAS IN INCREDIBLE PAIN.
HE ASKED FOR YOU.
FOR ME?
BUT WHY...?

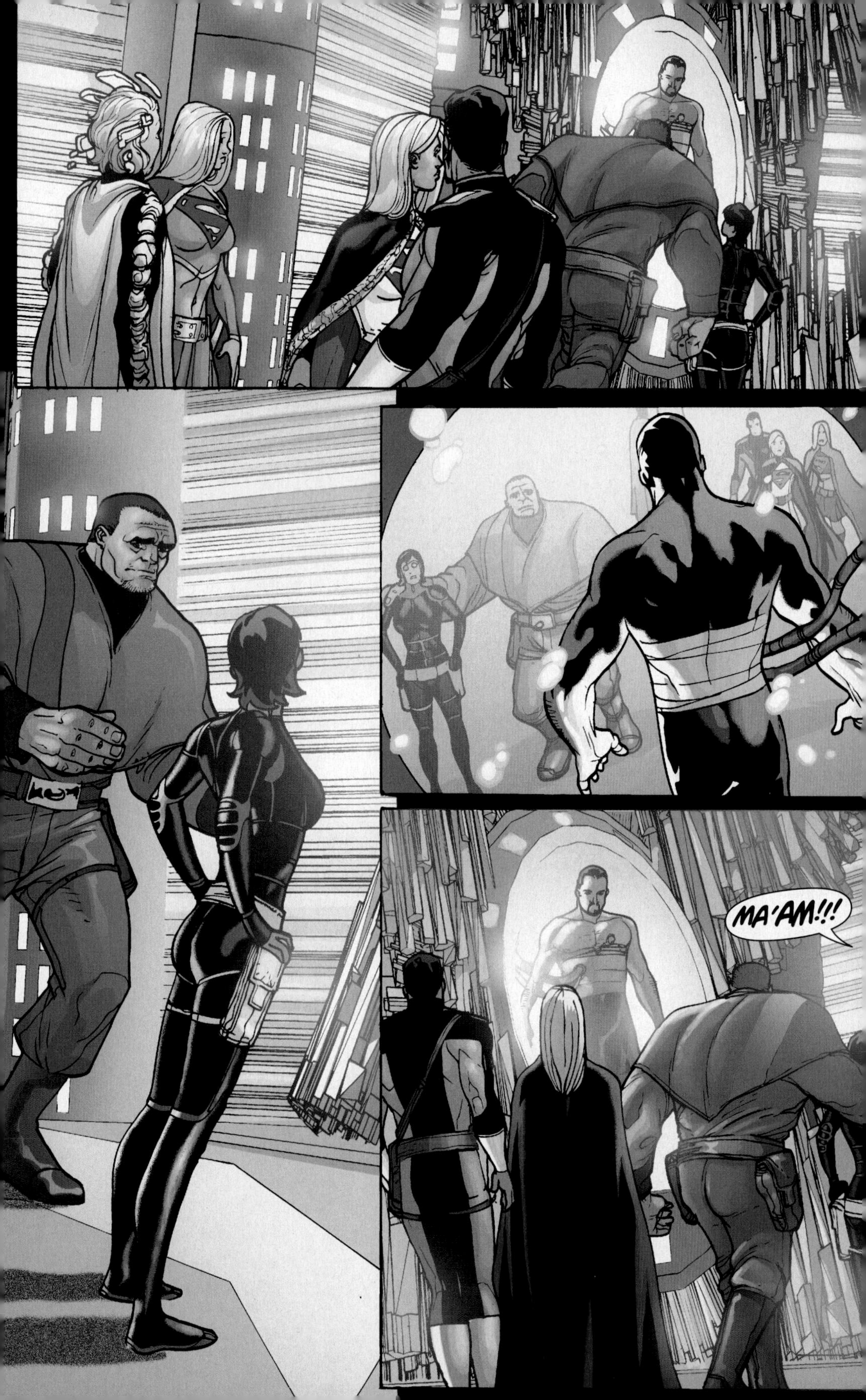
MA'AM!!!

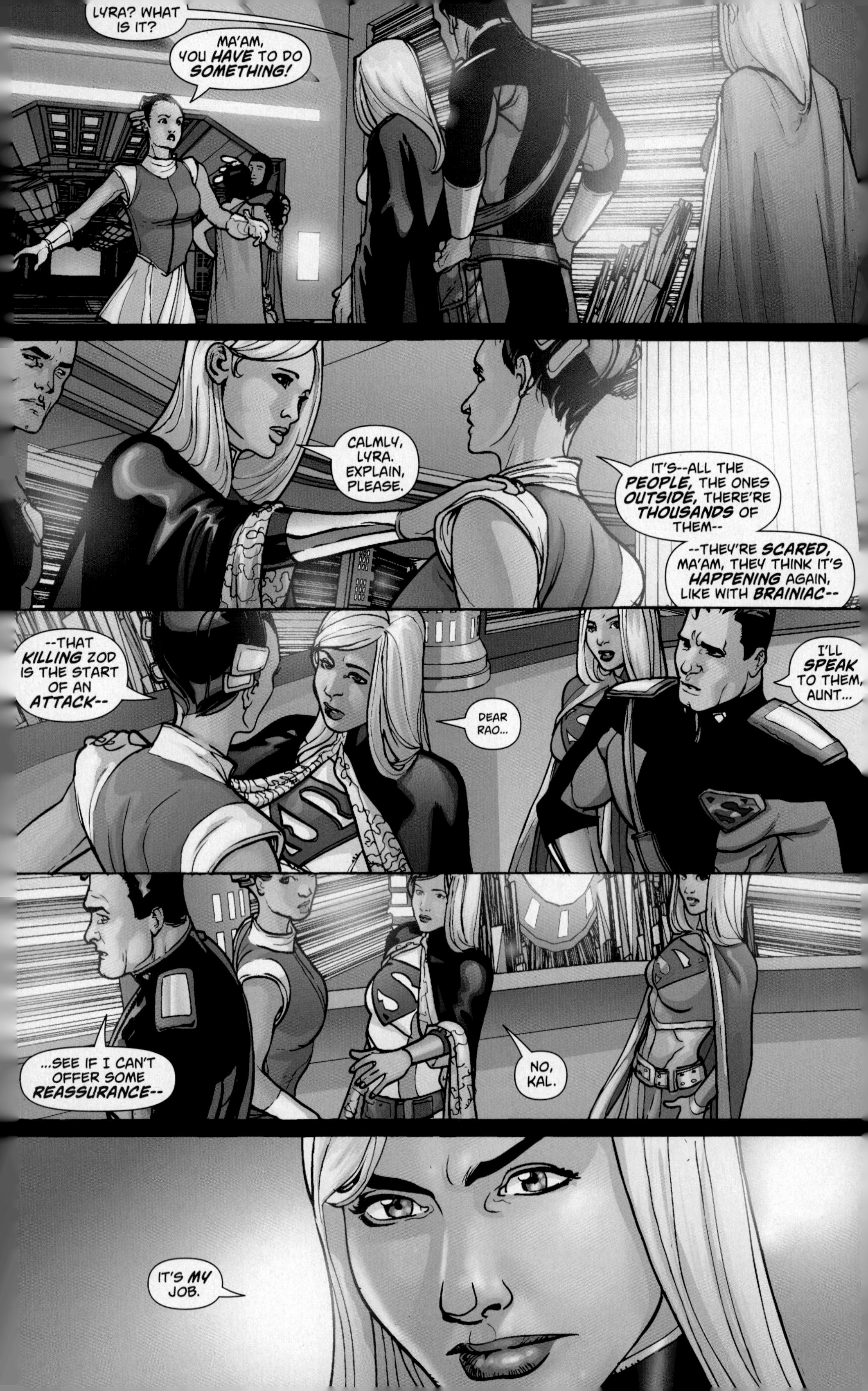
LYRA? WHAT IS IT?
MA'AM, YOU HAVE TO DO SOMETHING!
CALMLY, LYRA. EXPLAIN, PLEASE.
IT'S--ALL THE PEOPLE, THE ONES OUTSIDE, THERE'RE THOUSANDS OF THEM--
--THEY'RE SCARED, MA'AM, THEY THINK IT'S HAPPENING AGAIN, LIKE WITH BRAINIAC--
--THAT KILLING ZOD IS THE START OF AN ATTACK--
DEAR RAO...
I'LL SPEAK TO THEM, AUNT...
...SEE IF I CAN'T OFFER SOME REASSURANCE--
NO, KAL.
IT'S MY JOB.

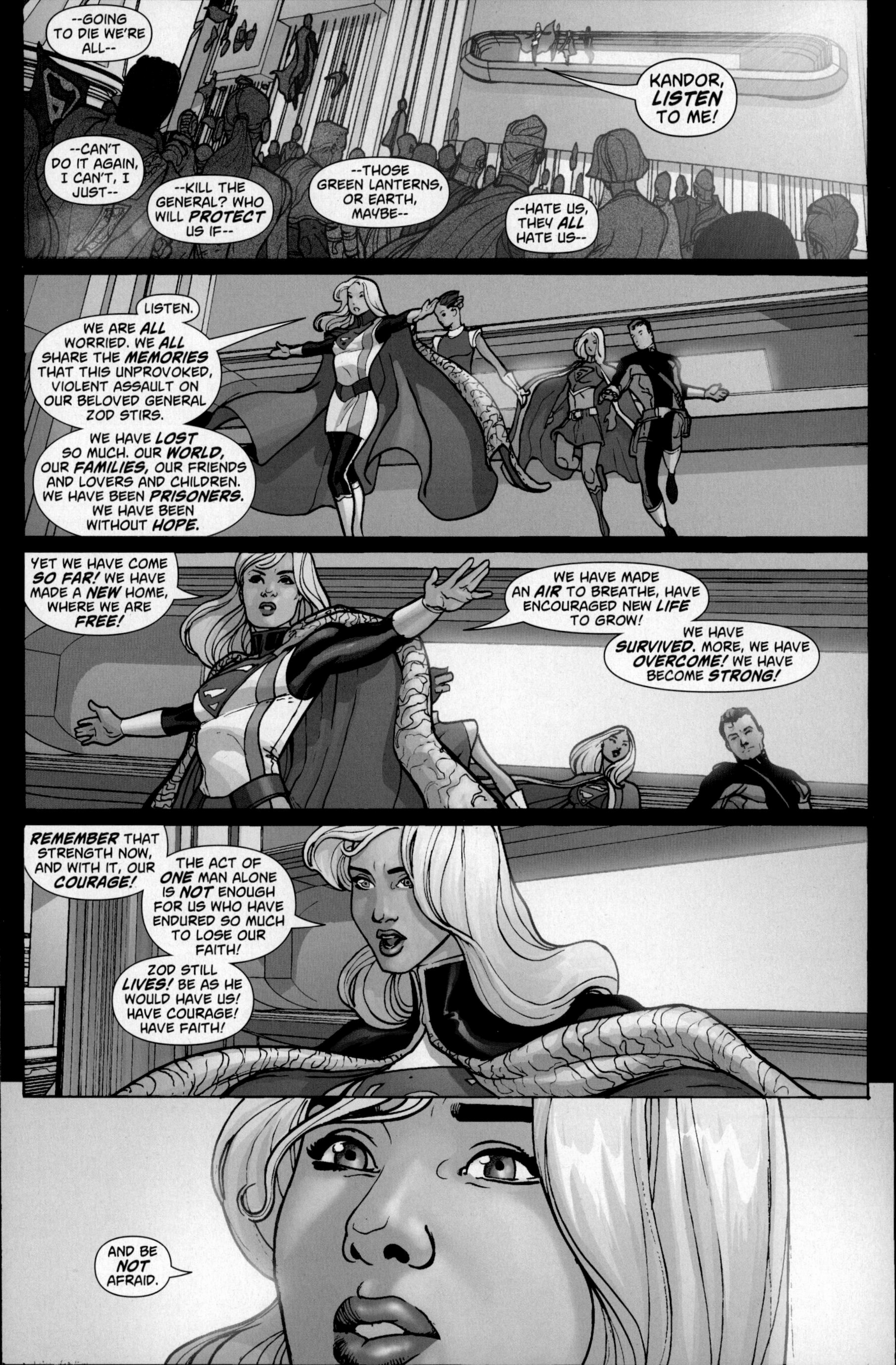
--GOING TO DIE WE'RE ALL--
KANDOR, LISTEN TO ME!
--CAN'T DO IT AGAIN, I CAN'T, I JUST--
--KILL THE GENERAL? WHO WILL PROTECT US IF--
--THOSE GREEN LANTERNS, OR EARTH, MAYBE--
--HATE US, THEY ALL HATE US--
LISTEN.
WE ARE ALL WORRIED. WE ALL SHARE THE MEMORIES THAT THIS UNPROVOKED, VIOLENT ASSAULT ON OUR BELOVED GENERAL ZOD STIRS.
WE HAVE LOST SO MUCH. OUR WORLD, OUR FAMILIES, OUR FRIENDS AND LOVERS AND CHILDREN. WE HAVE BEEN PRISONERS. WE HAVE BEEN WITHOUT HOPE.
YET WE HAVE COME SO FAR! WE HAVE MADE A NEW HOME, WHERE WE ARE FREE!
WE HAVE MADE AN AIR TO BREATHE, HAVE ENCOURAGED NEW LIFE TO GROW!
WE HAVE SURVIVED. MORE, WE HAVE OVERCOME! WE HAVE BECOME STRONG!
REMEMBER THAT STRENGTH NOW, AND WITH IT, OUR COURAGE!
THE ACT OF ONE MAN ALONE IS NOT ENOUGH FOR US WHO HAVE ENDURED SO MUCH TO LOSE OUR FAITH!
ZOD STILL LIVES! BE AS HE WOULD HAVE US! HAVE COURAGE! HAVE FAITH!
AND BE NOT AFRAID.

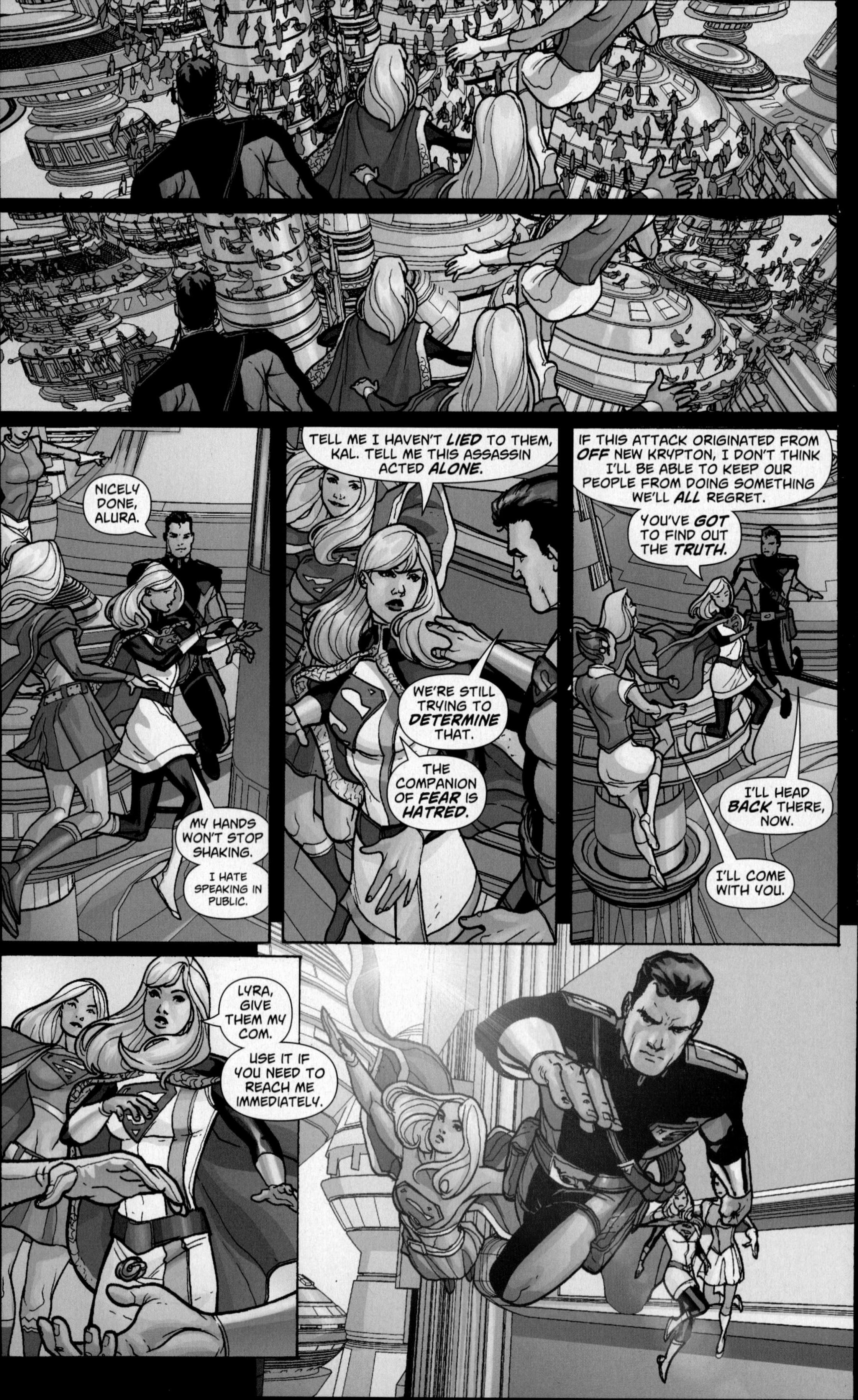
NICELY DONE, ALURA.
MY HANDS WON'T STOP SHAKING.
I HATE SPEAKING IN PUBLIC.
TELL ME I HAVEN'T LIED TO THEM, KAL. TELL ME THIS ASSASSIN ACTED ALONE.
WE'RE STILL TRYING TO DETERMINE THAT.
THE COMPANION OF FEAR IS HATRED.
IF THIS ATTACK ORIGINATED FROM OFF NEW KRYPTON, I DON'T THINK I'LL BE ABLE TO KEEP OUR PEOPLE FROM DOING SOMETHING WE'LL ALL REGRET.
YOU'VE GOT TO FIND OUT THE TRUTH.
I'LL HEAD BACK THERE, NOW.
I'LL COME WITH YOU.
LYRA, GIVE THEM MY COM.
USE IT IF YOU NEED TO REACH ME IMMEDIATELY.

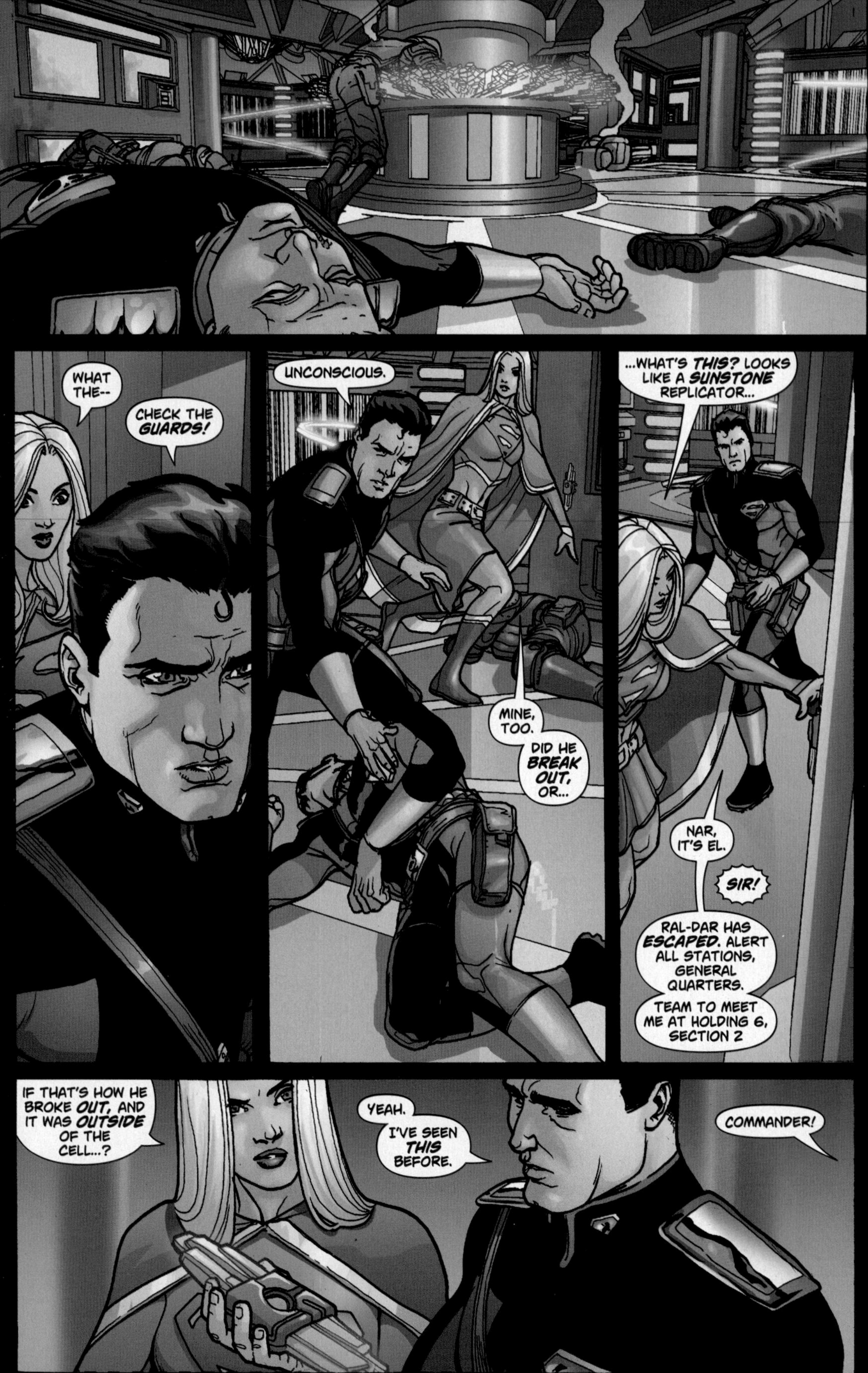
WHAT THE--
CHECK THE GUARDS!
UNCONSCIOUS.
MINE, TOO.
DID HE BREAK OUT, OR...
...WHAT'S THIS? LOOKS LIKE A SUNSTONE REPLICATOR...
NAR, IT'S EL.
SIR!
RAL-DAR HAS ESCAPED. ALERT ALL STATIONS, GENERAL QUARTERS.
TEAM TO MEET ME AT HOLDING 6, SECTION 2
IF THAT'S HOW HE BROKE OUT, AND IT WAS OUTSIDE OF THE CELL...?
YEAH.
I'VE SEEN THIS BEFORE.
COMMANDER!

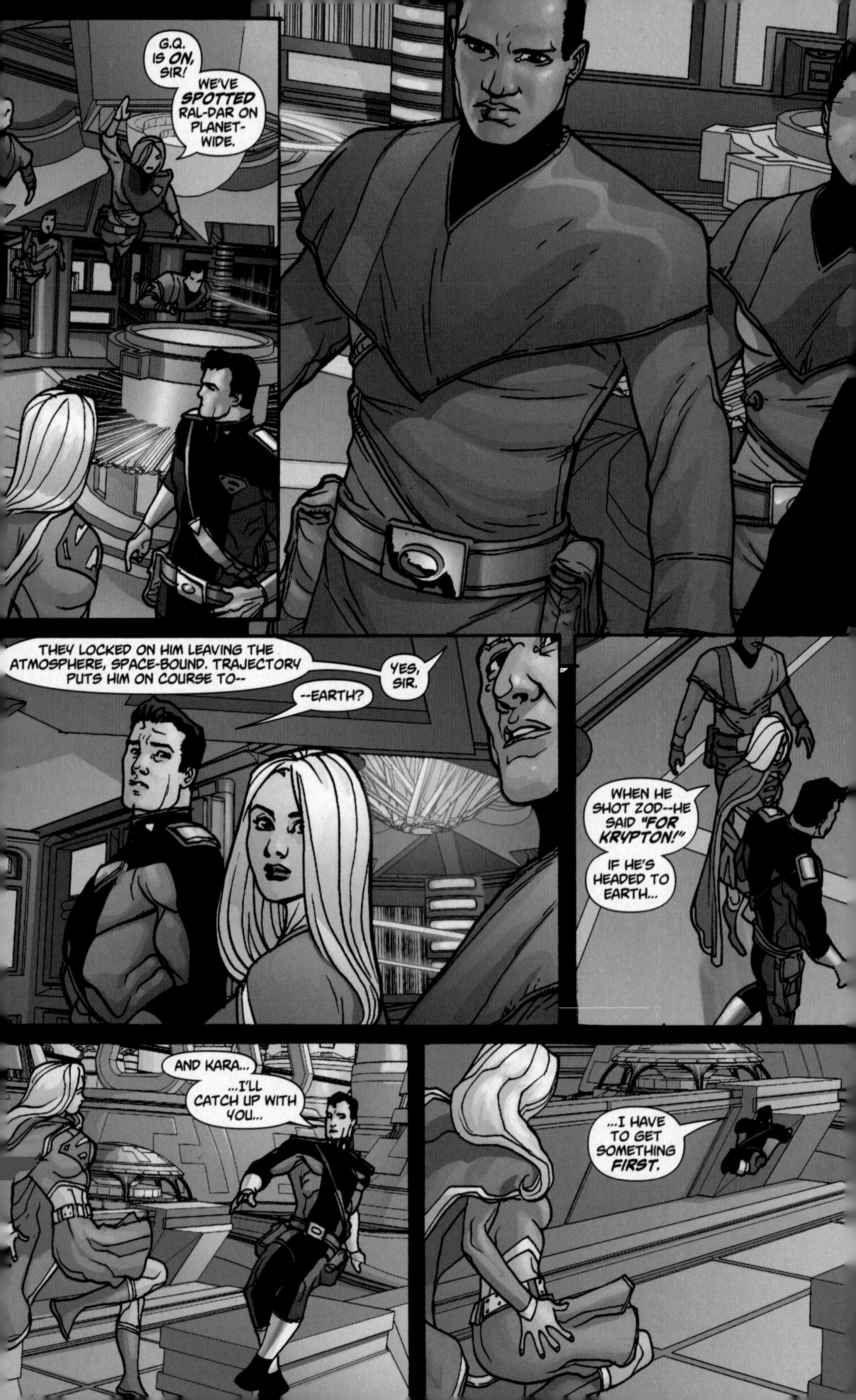
G.Q. IS *ON*, SIR!
WE'VE *SPOTTED* RAL-DAR ON PLANET-WIDE.
THEY LOCKED ON HIM LEAVING THE ATMOSPHERE, SPACE-BOUND. TRAJECTORY PUTS HIM ON COURSE TO--
YES, SIR.
--EARTH?
WHEN HE SHOT ZOD--HE SAID *"FOR KRYPTON!"*
IF HE'S HEADED TO EARTH...
AND KARA...
...I'LL CATCH UP WITH YOU...
...I HAVE TO GET SOMETHING *FIRST*.

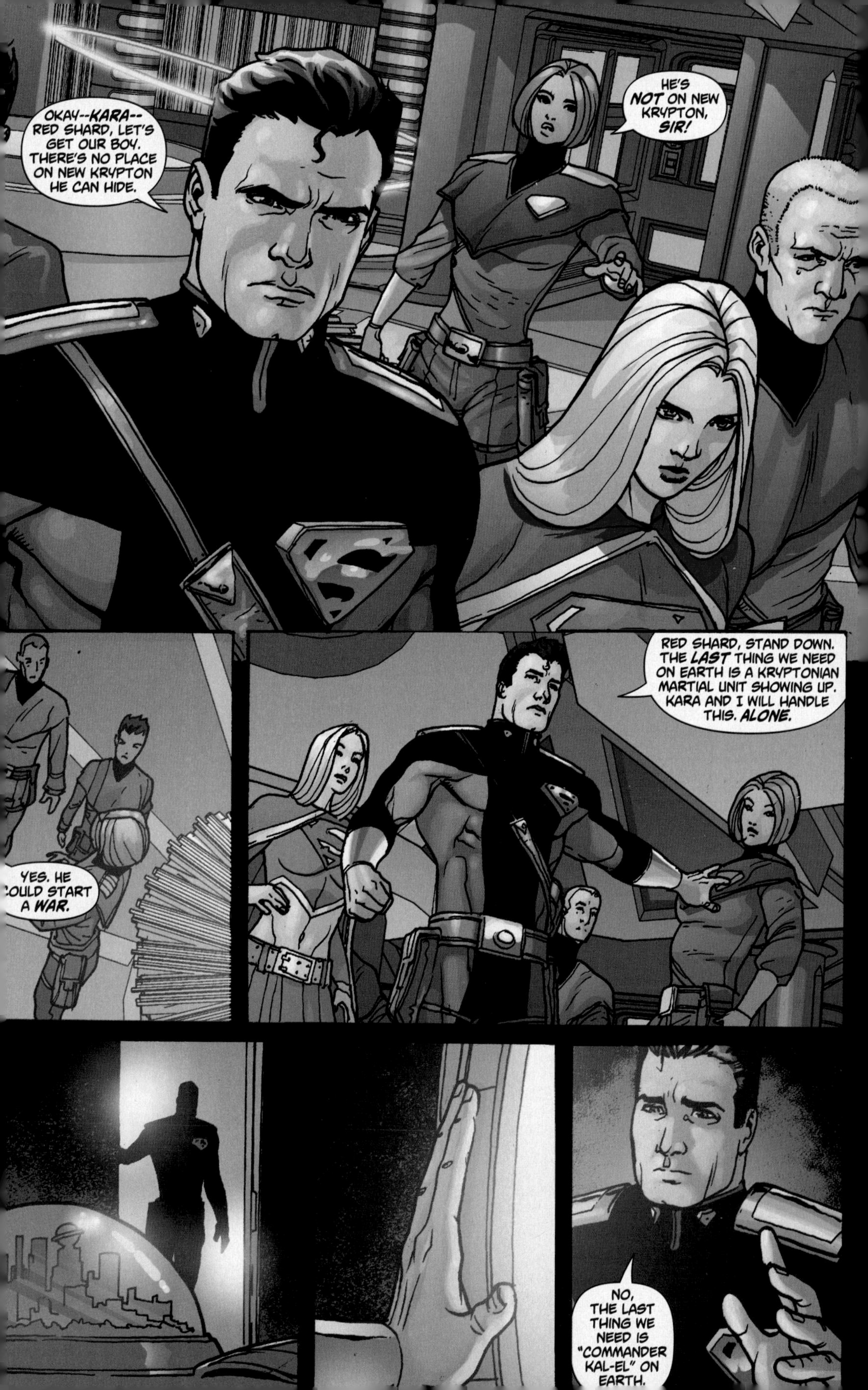
OKAY--KARA--
RED SHARD, LET'S GET OUR BOY. THERE'S NO PLACE ON NEW KRYPTON HE CAN HIDE.
HE'S NOT ON NEW KRYPTON, SIR!
YES. HE COULD START A WAR.
RED SHARD, STAND DOWN. THE LAST THING WE NEED ON EARTH IS A KRYPTONIAN MARTIAL UNIT SHOWING UP. KARA AND I WILL HANDLE THIS. ALONE.
NO, THE LAST THING WE NEED IS "COMMANDER KAL-EL" ON EARTH.

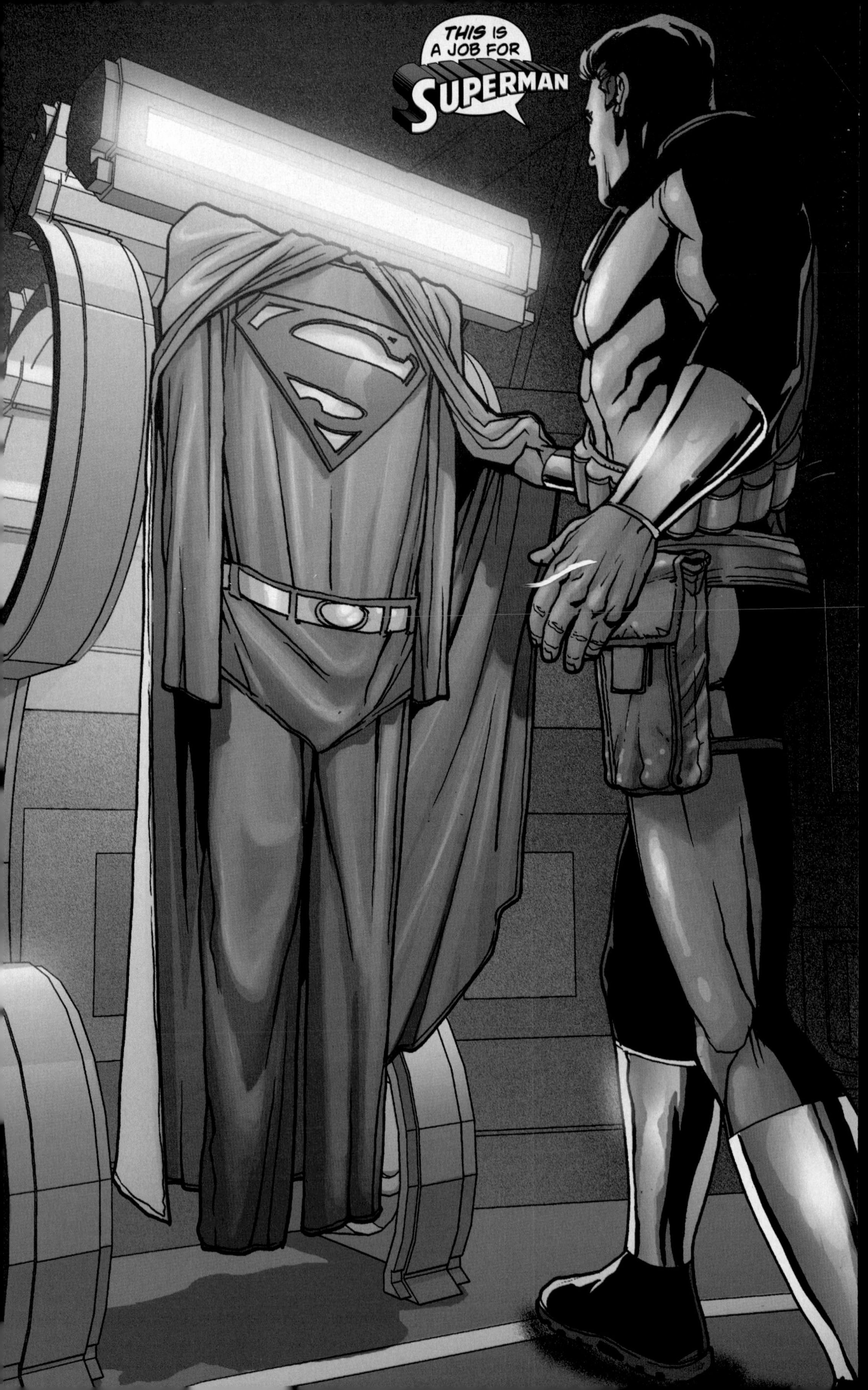
THIS IS A JOB FOR SUPERMAN

COVER ART BY FERNANDO DAGNINO & RAUL FERNANDEZ WITH MAZI

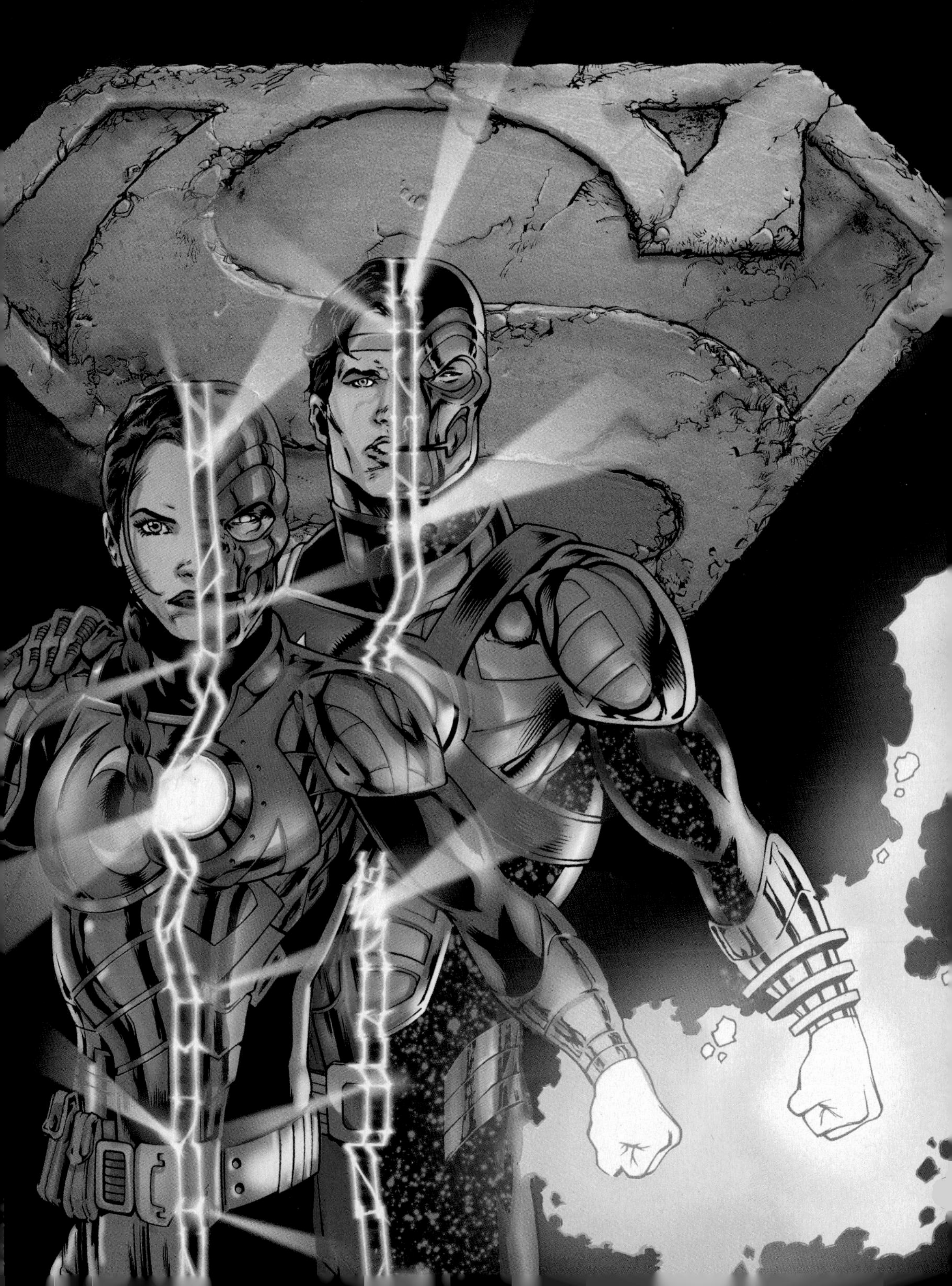

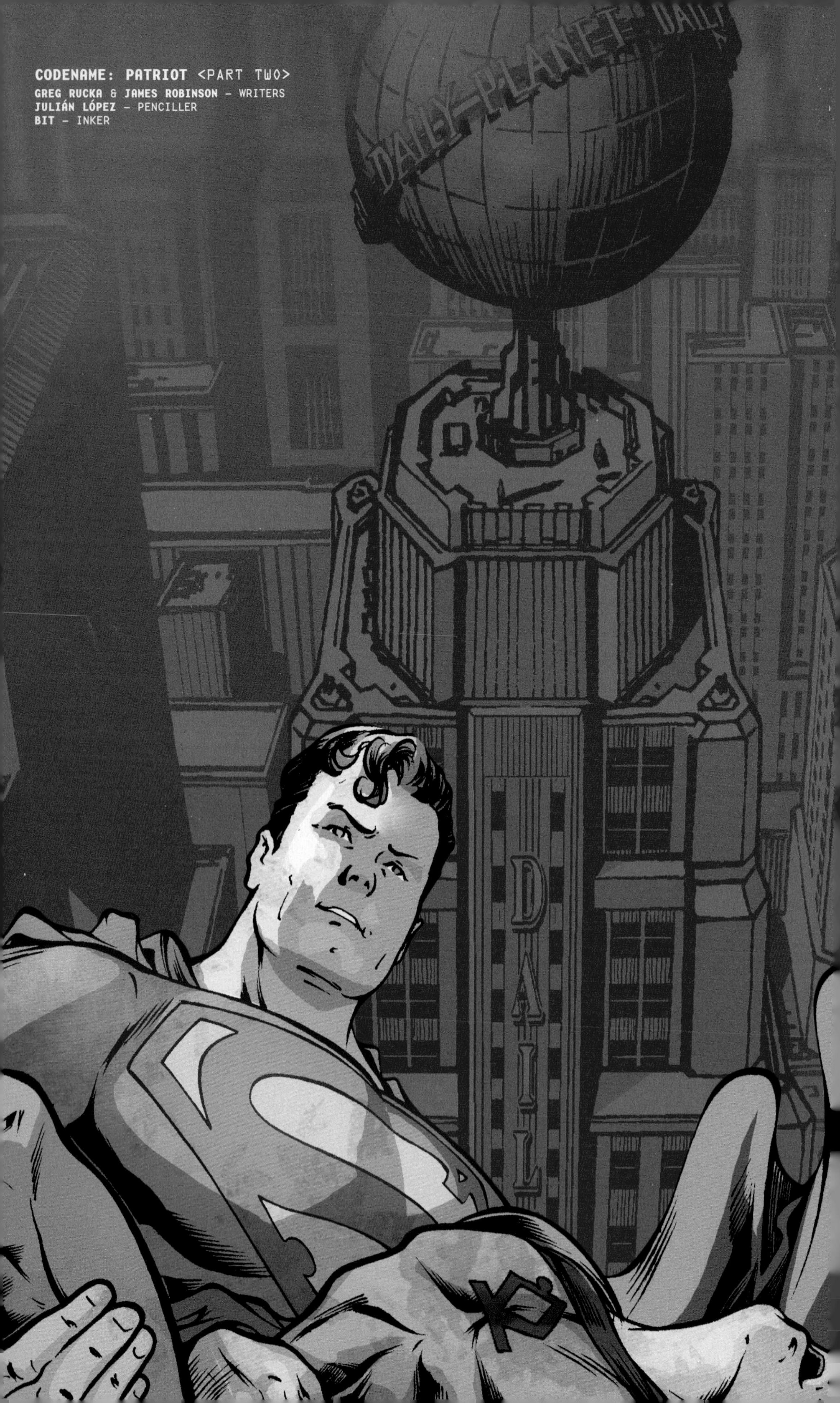

CODENAME: PATRIOT <PART TWO>
GREG RUCKA & JAMES ROBINSON – WRITERS
JULIÁN LÓPEZ – PENCILLER
BIT – INKER
DAILY PLANET DAILY
DAIL

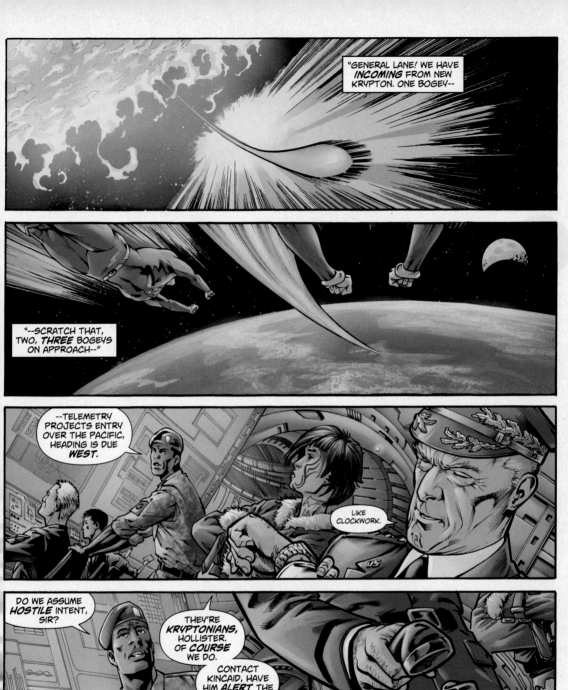

"GENERAL LANE! WE HAVE *INCOMING* FROM NEW KRYPTON. ONE BOGEY--"

"--SCRATCH THAT, TWO, *THREE* BOGEYS ON APPROACH--"

--TELEMETRY PROJECTS ENTRY OVER THE PACIFIC, HEADING IS DUE *WEST.*

LIKE CLOCKWORK.

DO WE ASSUME *HOSTILE* INTENT, SIR?

THEY'RE *KRYPTONIANS,* HOLLISTER. OF *COURSE* WE DO.

CONTACT KINCAID, HAVE HIM *ALERT* THE *MEDIA.*

COMMAND, OSCAR SEVEN-NINE-HOTEL-FIVE, THE WORD OF THE DAY IS "LEAPFROG."

WE HAVE *THREE* ALIENS ON AGGRESSIVE APPROACH, COLONEL...

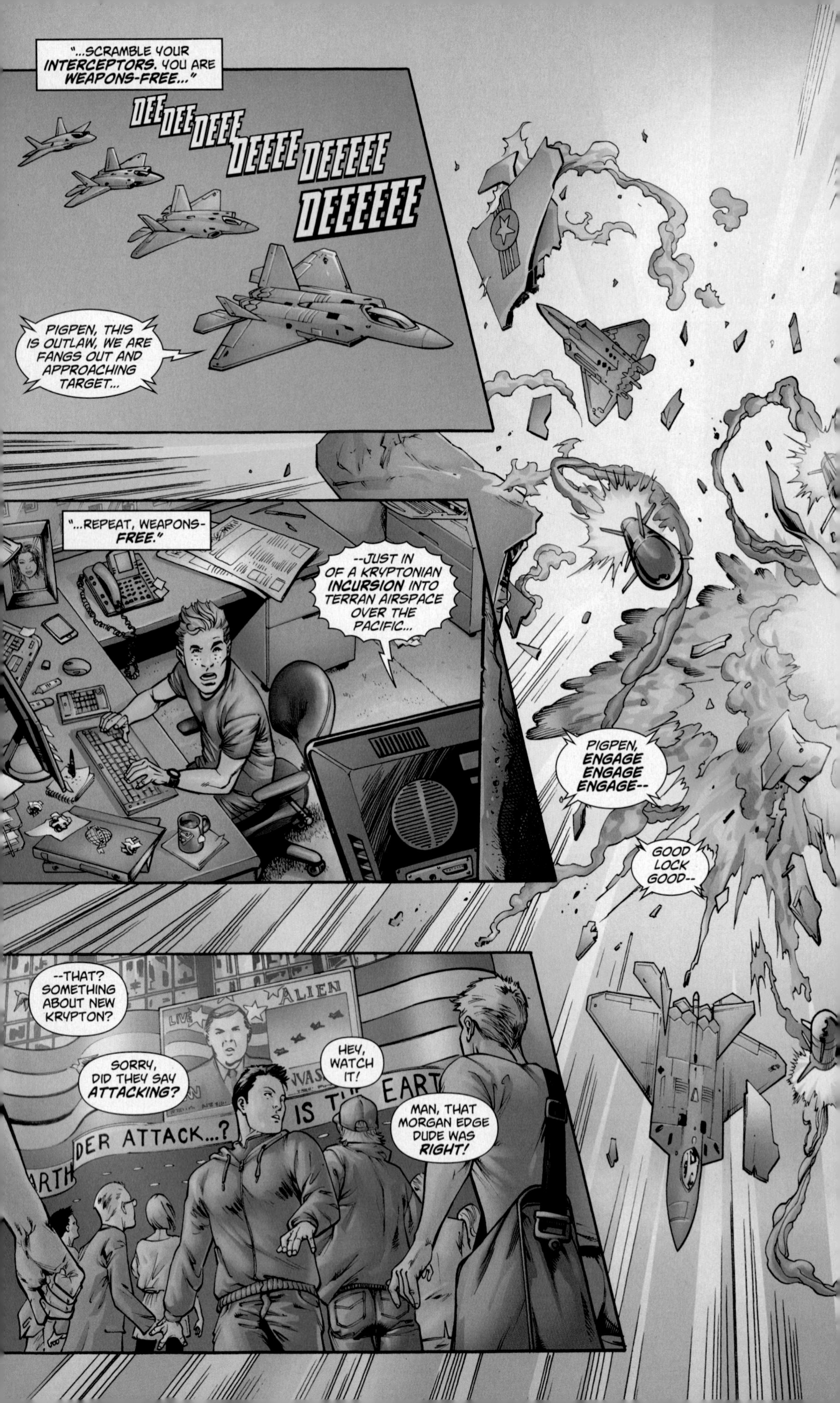
"...SCRAMBLE YOUR INTERCEPTORS. YOU ARE WEAPONS-FREE..."
DEE DEE DEEE DEEEE DEEEEE DEEEEEE
PIGPEN, THIS IS OUTLAW, WE ARE FANGS OUT AND APPROACHING TARGET...
"...REPEAT, WEAPONS-FREE."
--JUST IN OF A KRYPTONIAN INCURSION INTO TERRAN AIRSPACE OVER THE PACIFIC...
PIGPEN, ENGAGE ENGAGE ENGAGE--
GOOD LOCK GOOD--
--THAT? SOMETHING ABOUT NEW KRYPTON?
ALIEN
LIVE
SORRY, DID THEY SAY ATTACKING?
HEY, WATCH IT!
IS TH EART
DER ATTACK...?
ARTH
MAN, THAT MORGAN EDGE DUDE WAS RIGHT!

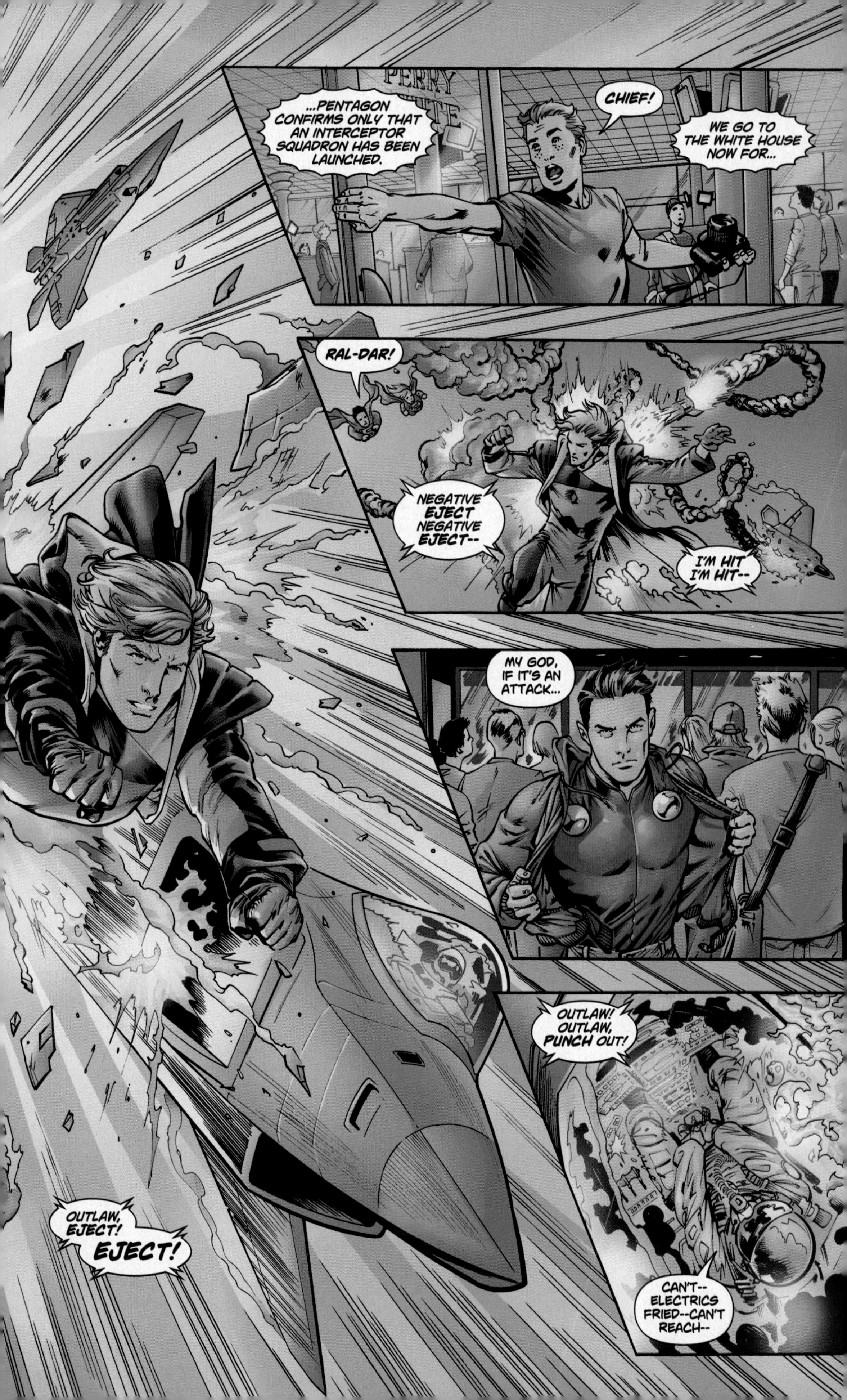
...PENTAGON CONFIRMS ONLY THAT AN INTERCEPTOR SQUADRON HAS BEEN LAUNCHED.
CHIEF!
WE GO TO THE WHITE HOUSE NOW FOR...
PERRY
RAL-DAR!
NEGATIVE EJECT NEGATIVE EJECT--
I'M HIT I'M HIT--
MY GOD, IF IT'S AN ATTACK...
OUTLAW! OUTLAW, PUNCH OUT!
CAN'T-- ELECTRICS FRIED--CAN'T REACH--
OUTLAW, EJECT! EJECT!

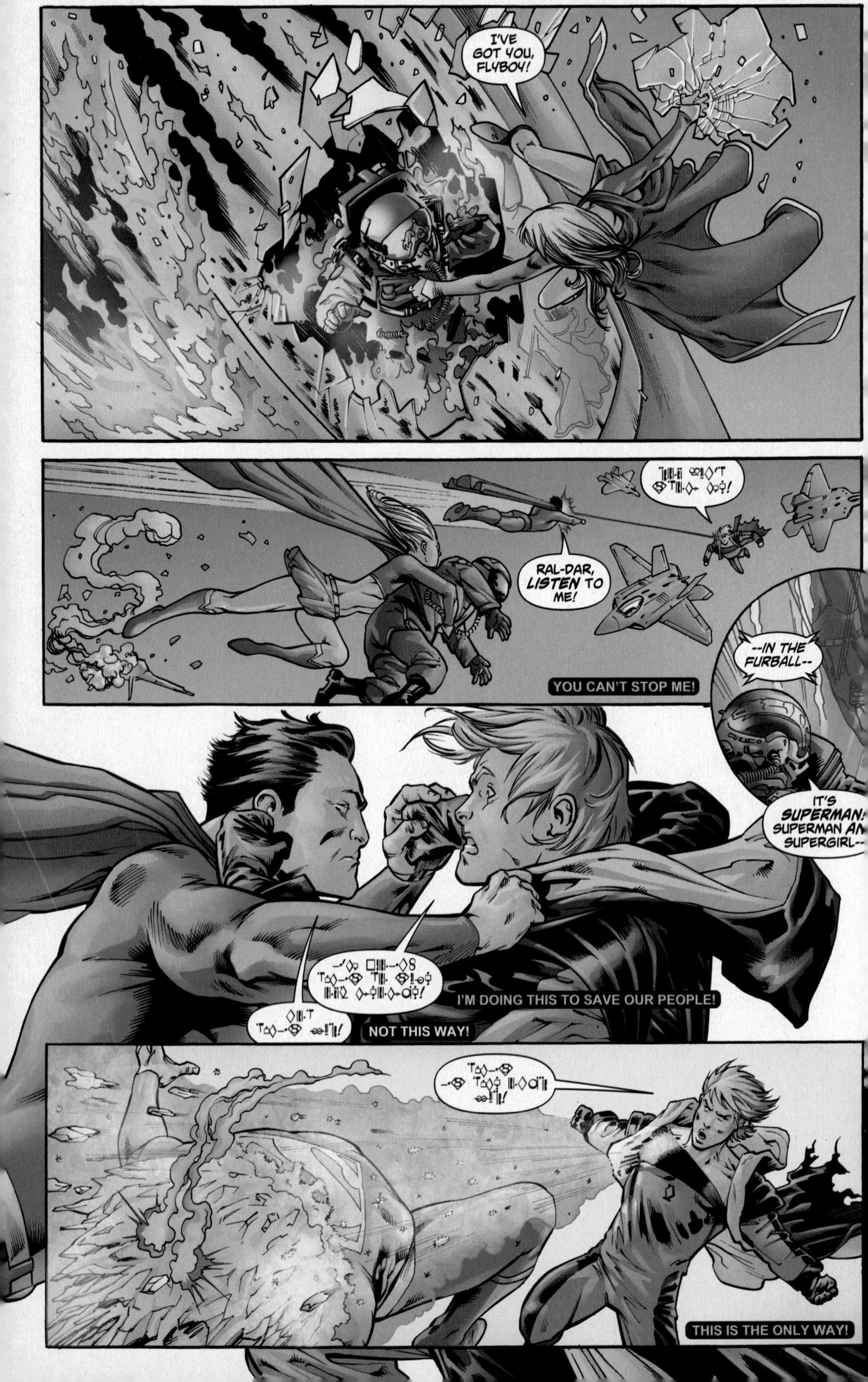

I'VE GOT YOU, FLYBOY!
RAL-DAR, LISTEN TO ME!
YOU CAN'T STOP ME!
--IN THE FURBALL--
IT'S SUPERMAN! SUPERMAN AN SUPERGIRL--
I'M DOING THIS TO SAVE OUR PEOPLE!
NOT THIS WAY!
THIS IS THE ONLY WAY!

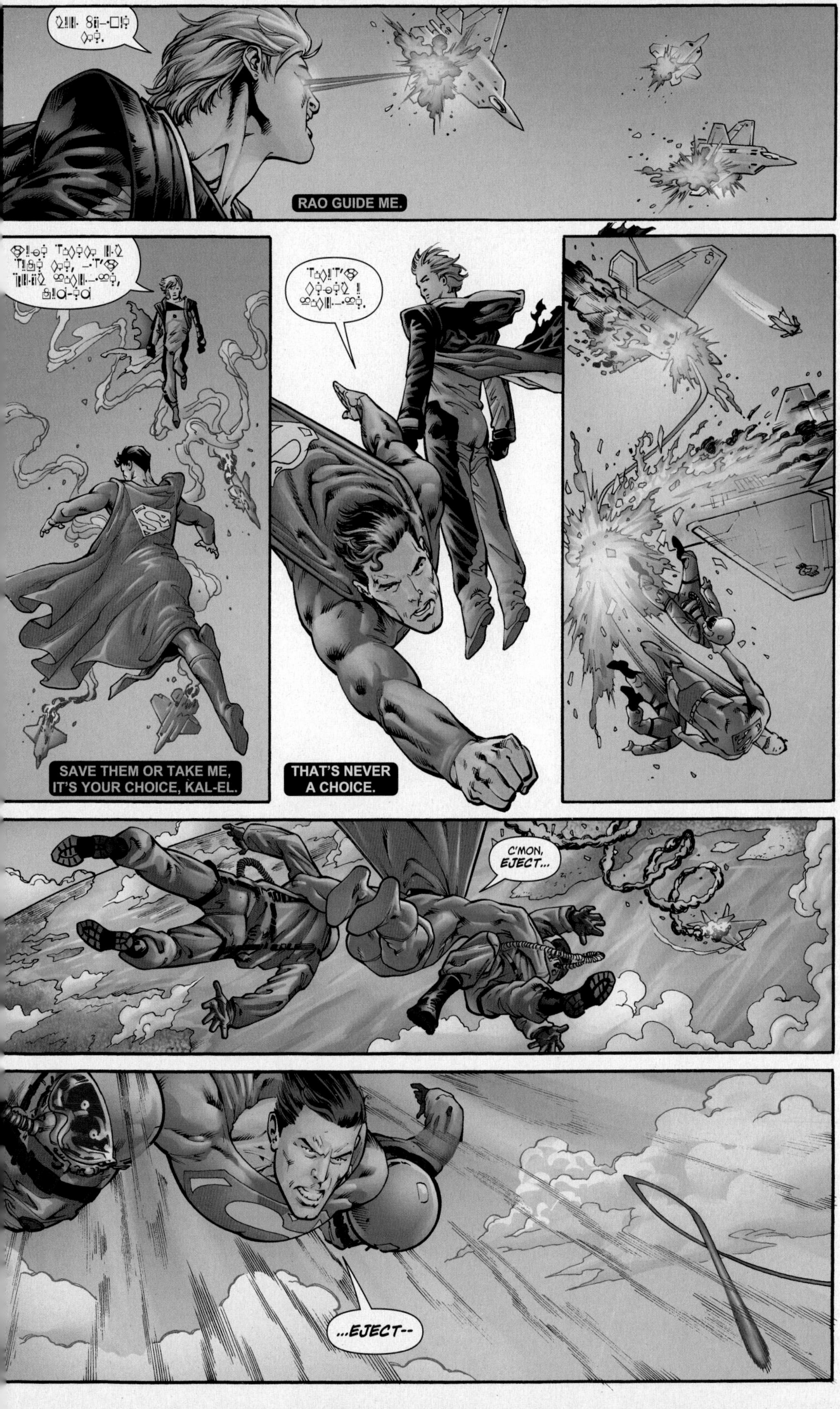
RAO GUIDE ME.
SAVE THEM OR TAKE ME, IT'S YOUR CHOICE, KAL-EL.
THAT'S NEVER A CHOICE.
C'MON, EJECT...
...EJECT--

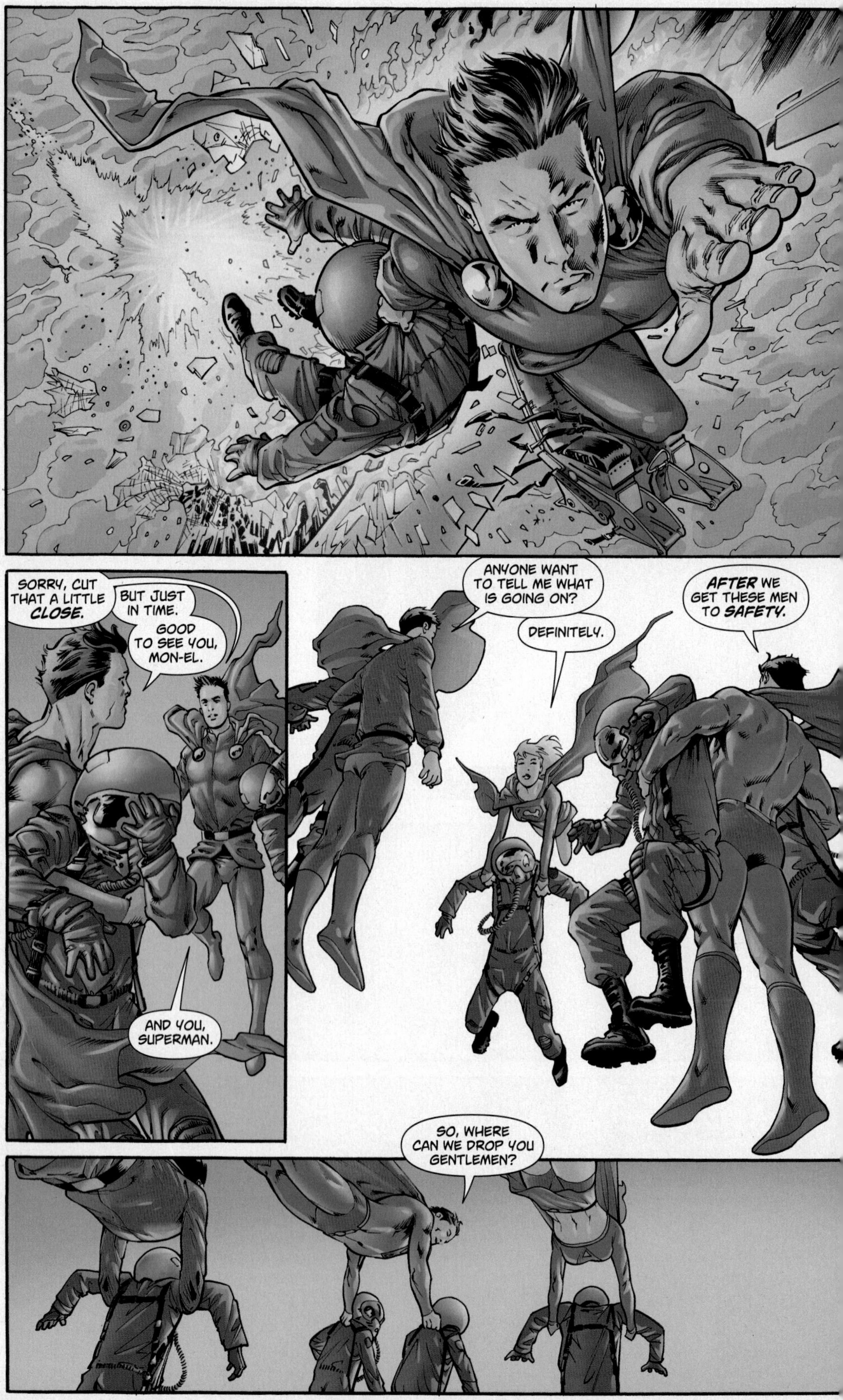

SORRY, CUT THAT A LITTLE CLOSE.
BUT JUST IN TIME.
GOOD TO SEE YOU, MON-EL.
AND YOU, SUPERMAN.
ANYONE WANT TO TELL ME WHAT IS GOING ON?
DEFINITELY.
AFTER WE GET THESE MEN TO SAFETY.
SO, WHERE CAN WE DROP YOU GENTLEMEN?

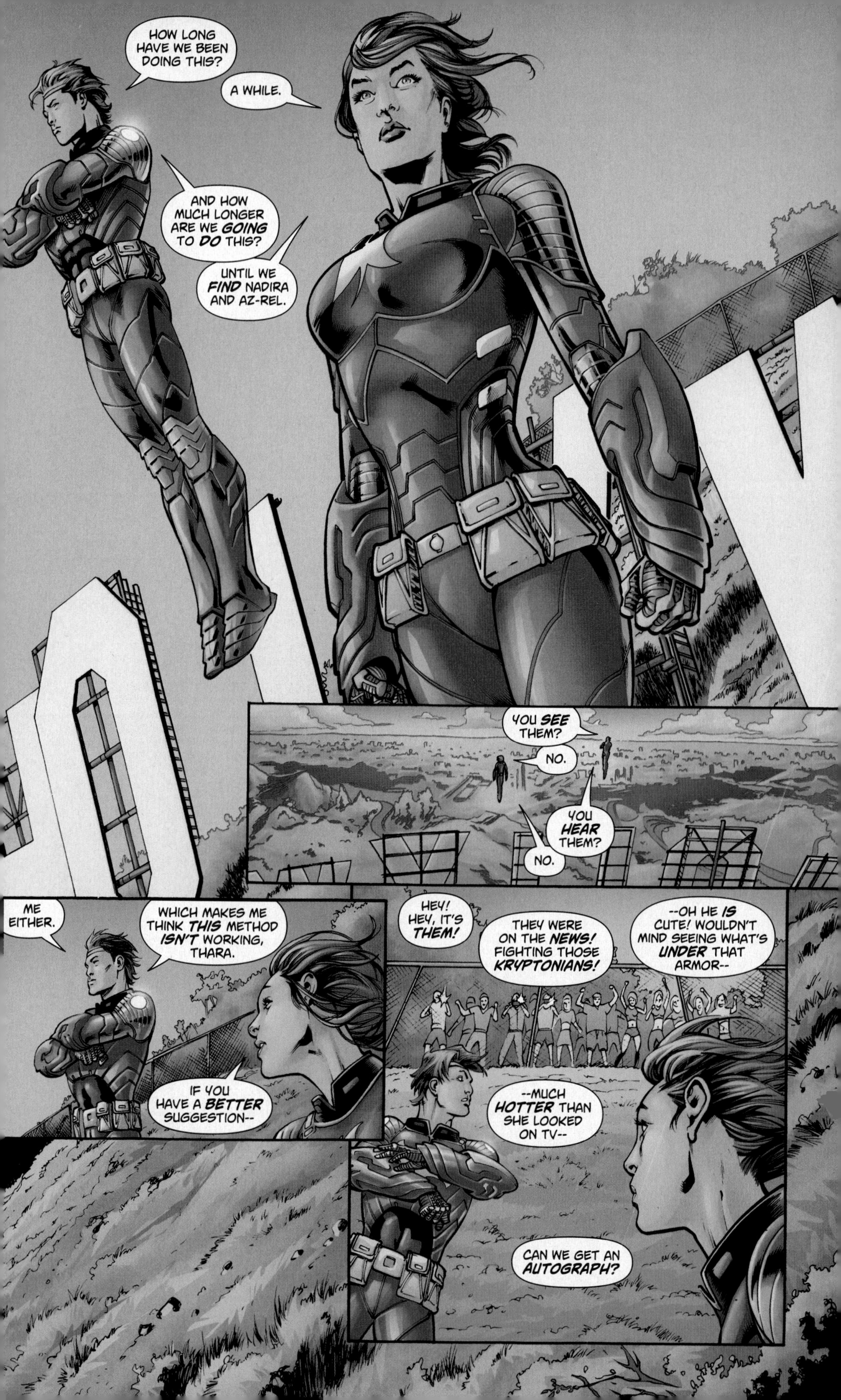

HOW LONG HAVE WE BEEN DOING THIS?
A WHILE.
AND HOW MUCH LONGER ARE WE GOING TO DO THIS?
UNTIL WE FIND NADIRA AND AZ-REL.
YOU SEE THEM?
NO.
YOU HEAR THEM?
NO.
ME EITHER.
WHICH MAKES ME THINK THIS METHOD ISN'T WORKING, THARA.
IF YOU HAVE A BETTER SUGGESTION--
HEY! HEY, IT'S THEM!
THEY WERE ON THE NEWS! FIGHTING THOSE KRYPTONIANS!
--OH HE IS CUTE! WOULDN'T MIND SEEING WHAT'S UNDER THAT ARMOR--
--MUCH HOTTER THAN SHE LOOKED ON TV--
CAN WE GET AN AUTOGRAPH?

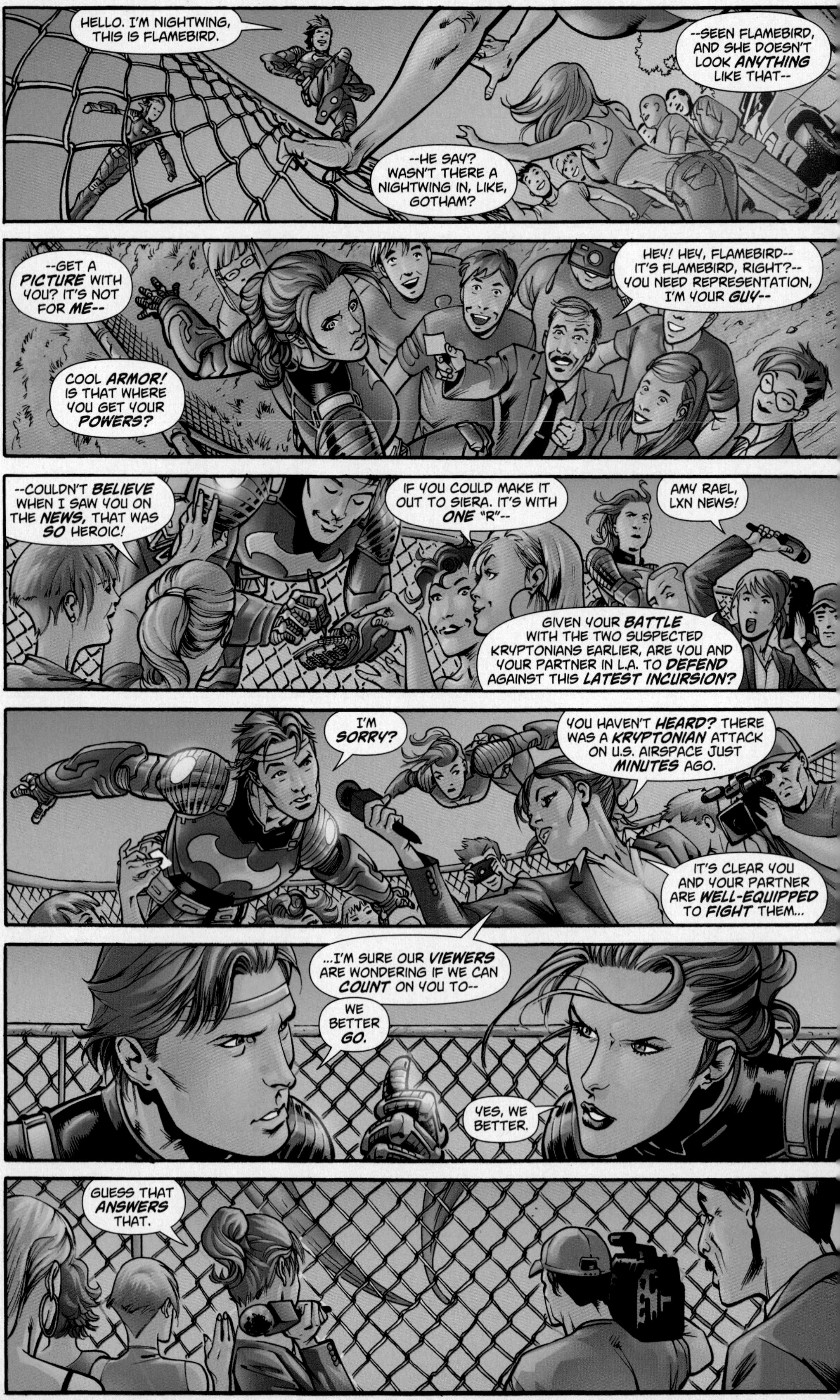
HELLO. I'M NIGHTWING, THIS IS FLAMEBIRD.
--SEEN FLAMEBIRD, AND SHE DOESN'T LOOK ANYTHING LIKE THAT--
--HE SAY? WASN'T THERE A NIGHTWING IN, LIKE, GOTHAM?
--GET A PICTURE WITH YOU? IT'S NOT FOR ME--
HEY! HEY, FLAMEBIRD-- IT'S FLAMEBIRD, RIGHT?-- YOU NEED REPRESENTATION, I'M YOUR GUY--
COOL ARMOR! IS THAT WHERE YOU GET YOUR POWERS?
--COULDN'T BELIEVE WHEN I SAW YOU ON THE NEWS, THAT WAS SO HEROIC!
IF YOU COULD MAKE IT OUT TO SIERA. IT'S WITH ONE "R"--
AMY RAEL, LXN NEWS!
GIVEN YOUR BATTLE WITH THE TWO SUSPECTED KRYPTONIANS EARLIER, ARE YOU AND YOUR PARTNER IN L.A. TO DEFEND AGAINST THIS LATEST INCURSION?
I'M SORRY?
YOU HAVEN'T HEARD? THERE WAS A KRYPTONIAN ATTACK ON U.S. AIRSPACE JUST MINUTES AGO.
IT'S CLEAR YOU AND YOUR PARTNER ARE WELL-EQUIPPED TO FIGHT THEM...
...I'M SURE OUR VIEWERS ARE WONDERING IF WE CAN COUNT ON YOU TO--
WE BETTER GO.
YES, WE BETTER.
GUESS THAT ANSWERS THAT.

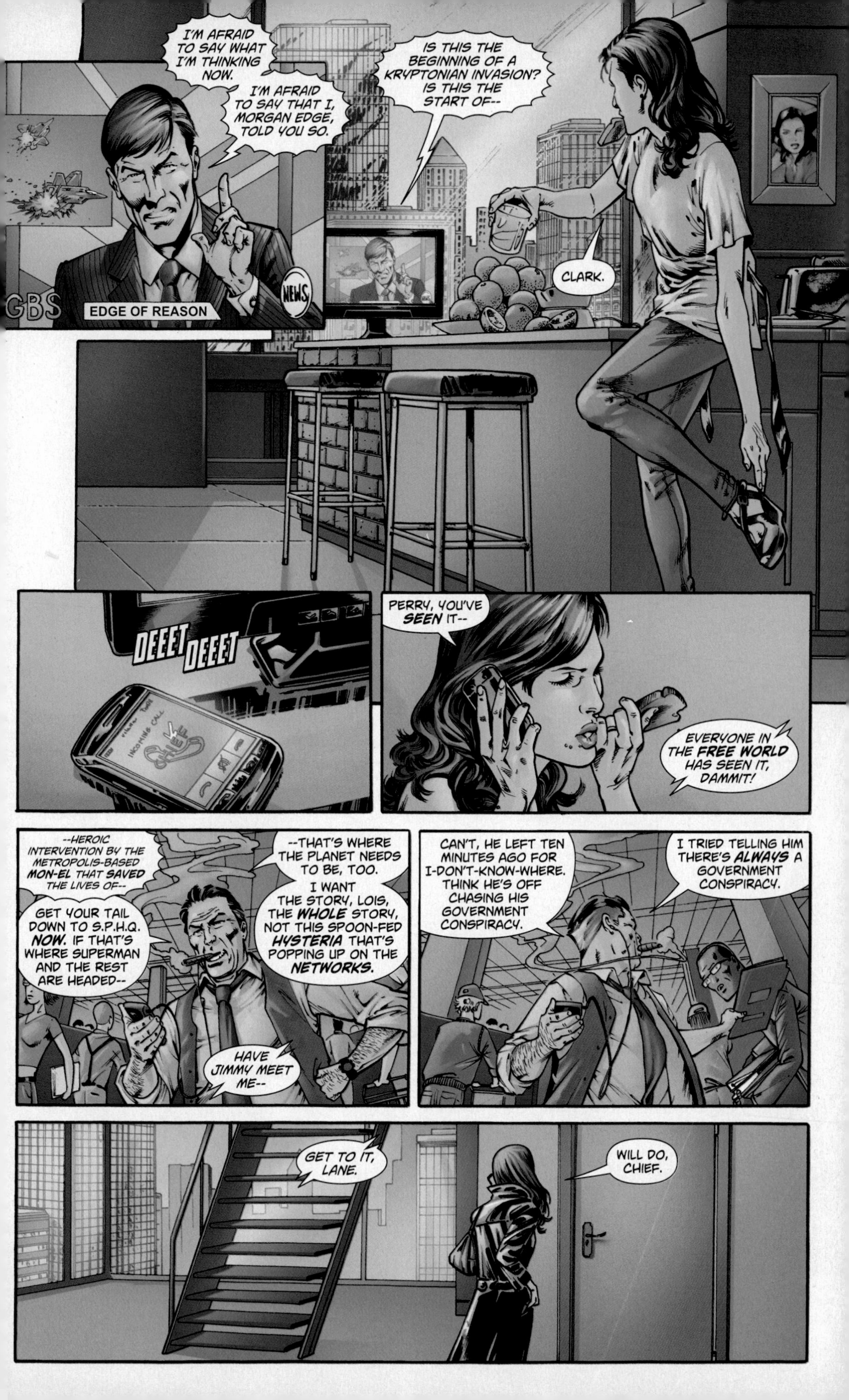
I'M AFRAID TO SAY WHAT I'M THINKING NOW.
I'M AFRAID TO SAY THAT I, MORGAN EDGE, TOLD YOU SO.
GBS
EDGE OF REASON
NEWS
IS THIS THE BEGINNING OF A KRYPTONIAN INVASION? IS THIS THE START OF--
CLARK.
DEEET DEEET
INCOMING CALL
PERRY, YOU'VE SEEN IT--
EVERYONE IN THE FREE WORLD HAS SEEN IT, DAMMIT!
--HEROIC INTERVENTION BY THE METROPOLIS-BASED MON-EL THAT SAVED THE LIVES OF--
GET YOUR TAIL DOWN TO S.P.H.Q. NOW. IF THAT'S WHERE SUPERMAN AND THE REST ARE HEADED--
--THAT'S WHERE THE PLANET NEEDS TO BE, TOO.
I WANT THE STORY, LOIS, THE WHOLE STORY, NOT THIS SPOON-FED HYSTERIA THAT'S POPPING UP ON THE NETWORKS.
HAVE JIMMY MEET ME--
CAN'T, HE LEFT TEN MINUTES AGO FOR I-DON'T-KNOW-WHERE. THINK HE'S OFF CHASING HIS GOVERNMENT CONSPIRACY.
I TRIED TELLING HIM THERE'S ALWAYS A GOVERNMENT CONSPIRACY.
GET TO IT, LANE.
WILL DO, CHIEF.

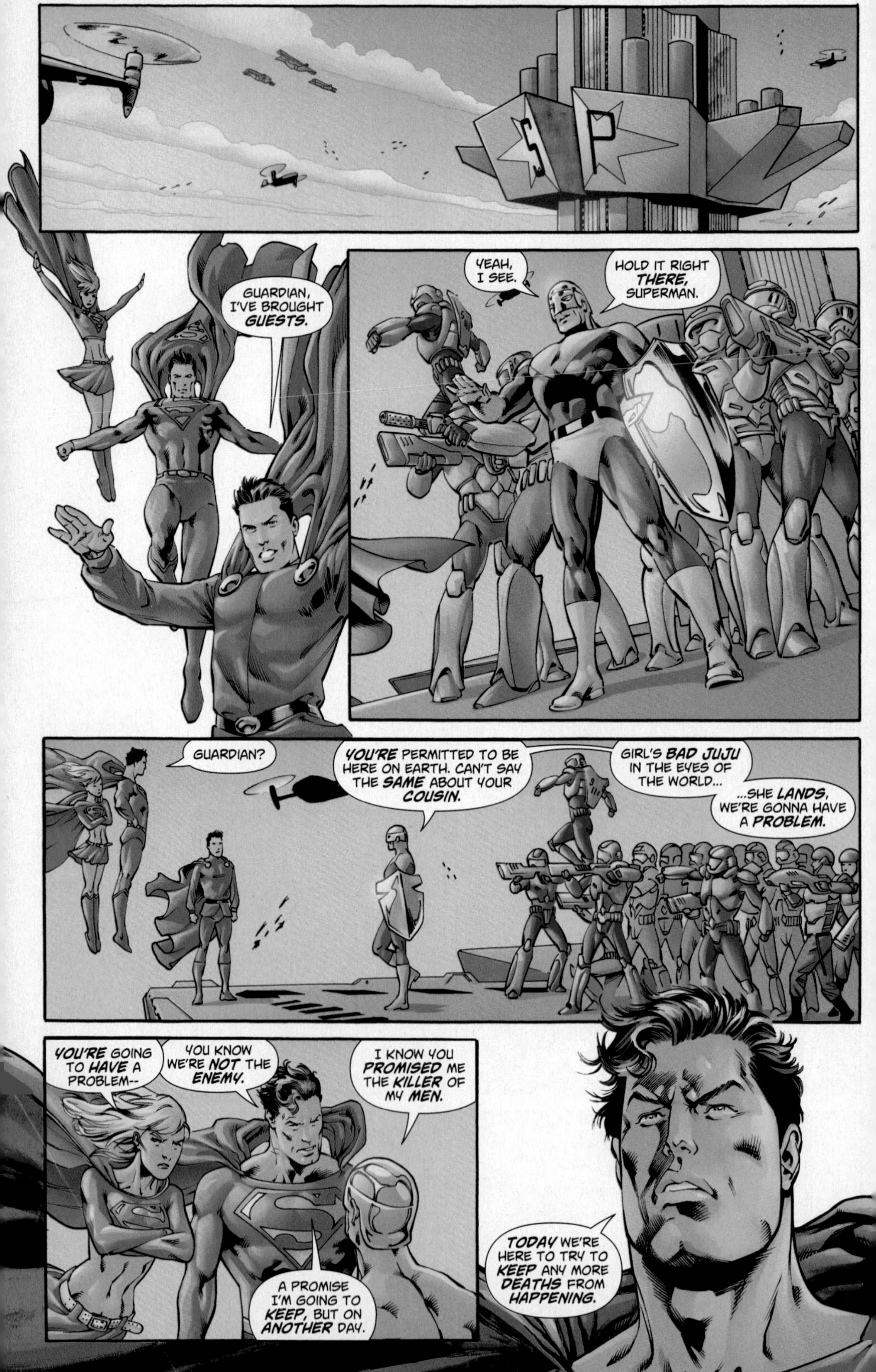
GUARDIAN, I'VE BROUGHT GUESTS.
YEAH, I SEE.
HOLD IT RIGHT THERE, SUPERMAN.
GUARDIAN?
YOU'RE PERMITTED TO BE HERE ON EARTH. CAN'T SAY THE SAME ABOUT YOUR COUSIN.
GIRL'S BAD JUJU IN THE EYES OF THE WORLD...
...SHE LANDS, WE'RE GONNA HAVE A PROBLEM.
YOU'RE GOING TO HAVE A PROBLEM--
YOU KNOW WE'RE NOT THE ENEMY.
I KNOW YOU PROMISED ME THE KILLER OF MY MEN.
A PROMISE I'M GOING TO KEEP, BUT ON ANOTHER DAY.
TODAY WE'RE HERE TO TRY TO KEEP ANY MORE DEATHS FROM HAPPENING.

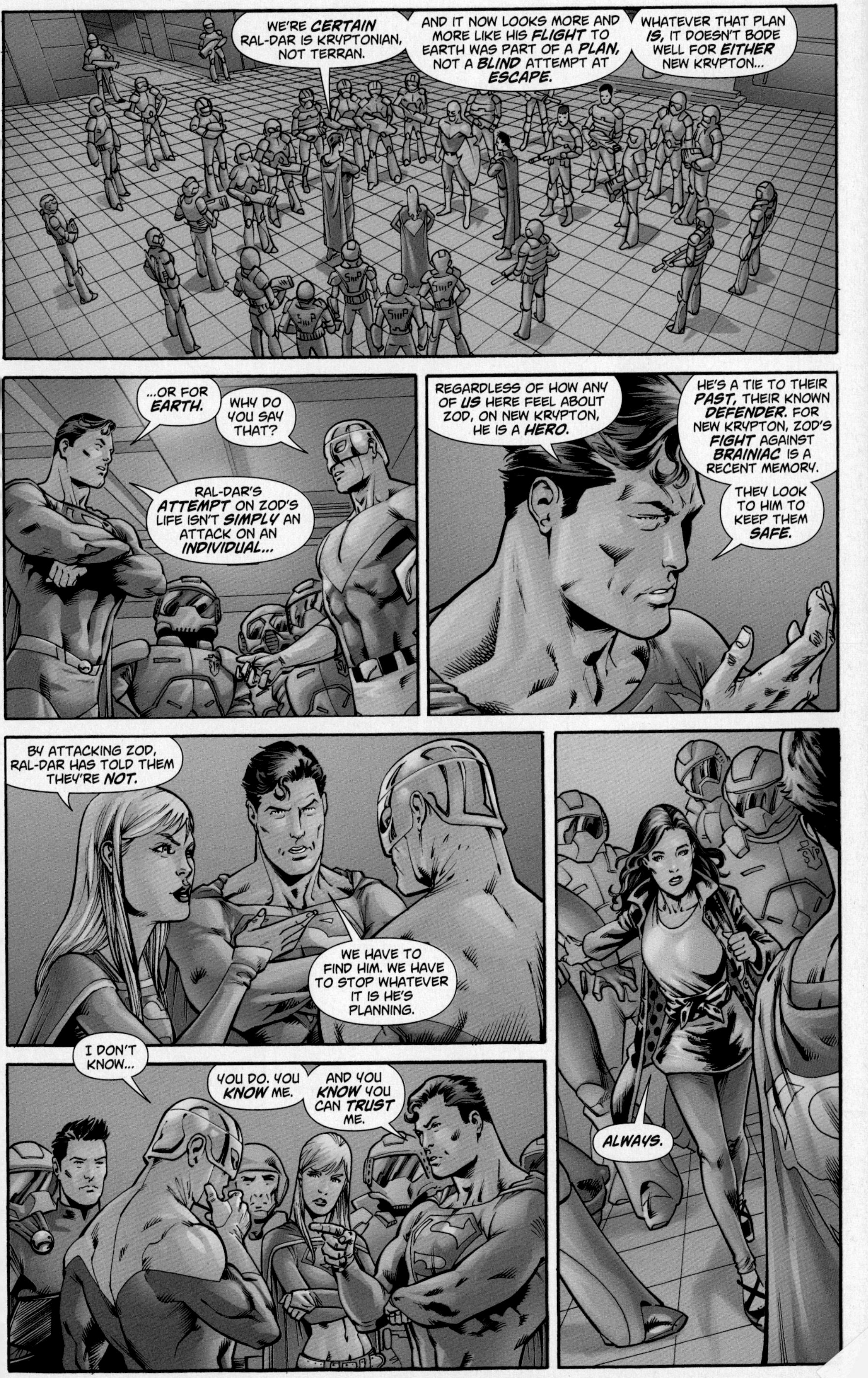
WE'RE CERTAIN RAL-DAR IS KRYPTONIAN, NOT TERRAN.
AND IT NOW LOOKS MORE AND MORE LIKE HIS FLIGHT TO EARTH WAS PART OF A PLAN, NOT A BLIND ATTEMPT AT ESCAPE.
WHATEVER THAT PLAN IS, IT DOESN'T BODE WELL FOR EITHER NEW KRYPTON...
...OR FOR EARTH.
WHY DO YOU SAY THAT?
RAL-DAR'S ATTEMPT ON ZOD'S LIFE ISN'T SIMPLY AN ATTACK ON AN INDIVIDUAL...
REGARDLESS OF HOW ANY OF US HERE FEEL ABOUT ZOD, ON NEW KRYPTON, HE IS A HERO.
HE'S A TIE TO THEIR PAST, THEIR KNOWN DEFENDER. FOR NEW KRYPTON, ZOD'S FIGHT AGAINST BRAINIAC IS A RECENT MEMORY.
THEY LOOK TO HIM TO KEEP THEM SAFE.
BY ATTACKING ZOD, RAL-DAR HAS TOLD THEM THEY'RE NOT.
WE HAVE TO FIND HIM. WE HAVE TO STOP WHATEVER IT IS HE'S PLANNING.
I DON'T KNOW...
YOU DO. YOU KNOW ME.
AND YOU KNOW YOU CAN TRUST ME.
ALWAYS.

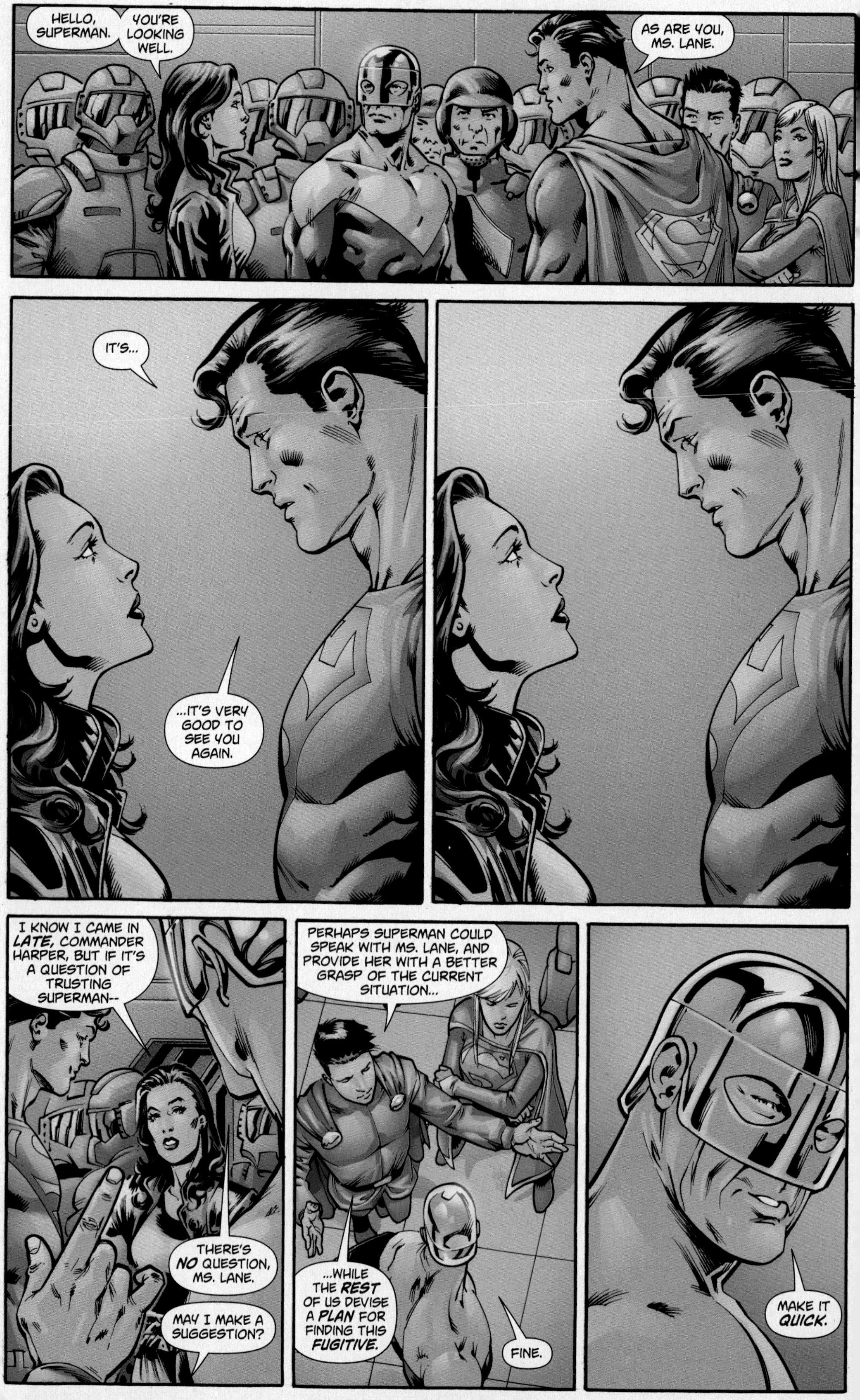
HELLO, SUPERMAN.
YOU'RE LOOKING WELL.
AS ARE YOU, MS. LANE.
IT'S...
...IT'S VERY GOOD TO SEE YOU AGAIN.
I KNOW I CAME IN LATE, COMMANDER HARPER, BUT IF IT'S A QUESTION OF TRUSTING SUPERMAN--
THERE'S NO QUESTION, MS. LANE.
MAY I MAKE A SUGGESTION?
PERHAPS SUPERMAN COULD SPEAK WITH MS. LANE, AND PROVIDE HER WITH A BETTER GRASP OF THE CURRENT SITUATION...
...WHILE THE REST OF US DEVISE A PLAN FOR FINDING THIS FUGITIVE.
FINE.
MAKE IT QUICK.

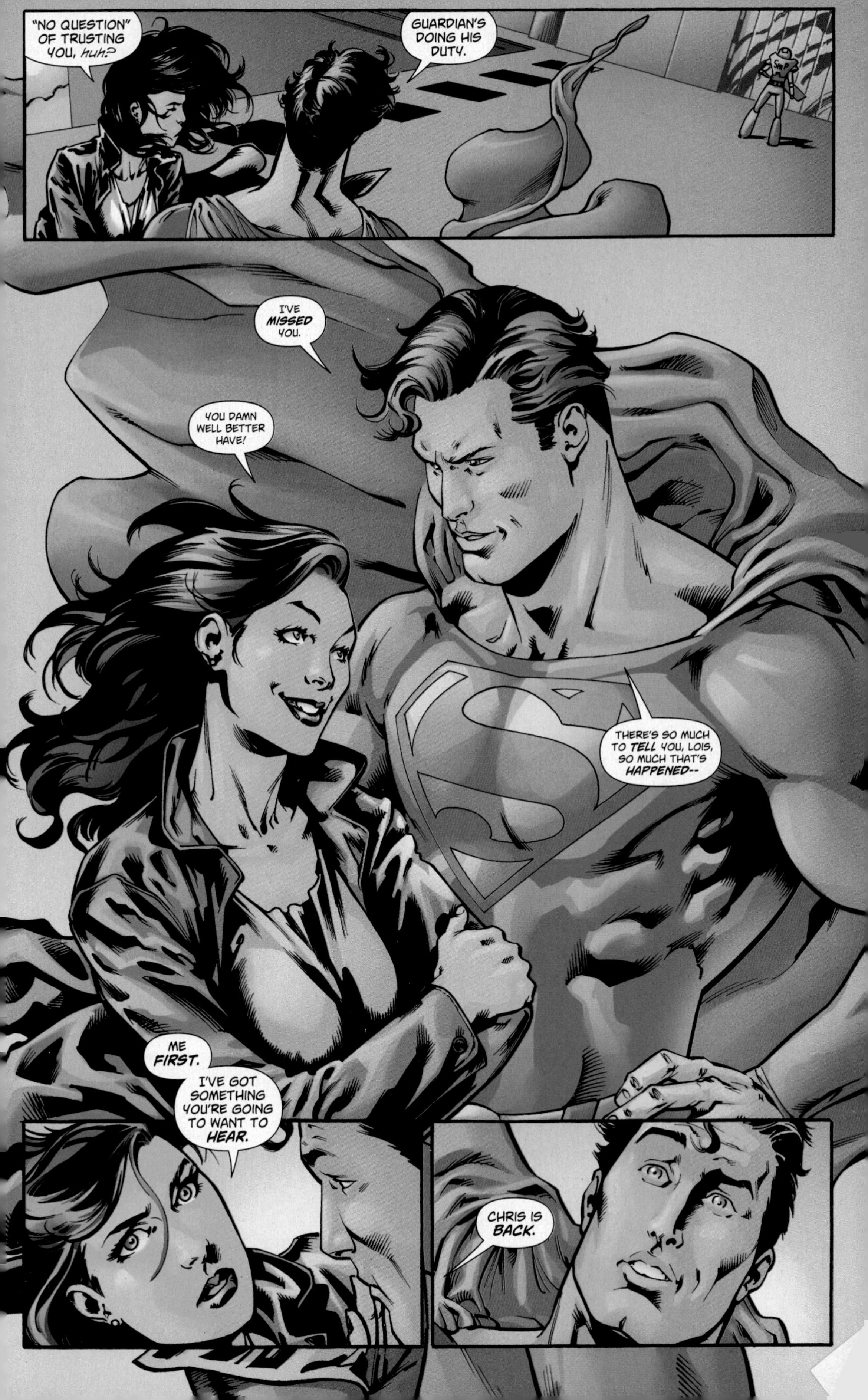
"NO QUESTION" OF TRUSTING YOU, *huh?*
GUARDIAN'S DOING HIS DUTY.
I'VE **MISSED** YOU.
YOU DAMN WELL BETTER HAVE!
THERE'S SO MUCH TO **TELL** YOU, LOIS, SO MUCH THAT'S **HAPPENED--**
ME **FIRST**.
I'VE GOT SOMETHING YOU'RE GOING TO WANT TO **HEAR**.
CHRIS IS **BACK**.

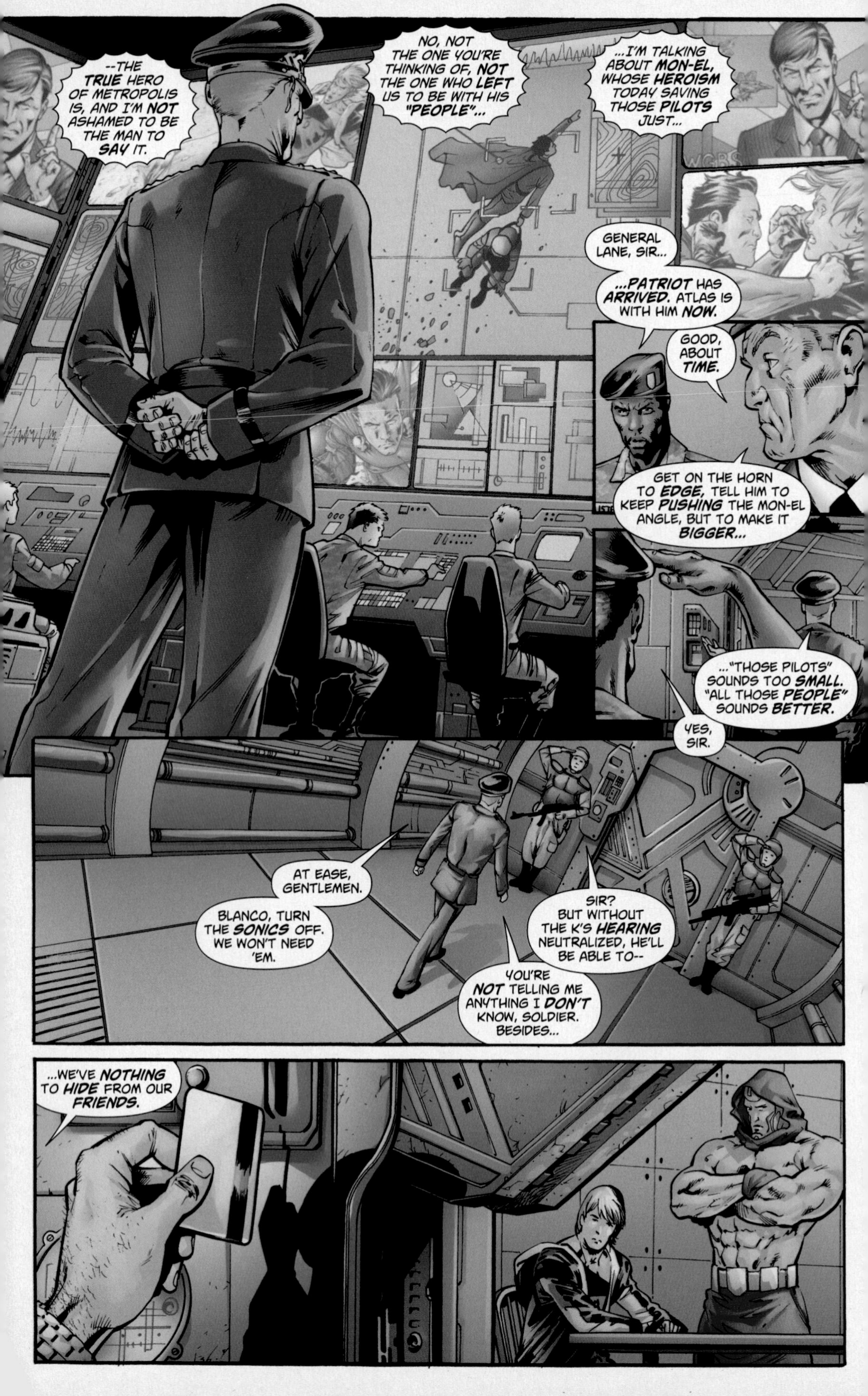

--THE TRUE HERO OF METROPOLIS IS, AND I'M NOT ASHAMED TO BE THE MAN TO SAY IT.
NO, NOT THE ONE YOU'RE THINKING OF, NOT THE ONE WHO LEFT US TO BE WITH HIS "PEOPLE"...
...I'M TALKING ABOUT MON-EL, WHOSE HEROISM TODAY SAVING THOSE PILOTS JUST...
WGBS
GENERAL LANE, SIR...
...PATRIOT HAS ARRIVED. ATLAS IS WITH HIM NOW.
GOOD, ABOUT TIME.
GET ON THE HORN TO EDGE, TELL HIM TO KEEP PUSHING THE MON-EL ANGLE, BUT TO MAKE IT BIGGER...
..."THOSE PILOTS" SOUNDS TOO SMALL. "ALL THOSE PEOPLE" SOUNDS BETTER.
YES, SIR.
AT EASE, GENTLEMEN.
BLANCO, TURN THE SONICS OFF. WE WON'T NEED 'EM.
SIR? BUT WITHOUT THE K'S HEARING NEUTRALIZED, HE'LL BE ABLE TO--
YOU'RE NOT TELLING ME ANYTHING I DON'T KNOW, SOLDIER. BESIDES...
...WE'VE NOTHING TO HIDE FROM OUR FRIENDS.

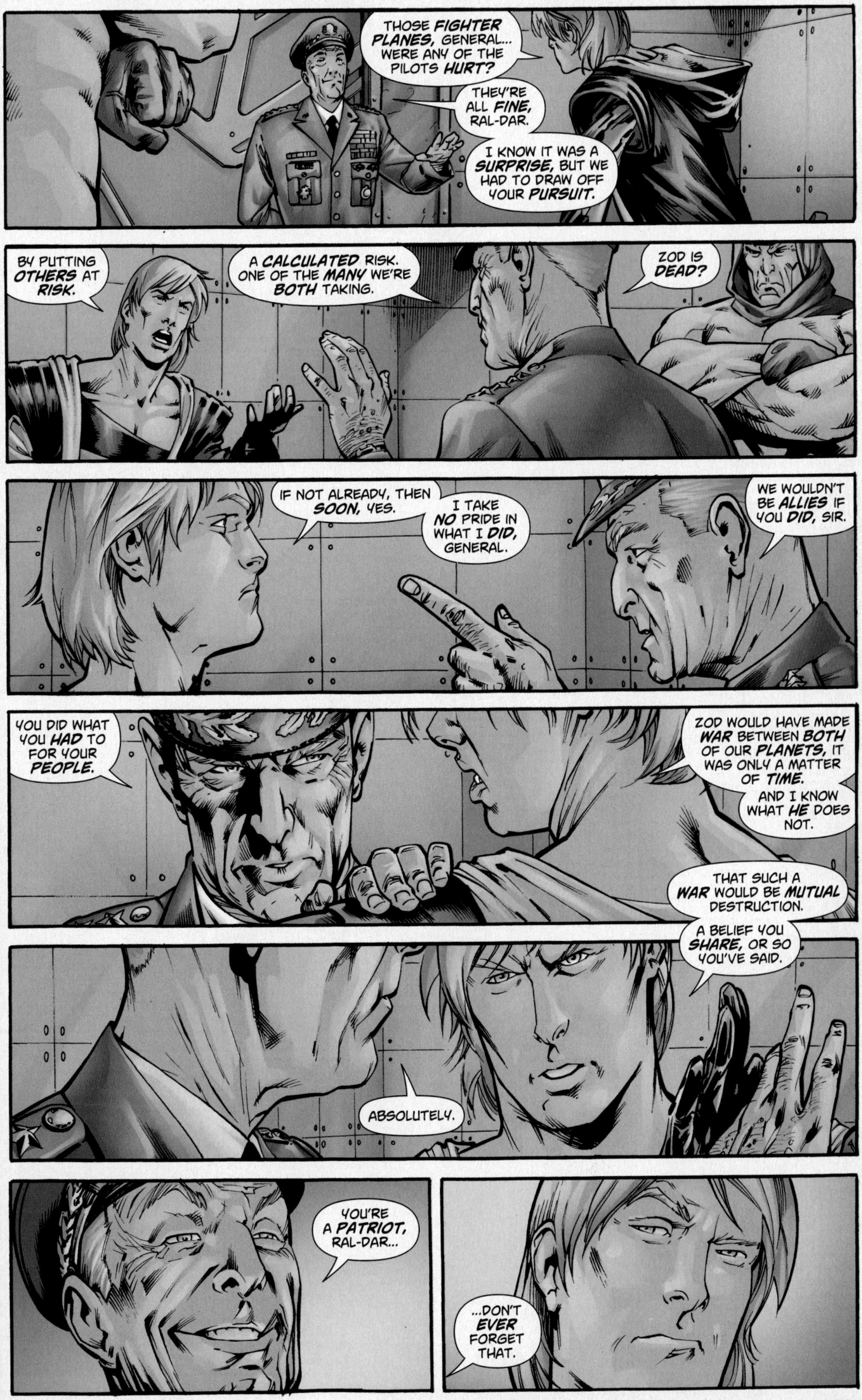

THOSE FIGHTER PLANES, GENERAL... WERE ANY OF THE PILOTS HURT?
THEY'RE ALL FINE, RAL-DAR.
I KNOW IT WAS A SURPRISE, BUT WE HAD TO DRAW OFF YOUR PURSUIT.
BY PUTTING OTHERS AT RISK.
A CALCULATED RISK. ONE OF THE MANY WE'RE BOTH TAKING.
ZOD IS DEAD?
IF NOT ALREADY, THEN SOON, YES.
I TAKE NO PRIDE IN WHAT I DID, GENERAL.
WE WOULDN'T BE ALLIES IF YOU DID, SIR.
YOU DID WHAT YOU HAD TO FOR YOUR PEOPLE.
ZOD WOULD HAVE MADE WAR BETWEEN BOTH OF OUR PLANETS, IT WAS ONLY A MATTER OF TIME.
AND I KNOW WHAT HE DOES NOT.
THAT SUCH A WAR WOULD BE MUTUAL DESTRUCTION.
A BELIEF YOU SHARE, OR SO YOU'VE SAID.
ABSOLUTELY.
YOU'RE A PATRIOT, RAL-DAR...
...DON'T EVER FORGET THAT.

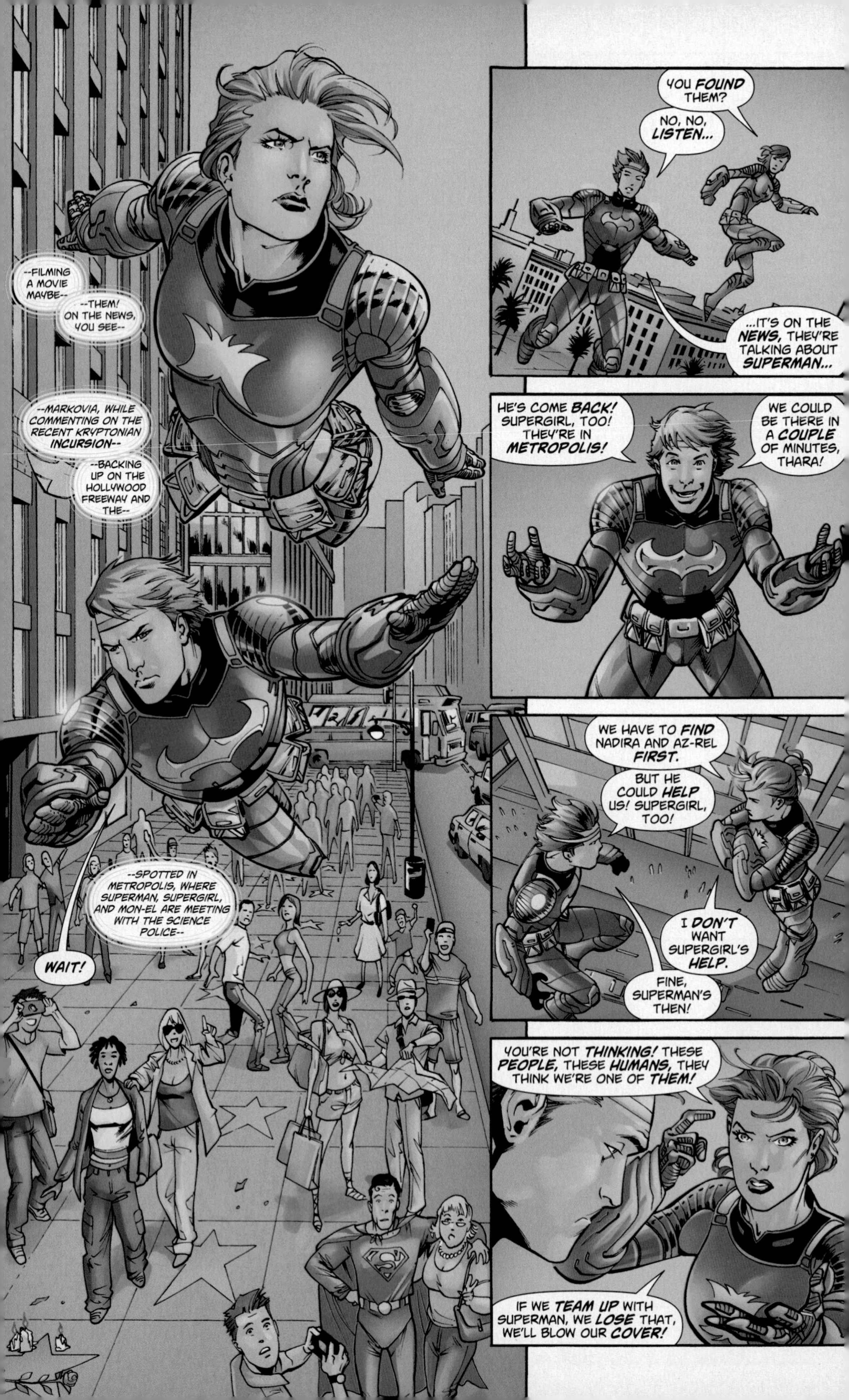

--FILMING A MOVIE MAYBE--
--THEM! ON THE NEWS, YOU SEE--
--MARKOVIA, WHILE COMMENTING ON THE RECENT KRYPTONIAN INCURSION--
--BACKING UP ON THE HOLLYWOOD FREEWAY AND THE--
--SPOTTED IN METROPOLIS, WHERE SUPERMAN, SUPERGIRL, AND MON-EL ARE MEETING WITH THE SCIENCE POLICE--
WAIT!
YOU FOUND THEM?
NO, NO, LISTEN...
...IT'S ON THE NEWS, THEY'RE TALKING ABOUT SUPERMAN...
HE'S COME BACK! SUPERGIRL, TOO! THEY'RE IN METROPOLIS!
WE COULD BE THERE IN A COUPLE OF MINUTES, THARA!
WE HAVE TO FIND NADIRA AND AZ-REL FIRST.
BUT HE COULD HELP US! SUPERGIRL, TOO!
I DON'T WANT SUPERGIRL'S HELP.
FINE, SUPERMAN'S THEN!
YOU'RE NOT THINKING! THESE PEOPLE, THESE HUMANS, THEY THINK WE'RE ONE OF THEM!
IF WE TEAM UP WITH SUPERMAN, WE LOSE THAT, WE'LL BLOW OUR COVER!

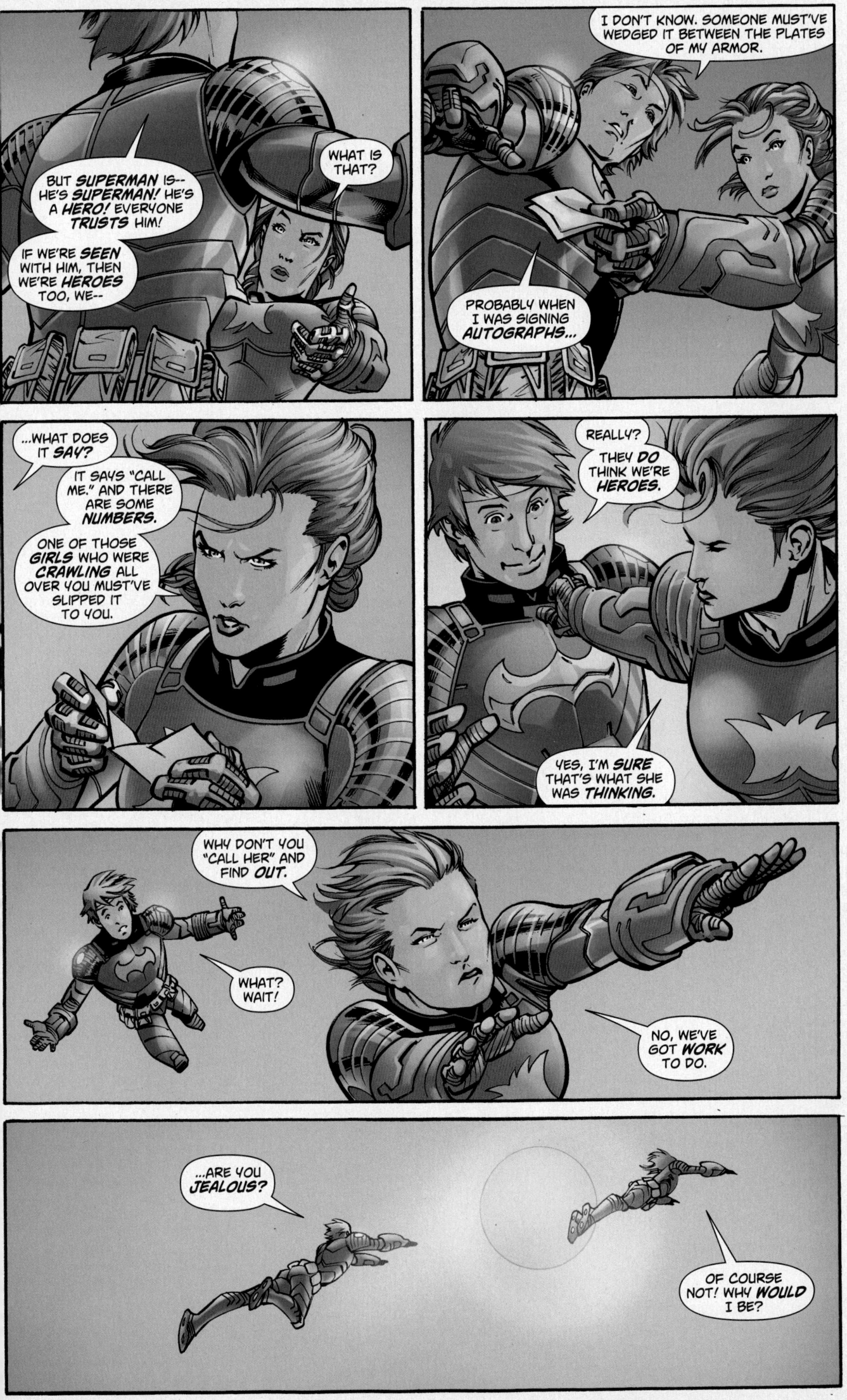
BUT SUPERMAN IS-- HE'S SUPERMAN! HE'S A HERO! EVERYONE TRUSTS HIM!
IF WE'RE SEEN WITH HIM, THEN WE'RE HEROES TOO, WE--
WHAT IS THAT?
I DON'T KNOW. SOMEONE MUST'VE WEDGED IT BETWEEN THE PLATES OF MY ARMOR.
PROBABLY WHEN I WAS SIGNING AUTOGRAPHS...
...WHAT DOES IT SAY?
IT SAYS "CALL ME." AND THERE ARE SOME NUMBERS.
ONE OF THOSE GIRLS WHO WERE CRAWLING ALL OVER YOU MUST'VE SLIPPED IT TO YOU.
REALLY? THEY DO THINK WE'RE HEROES.
YES, I'M SURE THAT'S WHAT SHE WAS THINKING.
WHY DON'T YOU "CALL HER" AND FIND OUT.
WHAT? WAIT!
NO, WE'VE GOT WORK TO DO.
...ARE YOU JEALOUS?
OF COURSE NOT! WHY WOULD I BE?

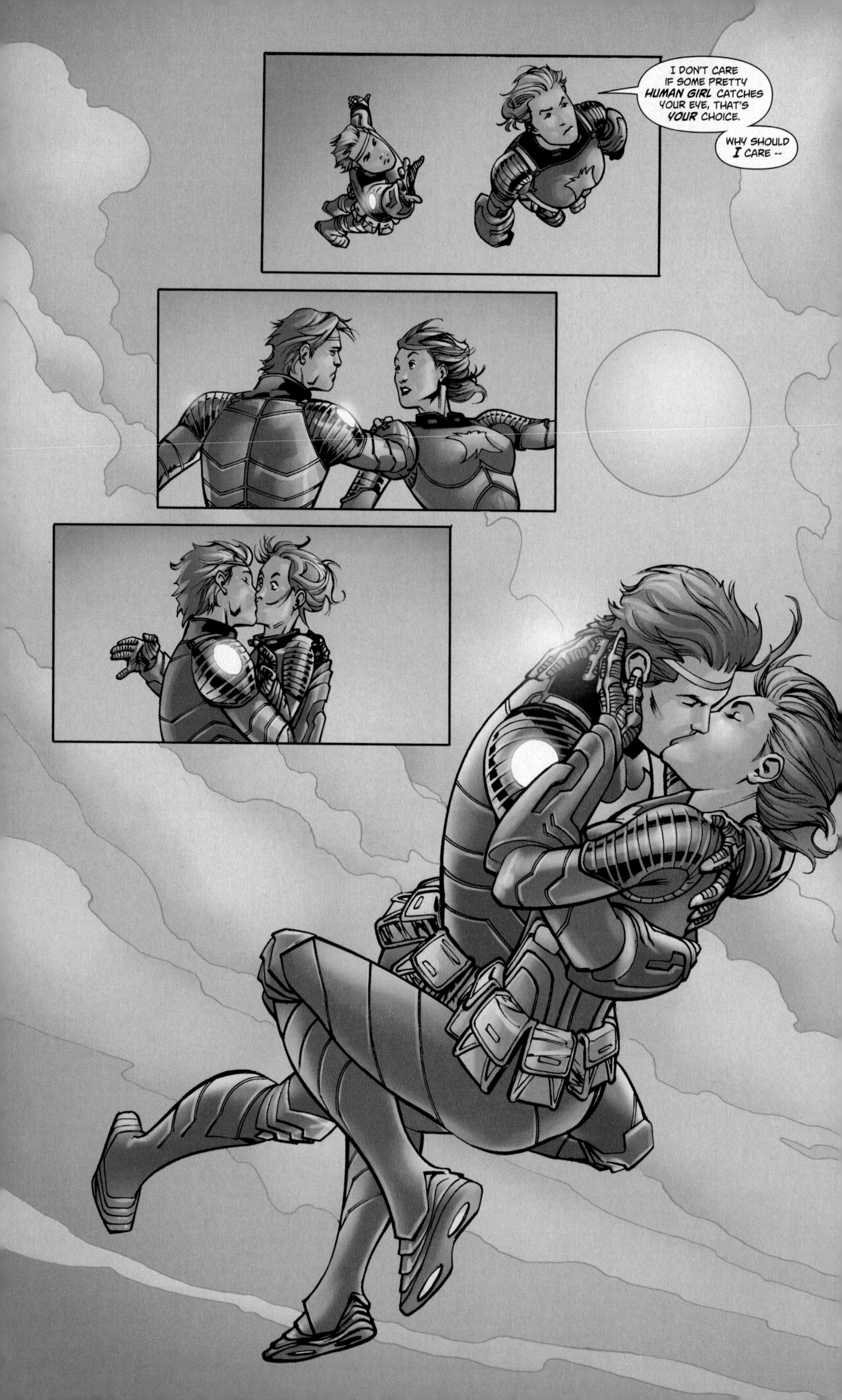
I DON'T CARE IF SOME PRETTY **HUMAN GIRL** CATCHES YOUR EYE, THAT'S **YOUR** CHOICE.
WHY SHOULD **I** CARE --

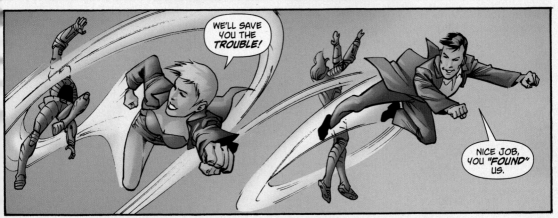

WE SHOULD KEEP LOOKING...

...YEAH, WE SHOULD--

WE'LL SAVE YOU THE *TROUBLE!*

NICE JOB, YOU *"FOUND"* US.

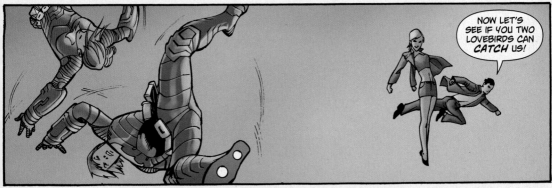

NOW LET'S SEE IF YOU TWO LOVEBIRDS CAN *CATCH* US!

WITH *PLEASURE.*

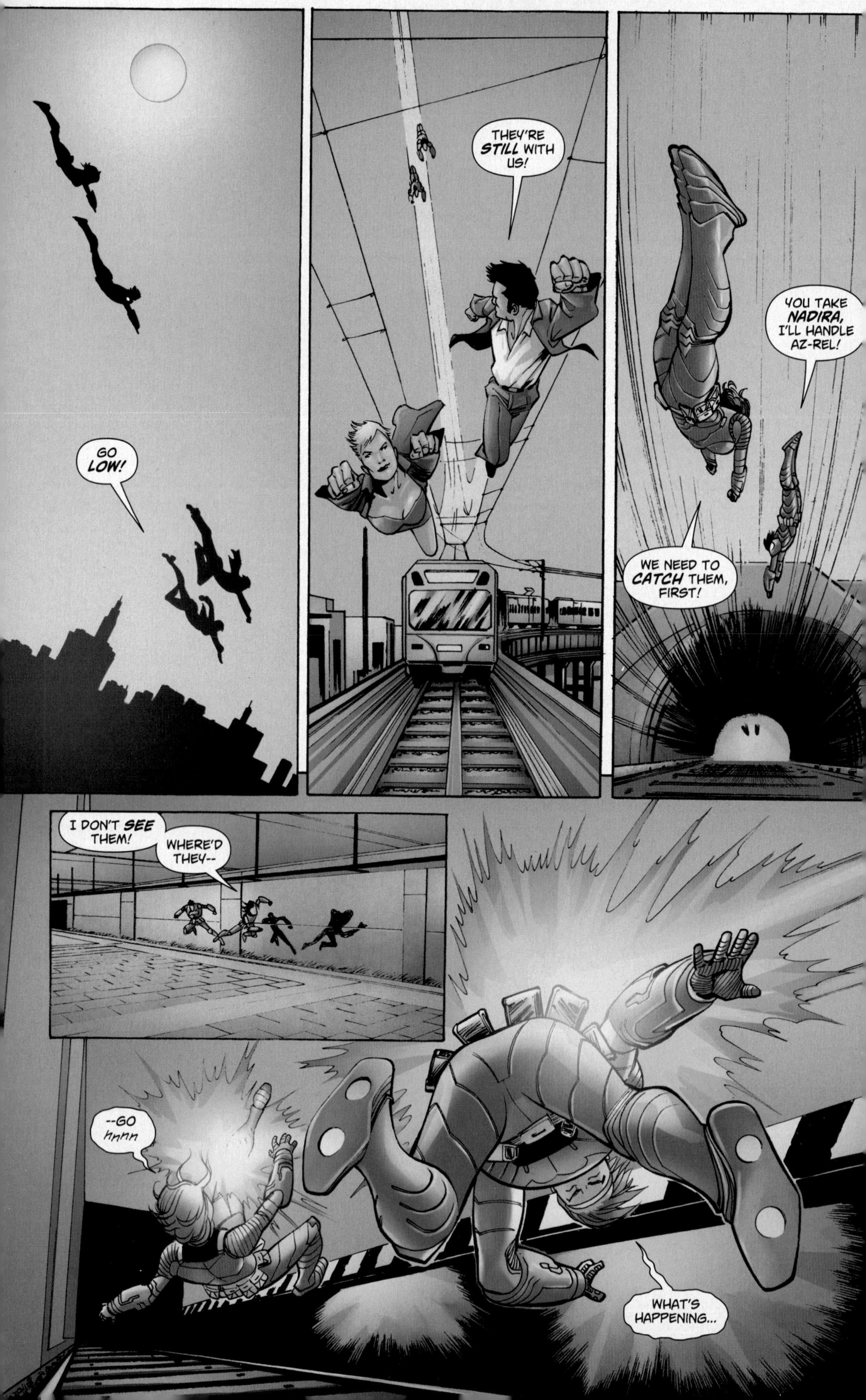
GO LOW!
THEY'RE STILL WITH US!
YOU TAKE NADIRA, I'LL HANDLE AZ-REL!
WE NEED TO CATCH THEM, FIRST!
I DON'T SEE THEM!
WHERE'D THEY--
--GO hnnn
WHAT'S HAPPENING...

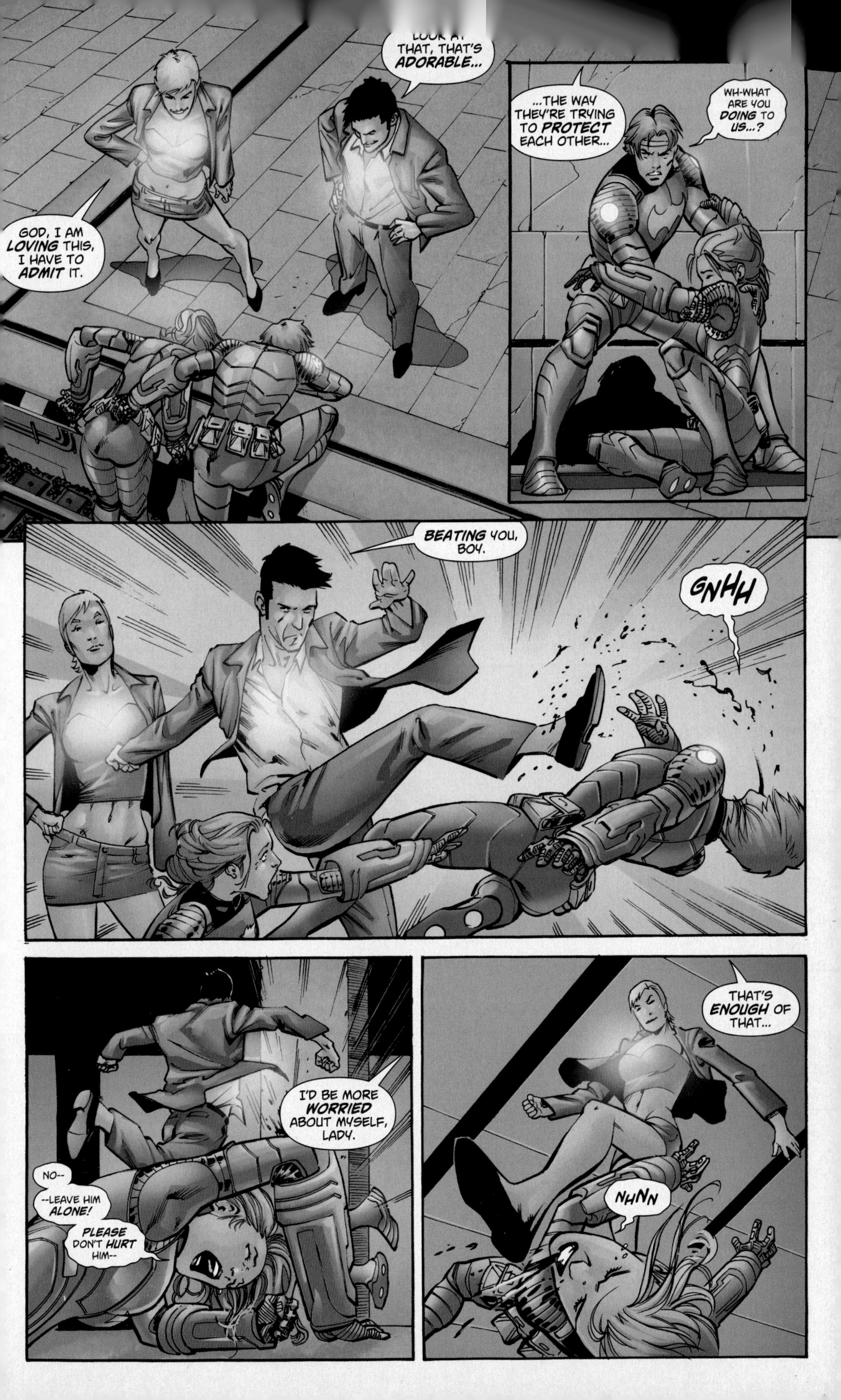

LOOK AT THAT, THAT'S ADORABLE...
GOD, I AM LOVING THIS, I HAVE TO ADMIT IT.
...THE WAY THEY'RE TRYING TO PROTECT EACH OTHER...
WH-WHAT ARE YOU DOING TO US...?
BEATING YOU, BOY.
GNHH
I'D BE MORE WORRIED ABOUT MYSELF, LADY.
NO--
--LEAVE HIM ALONE!
PLEASE DON'T HURT HIM--
THAT'S ENOUGH OF THAT...
NHNN

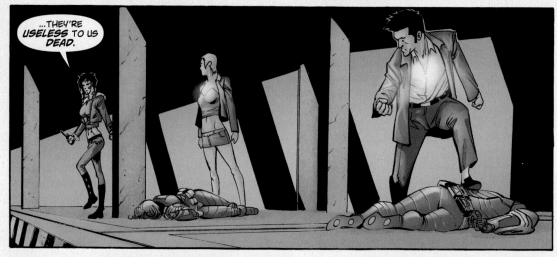

...THEY'RE *USELESS* TO US *DEAD.*

MY WORK I UNWORK...

INFORM GENERAL LANE THAT PHASE TWO IS *COMPLETE.*

MOVING TO PHASE *THREE.*

<SUPERGIRL 44>
COVER ART BY **FERNANDO DAGNINO** & **RAÚL FERNANDEZ** WITH **MAZI**

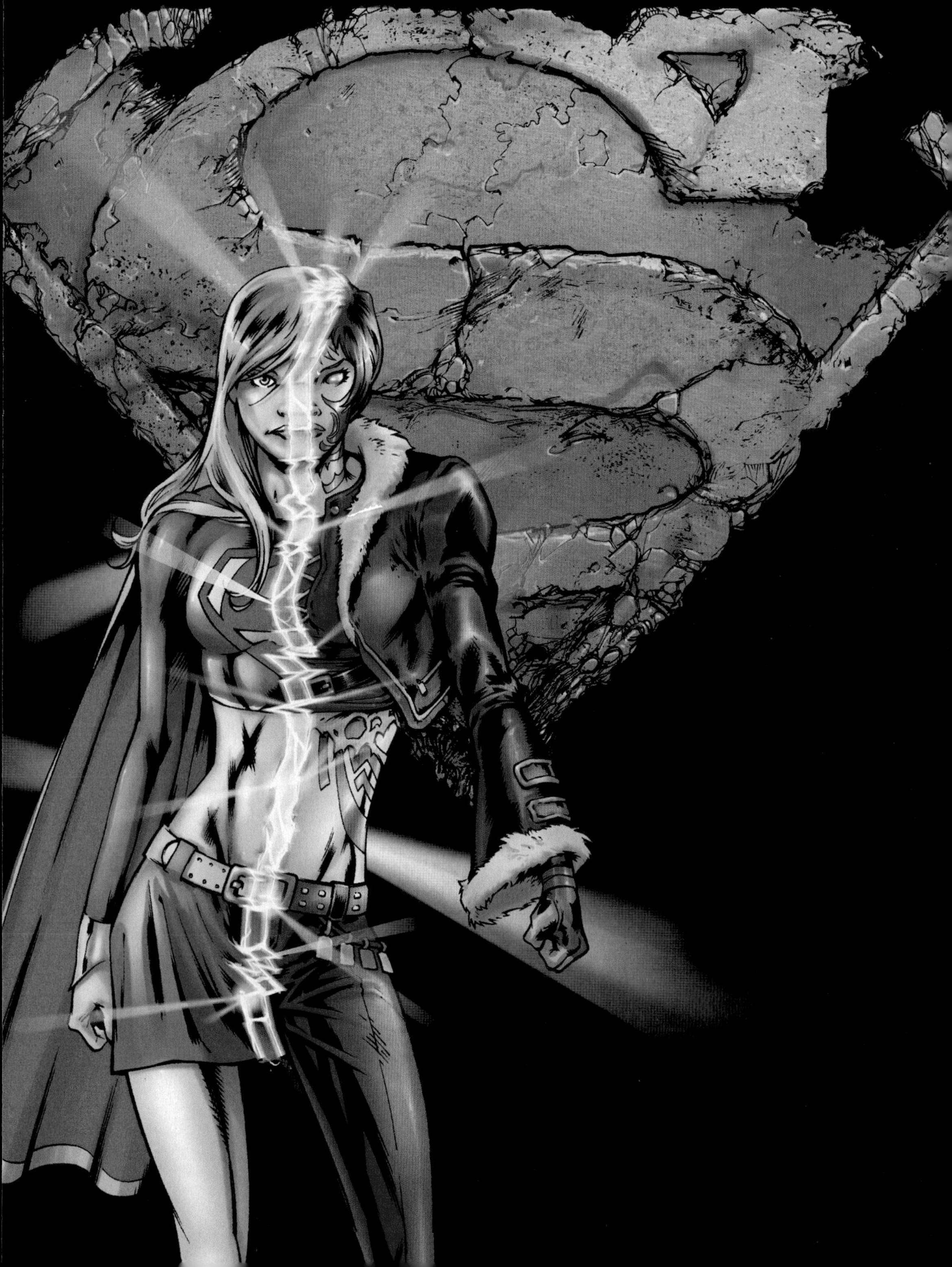

CODENAME: PATRIOT <PART THREE>

STERLING GATES – WRITER
JAMAL IGLE – PENCILLER
JON SIBAL – INKER

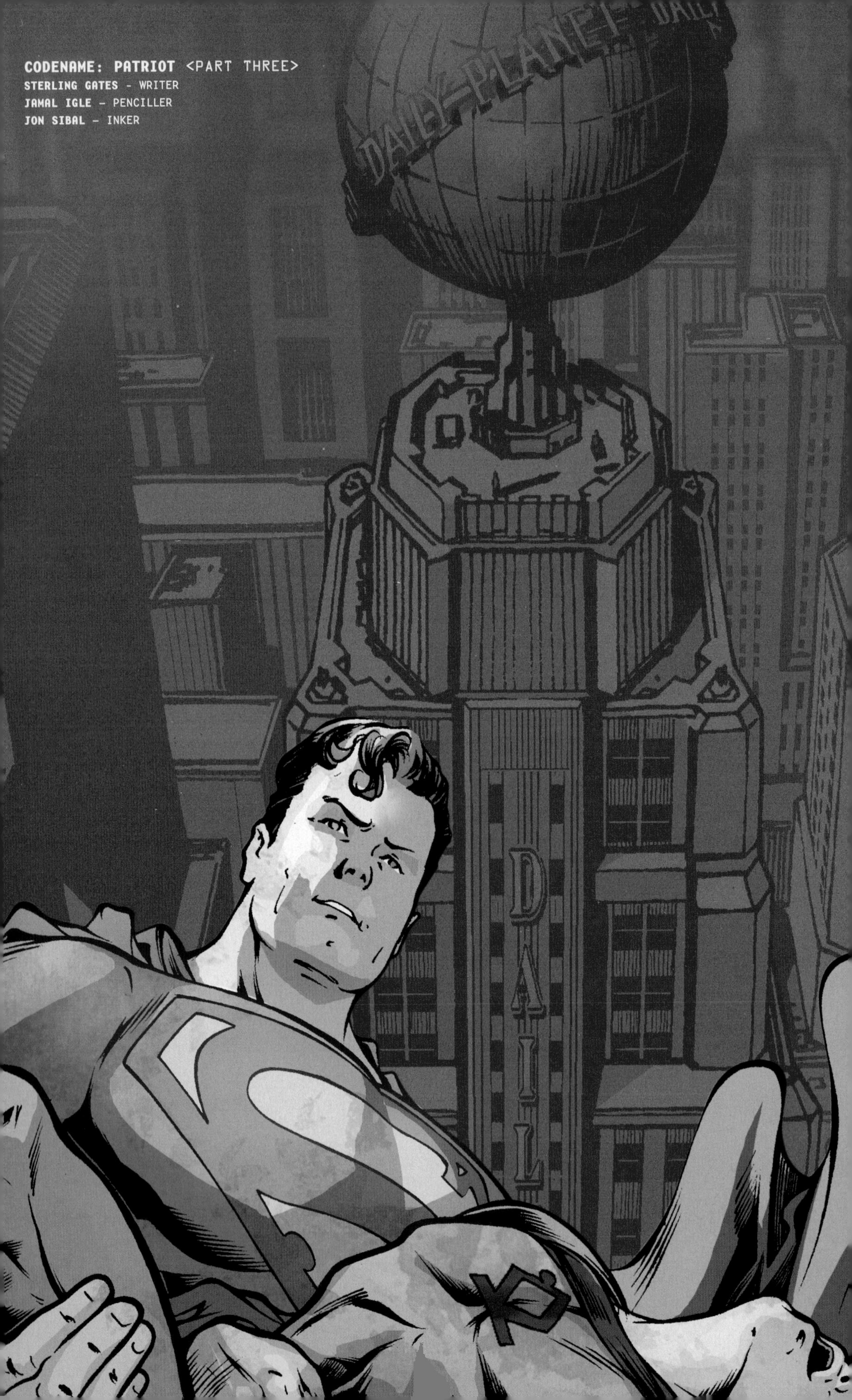

DAILY PLANET

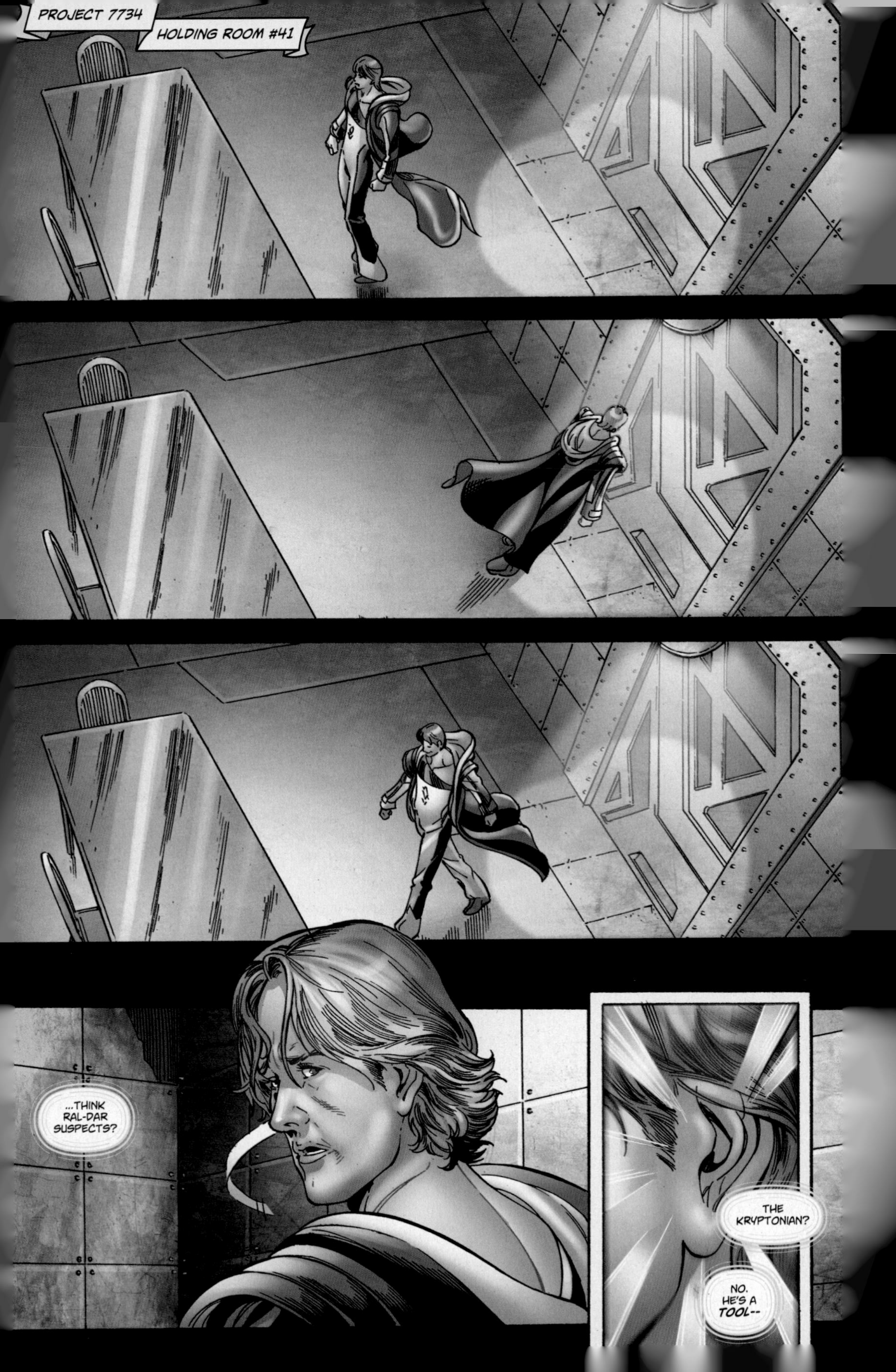
PROJECT 7734
HOLDING ROOM #41
...THINK RAL-DAR SUSPECTS?
THE KRYPTONIAN?
NO. HE'S A TOOL--

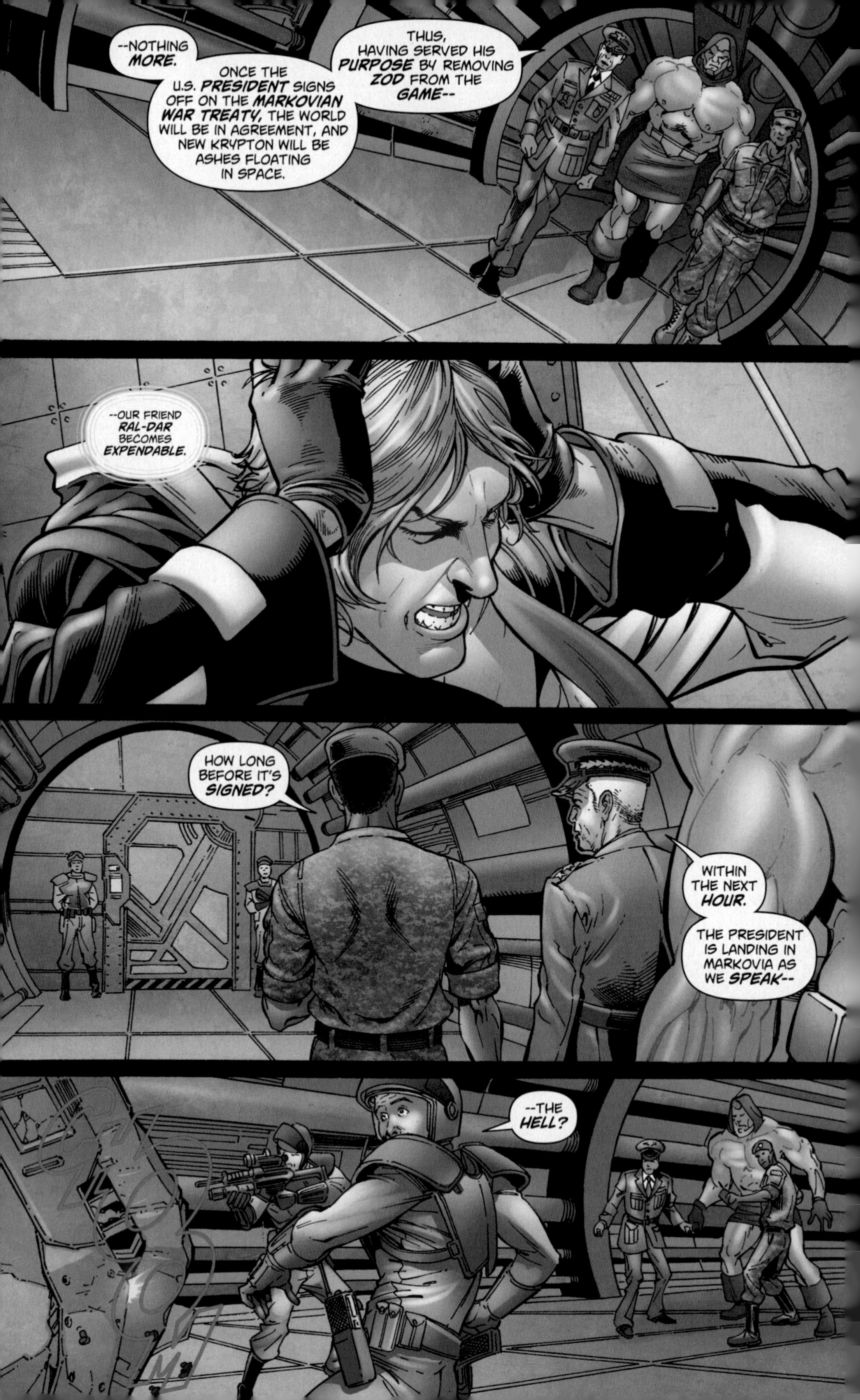
--NOTHING MORE.
ONCE THE U.S. PRESIDENT SIGNS OFF ON THE MARKOVIAN WAR TREATY, THE WORLD WILL BE IN AGREEMENT, AND NEW KRYPTON WILL BE ASHES FLOATING IN SPACE.
THUS, HAVING SERVED HIS PURPOSE BY REMOVING ZOD FROM THE GAME--
--OUR FRIEND RAL-DAR BECOMES EXPENDABLE.
HOW LONG BEFORE IT'S SIGNED?
WITHIN THE NEXT HOUR.
THE PRESIDENT IS LANDING IN MARKOVIA AS WE SPEAK--
--THE HELL?

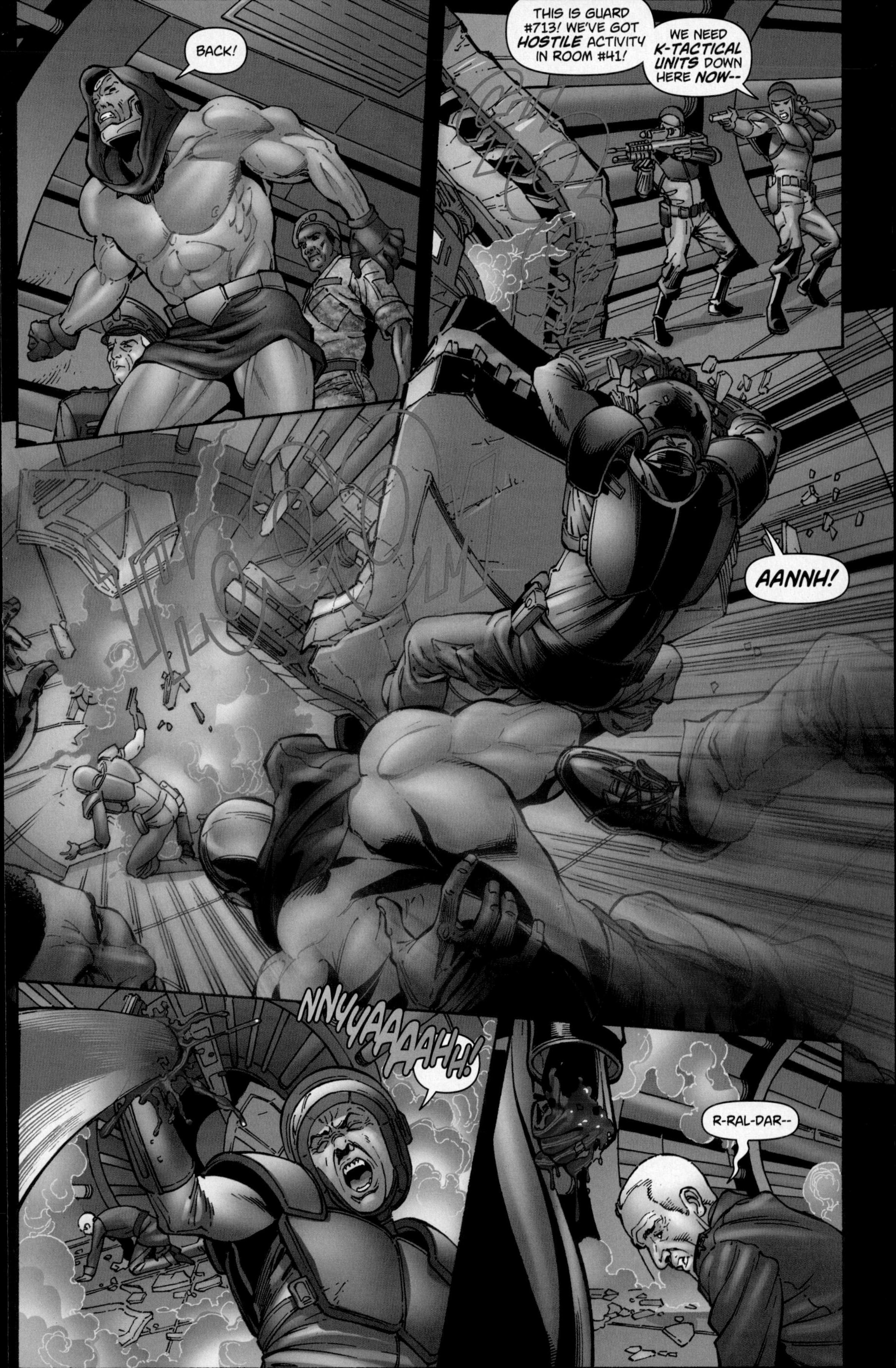
BACK!
THIS IS GUARD #713! WE'VE GOT HOSTILE ACTIVITY IN ROOM #41!
WE NEED K-TACTICAL UNITS DOWN HERE NOW--
AANNH!
NNYYAAAAAHH!
R-RAL-DAR--

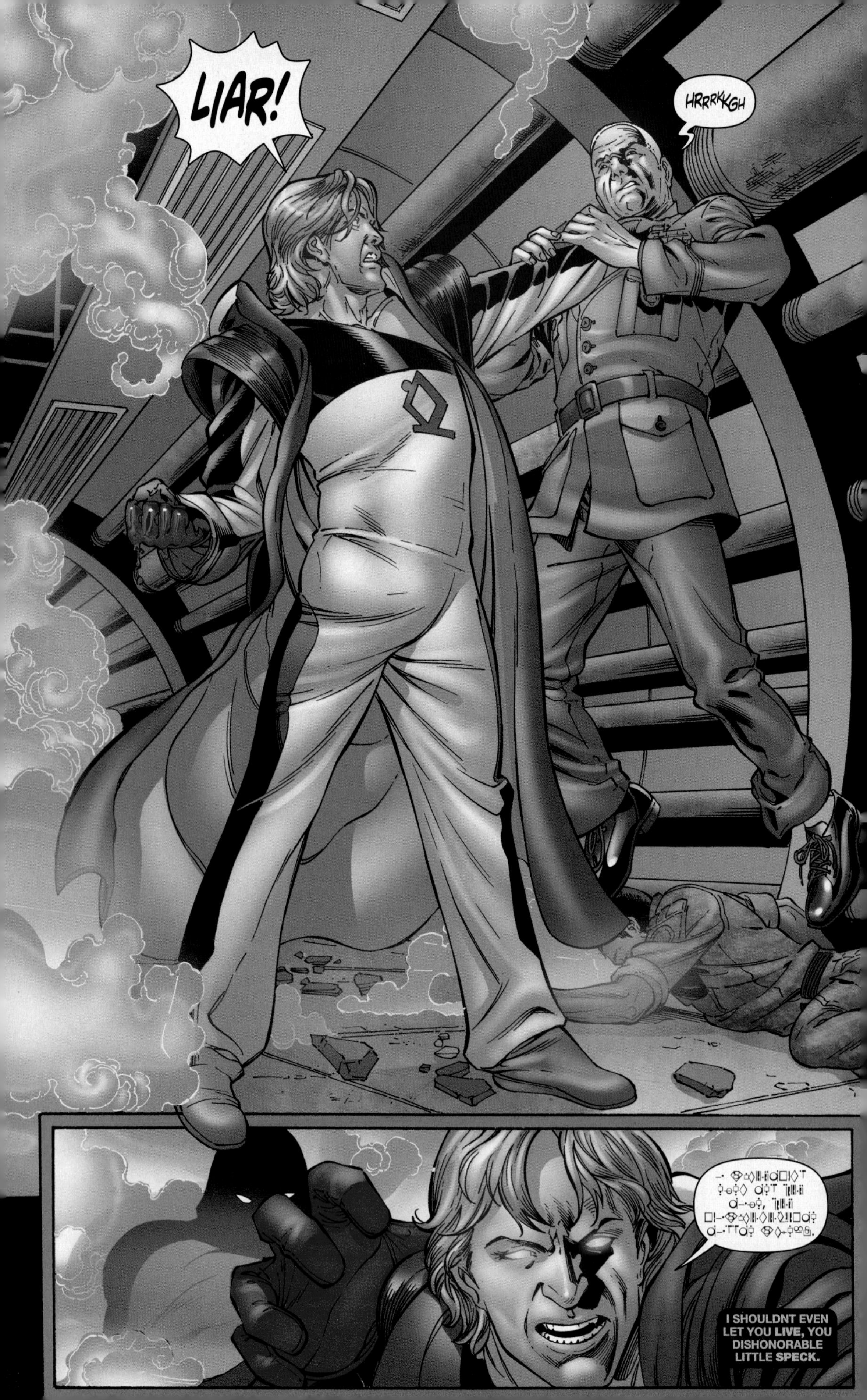
LIAR!
HRRRKKGH
I SHOULDNT EVEN LET YOU LIVE, YOU DISHONORABLE LITTLE SPECK.

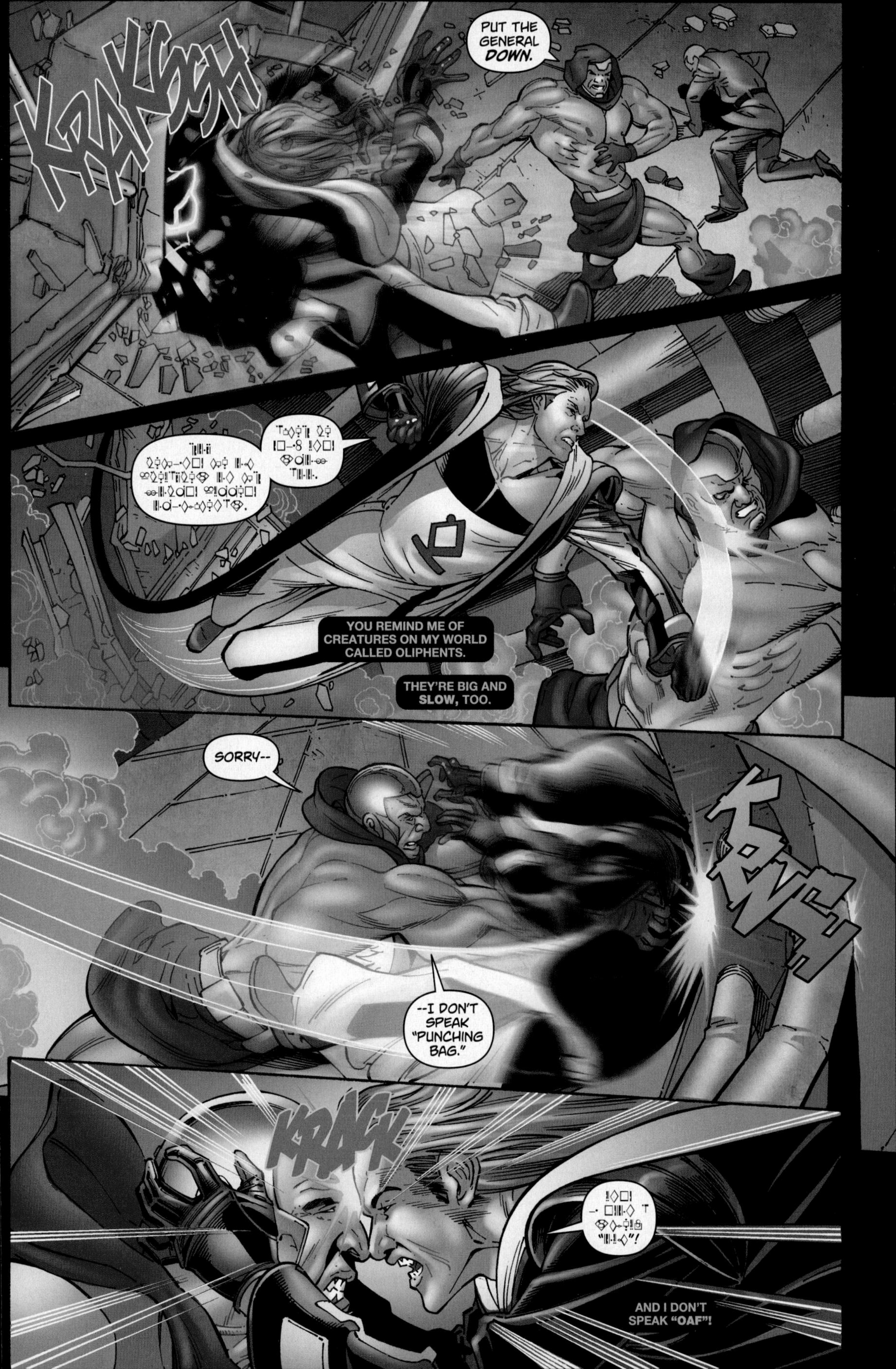
KRAKSCH
PUT THE GENERAL DOWN.
YOU REMIND ME OF CREATURES ON MY WORLD CALLED OLIPHENTS.
THEY'RE BIG AND SLOW, TOO.
SORRY--
--I DON'T SPEAK "PUNCHING BAG."
KRACK
AND I DON'T SPEAK "OAF"!

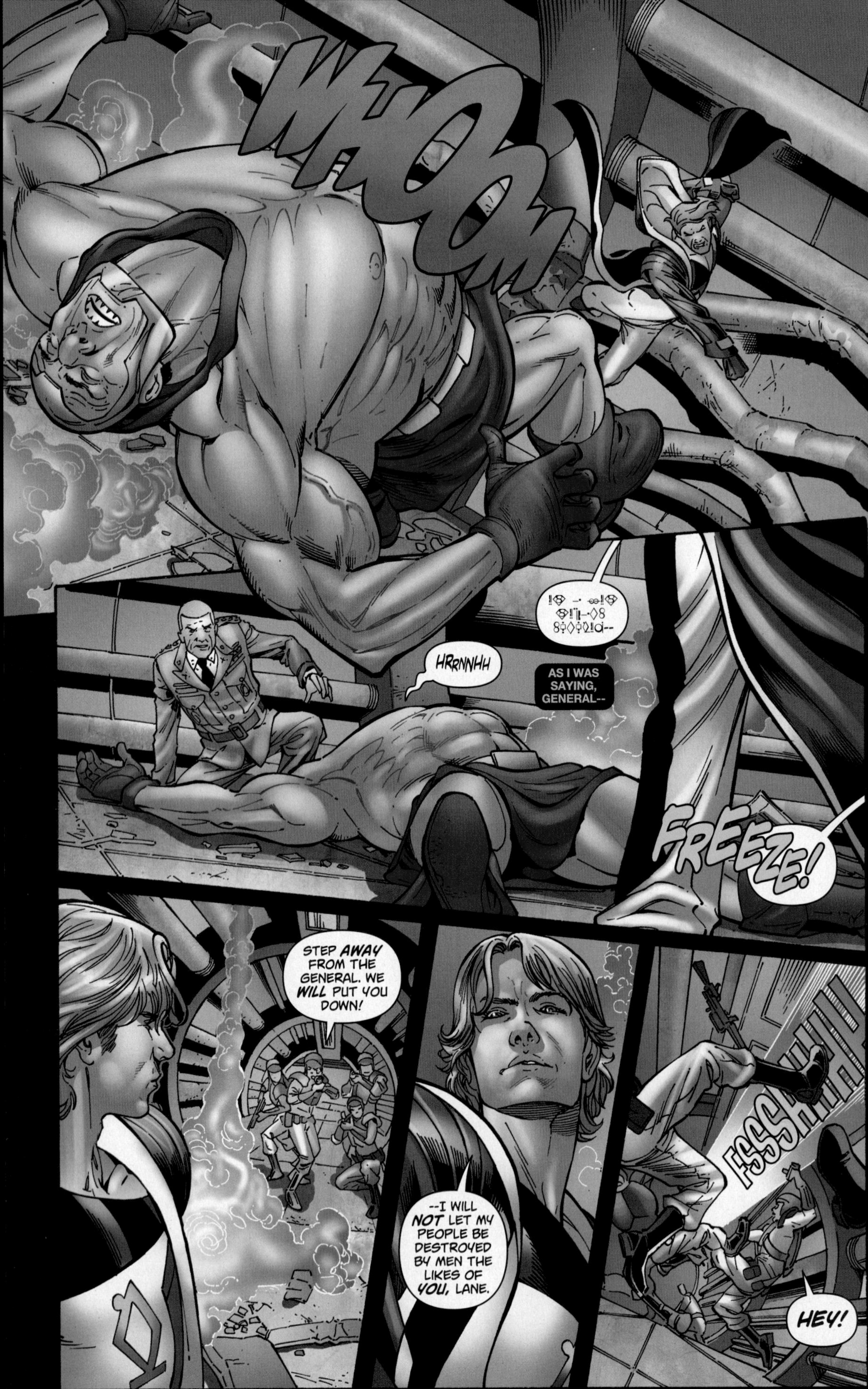
WHOOM
HRrNNHH
AS I WAS SAYING, GENERAL--
FREEZE!
STEP AWAY FROM THE GENERAL. WE WILL PUT YOU DOWN!
--I WILL NOT LET MY PEOPLE BE DESTROYED BY MEN THE LIKES OF YOU, LANE.
FSSSHHHH
HEY!

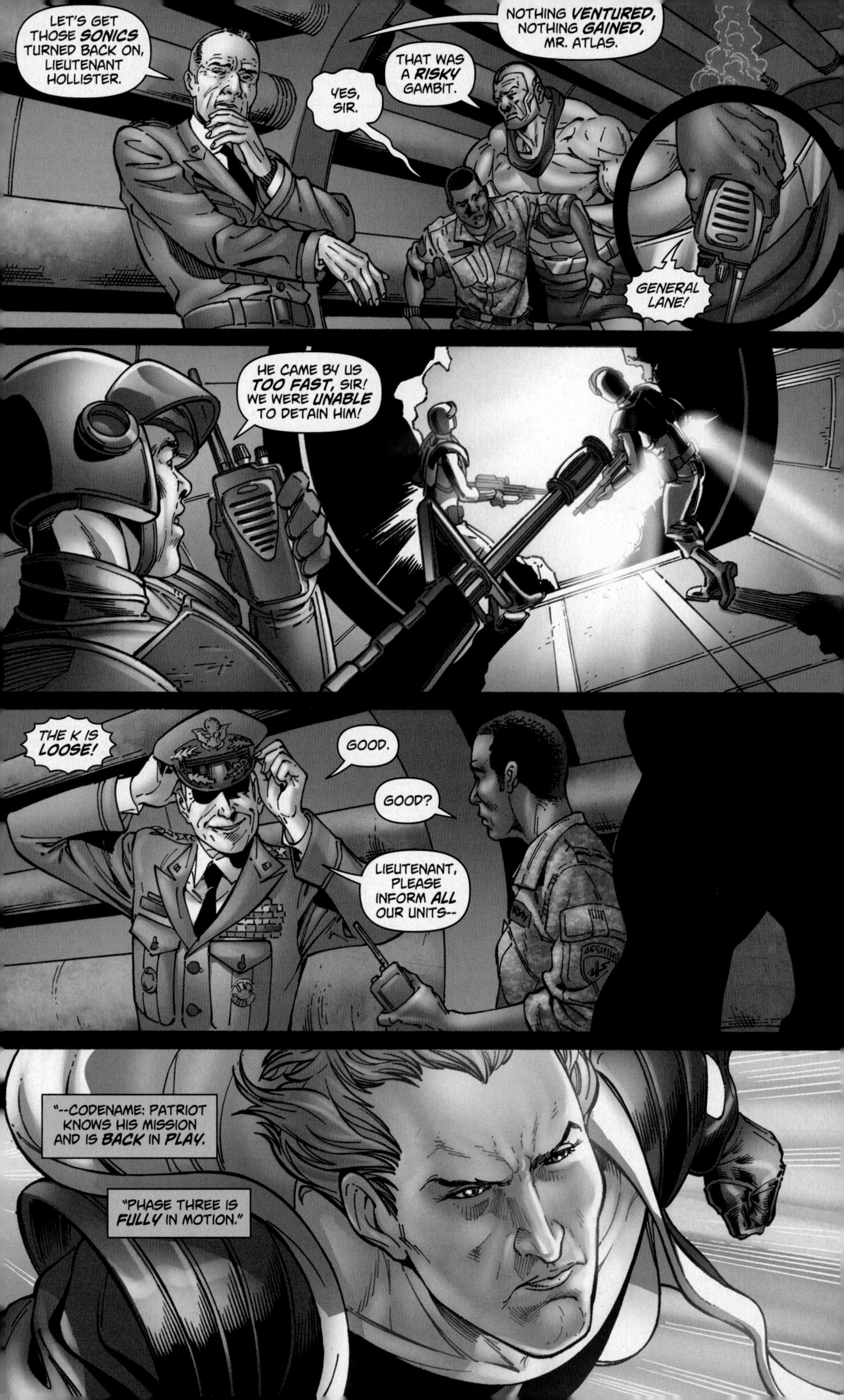
LET'S GET THOSE SONICS TURNED BACK ON, LIEUTENANT HOLLISTER.
NOTHING VENTURED, NOTHING GAINED, MR. ATLAS.
THAT WAS A RISKY GAMBIT.
YES, SIR.
GENERAL LANE!
HE CAME BY US TOO FAST, SIR! WE WERE UNABLE TO DETAIN HIM!
THE K IS LOOSE!
GOOD.
GOOD?
LIEUTENANT, PLEASE INFORM ALL OUR UNITS--
"--CODENAME: PATRIOT KNOWS HIS MISSION AND IS BACK IN PLAY.
"PHASE THREE IS FULLY IN MOTION."

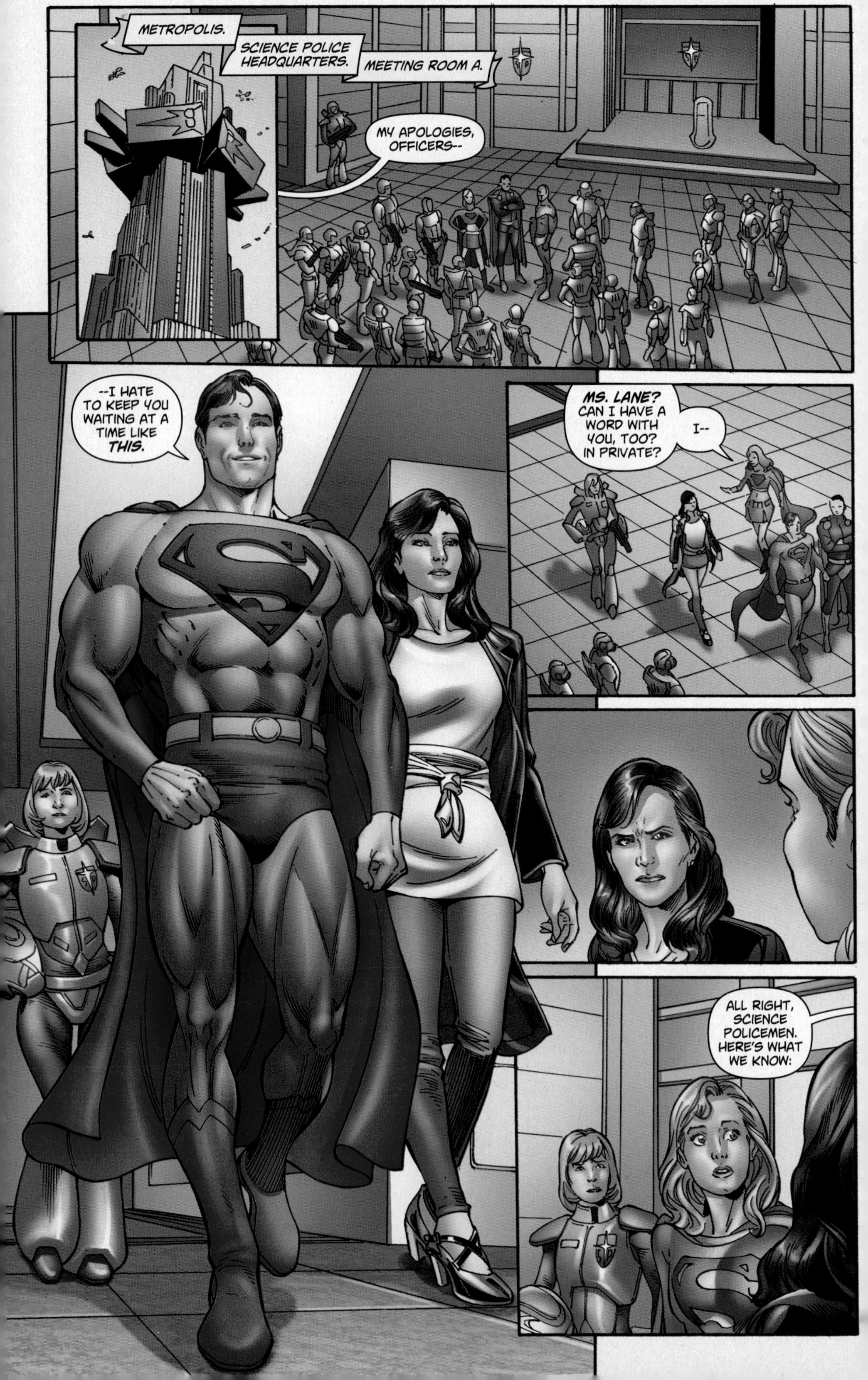
METROPOLIS.
SCIENCE POLICE HEADQUARTERS.
MEETING ROOM A.
MY APOLOGIES, OFFICERS--
--I HATE TO KEEP YOU WAITING AT A TIME LIKE THIS.
MS. LANE? CAN I HAVE A WORD WITH YOU, TOO? IN PRIVATE?
I--
ALL RIGHT, SCIENCE POLICEMEN. HERE'S WHAT WE KNOW:

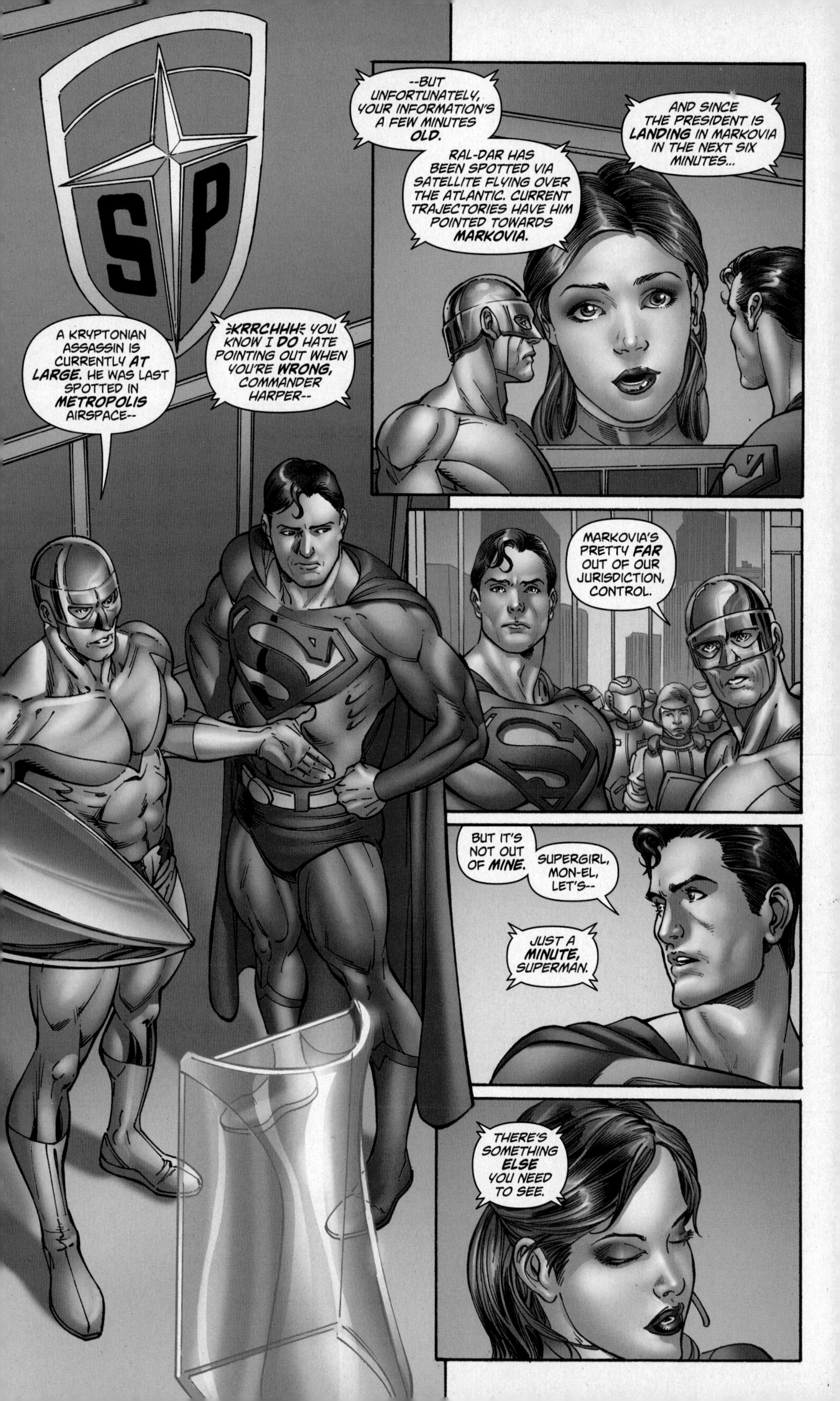
A KRYPTONIAN ASSASSIN IS CURRENTLY AT LARGE. HE WAS LAST SPOTTED IN METROPOLIS AIRSPACE--
KRRCHHH YOU KNOW I DO HATE POINTING OUT WHEN YOU'RE WRONG, COMMANDER HARPER--
--BUT UNFORTUNATELY, YOUR INFORMATION'S A FEW MINUTES OLD.
RAL-DAR HAS BEEN SPOTTED VIA SATELLITE FLYING OVER THE ATLANTIC. CURRENT TRAJECTORIES HAVE HIM POINTED TOWARDS MARKOVIA.
AND SINCE THE PRESIDENT IS LANDING IN MARKOVIA IN THE NEXT SIX MINUTES...
MARKOVIA'S PRETTY FAR OUT OF OUR JURISDICTION, CONTROL.
BUT IT'S NOT OUT OF MINE.
SUPERGIRL, MON-EL, LET'S--
JUST A MINUTE, SUPERMAN.
THERE'S SOMETHING ELSE YOU NEED TO SEE.

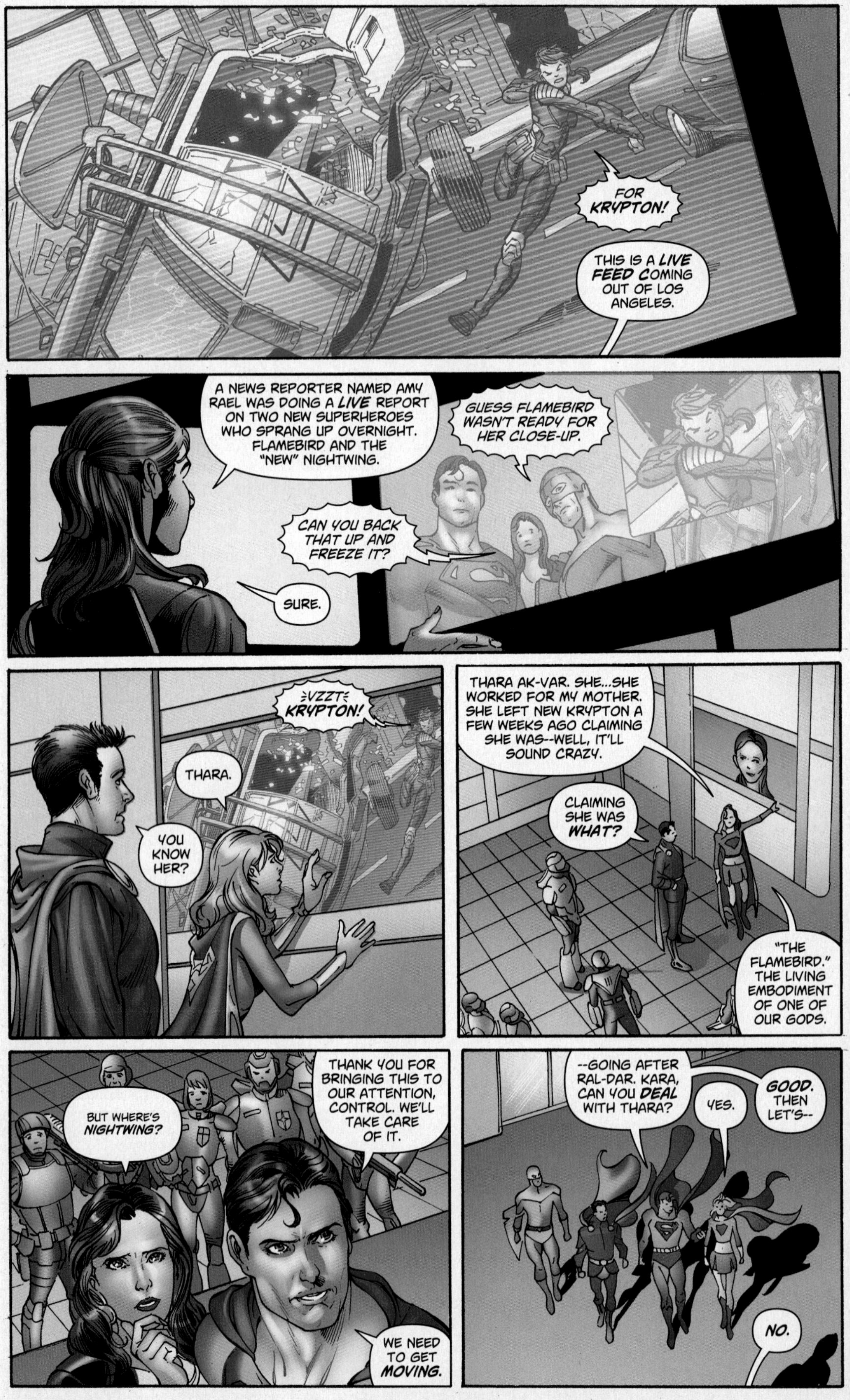
FOR KRYPTON!
THIS IS A LIVE FEED COMING OUT OF LOS ANGELES.
A NEWS REPORTER NAMED AMY RAEL WAS DOING A LIVE REPORT ON TWO NEW SUPERHEROES WHO SPRANG UP OVERNIGHT. FLAMEBIRD AND THE "NEW" NIGHTWING.
GUESS FLAMEBIRD WASN'T READY FOR HER CLOSE-UP.
CAN YOU BACK THAT UP AND FREEZE IT?
SURE.
VZZT KRYPTON!
THARA.
YOU KNOW HER?
THARA AK-VAR. SHE...SHE WORKED FOR MY MOTHER. SHE LEFT NEW KRYPTON A FEW WEEKS AGO CLAIMING SHE WAS--WELL, IT'LL SOUND CRAZY.
CLAIMING SHE WAS WHAT?
"THE FLAMEBIRD." THE LIVING EMBODIMENT OF ONE OF OUR GODS.
BUT WHERE'S NIGHTWING?
THANK YOU FOR BRINGING THIS TO OUR ATTENTION, CONTROL. WE'LL TAKE CARE OF IT.
WE NEED TO GET MOVING.
--GOING AFTER RAL-DAR. KARA, CAN YOU DEAL WITH THARA?
YES.
GOOD. THEN LET'S--
NO.

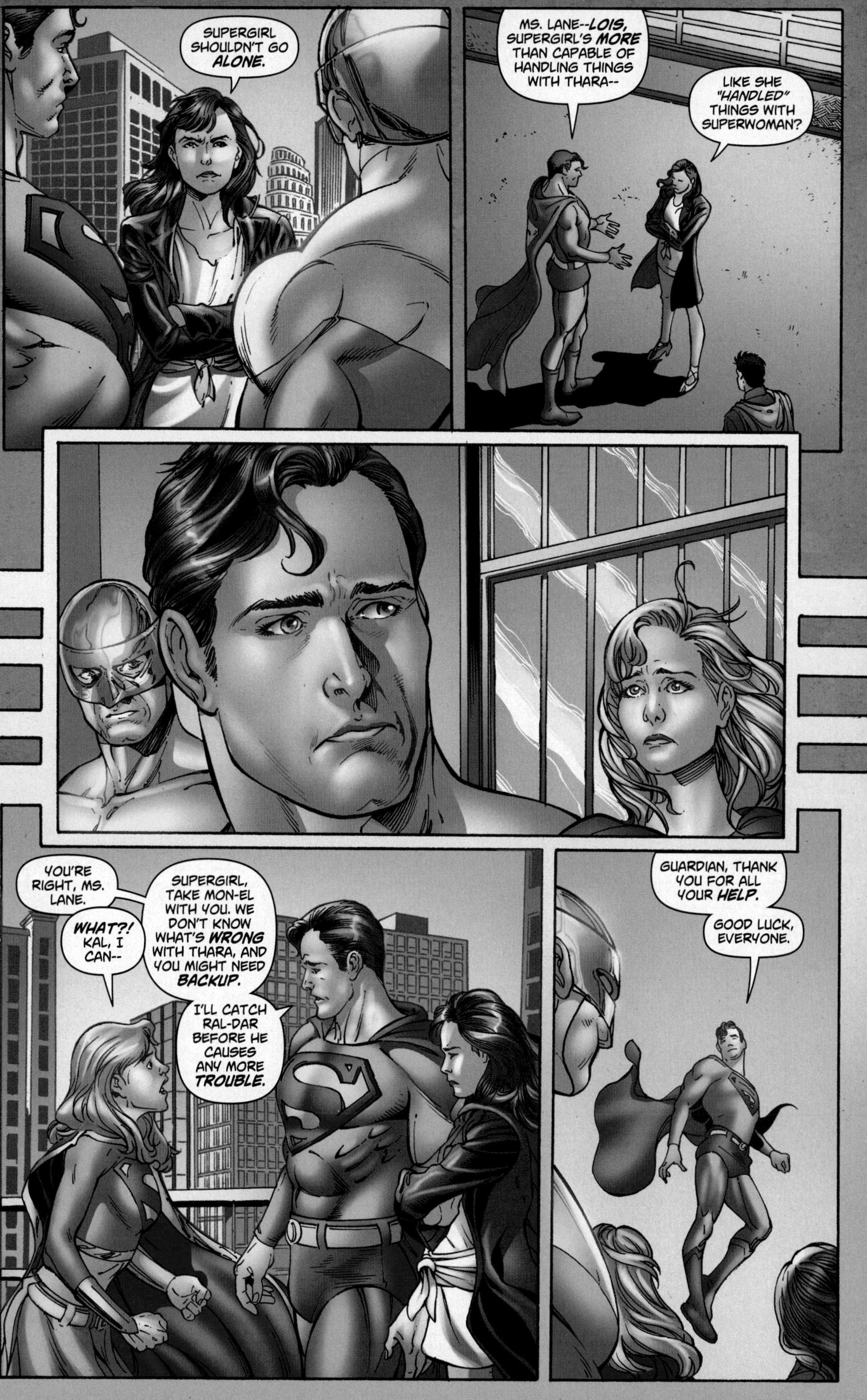
SUPERGIRL SHOULDN'T GO ALONE.
MS. LANE--LOIS, SUPERGIRL'S MORE THAN CAPABLE OF HANDLING THINGS WITH THARA--
LIKE SHE "HANDLED" THINGS WITH SUPERWOMAN?
YOU'RE RIGHT, MS. LANE.
WHAT?! KAL, I CAN--
SUPERGIRL, TAKE MON-EL WITH YOU. WE DON'T KNOW WHAT'S WRONG WITH THARA, AND YOU MIGHT NEED BACKUP.
I'LL CATCH RAL-DAR BEFORE HE CAUSES ANY MORE TROUBLE.
GUARDIAN, THANK YOU FOR ALL YOUR HELP.
GOOD LUCK, EVERYONE.

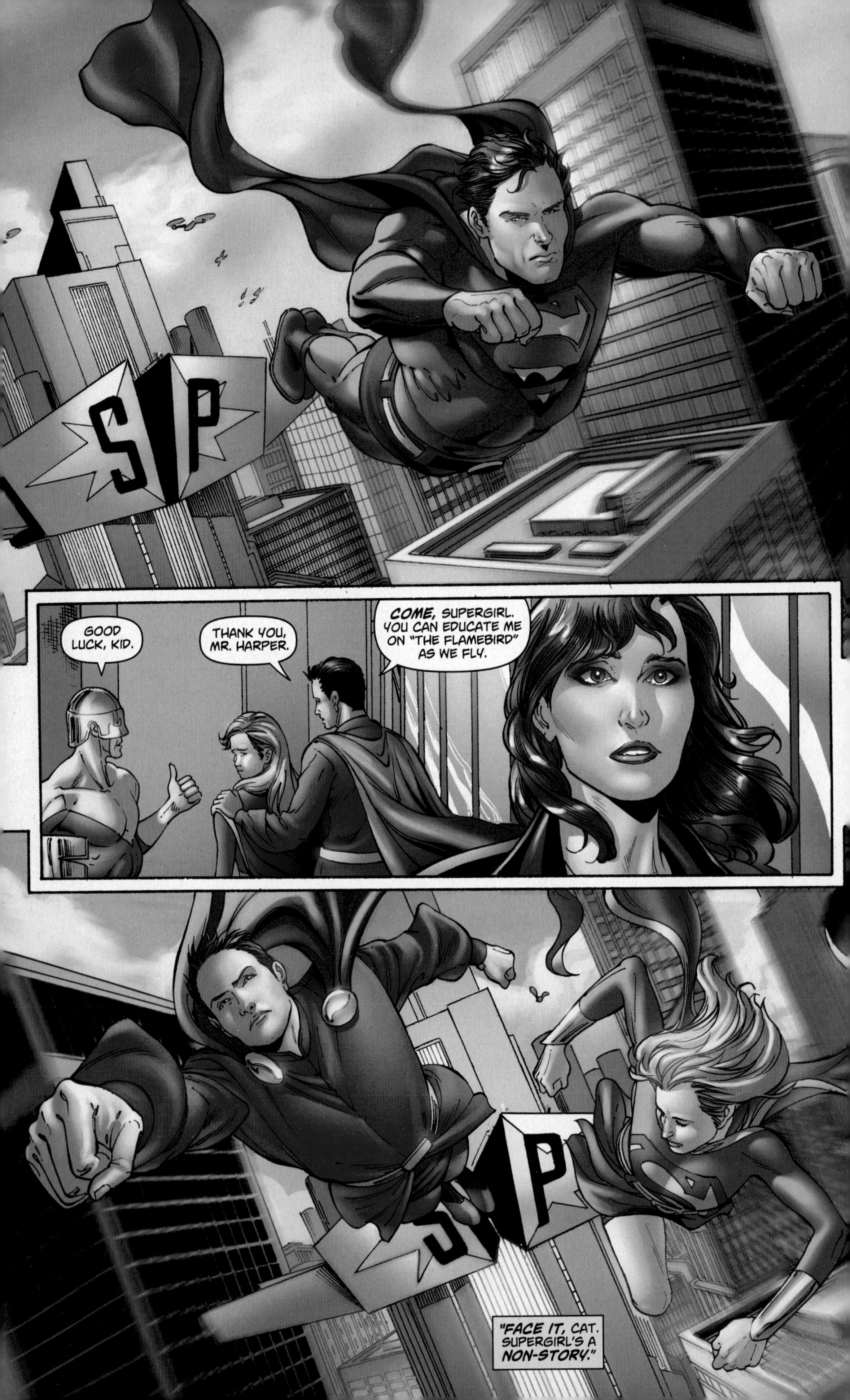

GOOD LUCK, KID.
THANK YOU, MR. HARPER.
COME, SUPERGIRL. YOU CAN EDUCATE ME ON "THE FLAMEBIRD" AS WE FLY.
"FACE IT, CAT. SUPERGIRL'S A NON-STORY."

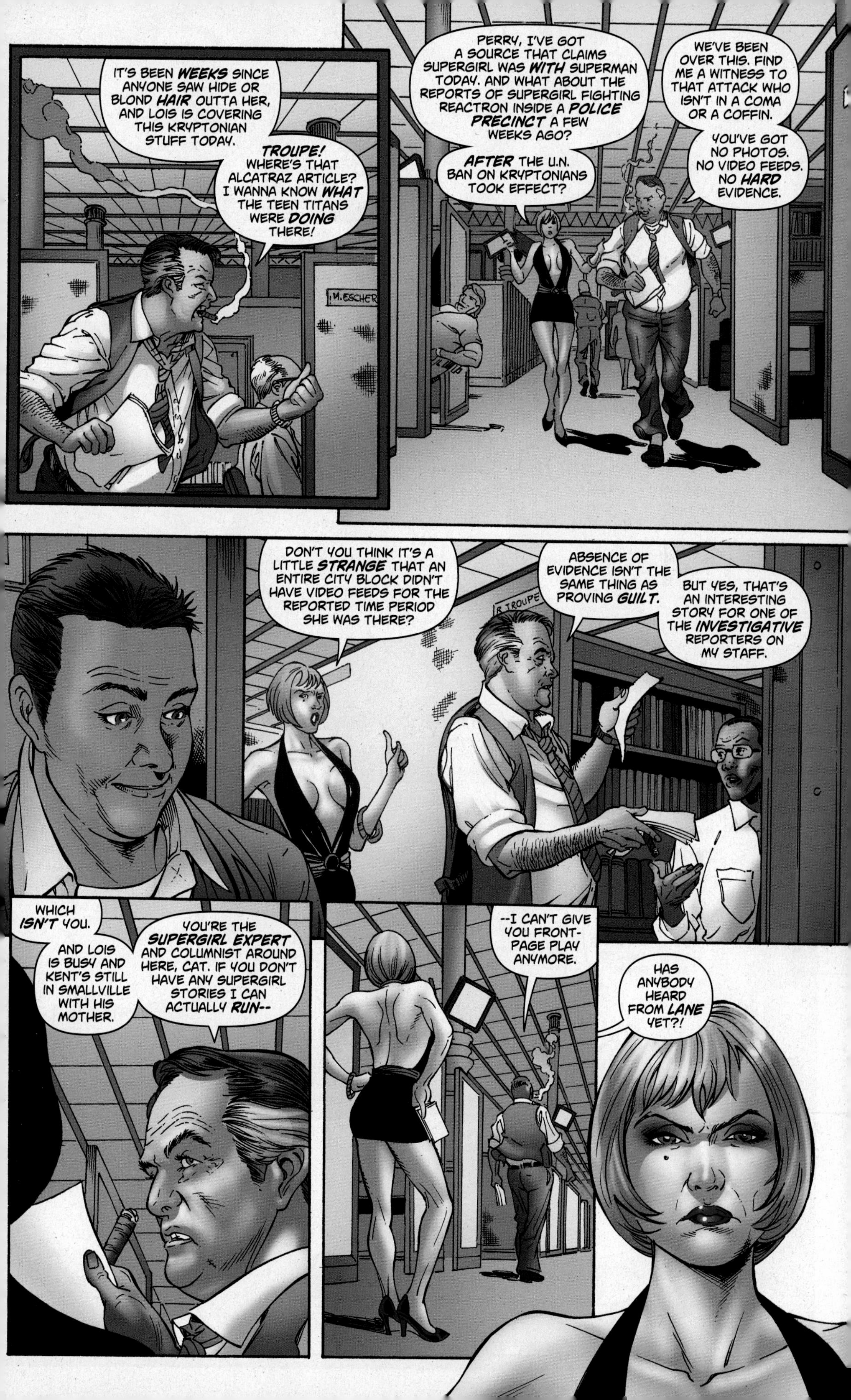
IT'S BEEN WEEKS SINCE ANYONE SAW HIDE OR BLOND HAIR OUTTA HER, AND LOIS IS COVERING THIS KRYPTONIAN STUFF TODAY.
TROUPE! WHERE'S THAT ALCATRAZ ARTICLE? I WANNA KNOW WHAT THE TEEN TITANS WERE DOING THERE!
M. ESCHER
PERRY, I'VE GOT A SOURCE THAT CLAIMS SUPERGIRL WAS WITH SUPERMAN TODAY. AND WHAT ABOUT THE REPORTS OF SUPERGIRL FIGHTING REACTRON INSIDE A POLICE PRECINCT A FEW WEEKS AGO?
AFTER THE U.N. BAN ON KRYPTONIANS TOOK EFFECT?
WE'VE BEEN OVER THIS. FIND ME A WITNESS TO THAT ATTACK WHO ISN'T IN A COMA OR A COFFIN.
YOU'VE GOT NO PHOTOS. NO VIDEO FEEDS. NO HARD EVIDENCE.
DON'T YOU THINK IT'S A LITTLE STRANGE THAT AN ENTIRE CITY BLOCK DIDN'T HAVE VIDEO FEEDS FOR THE REPORTED TIME PERIOD SHE WAS THERE?
B. TROUPE
ABSENCE OF EVIDENCE ISN'T THE SAME THING AS PROVING GUILT.
BUT YES, THAT'S AN INTERESTING STORY FOR ONE OF THE INVESTIGATIVE REPORTERS ON MY STAFF.
WHICH ISN'T YOU.
AND LOIS IS BUSY AND KENT'S STILL IN SMALLVILLE WITH HIS MOTHER.
YOU'RE THE SUPERGIRL EXPERT AND COLUMNIST AROUND HERE, CAT. IF YOU DON'T HAVE ANY SUPERGIRL STORIES I CAN ACTUALLY RUN--
--I CAN'T GIVE YOU FRONT-PAGE PLAY ANYMORE.
HAS ANYBODY HEARD FROM LANE YET?!

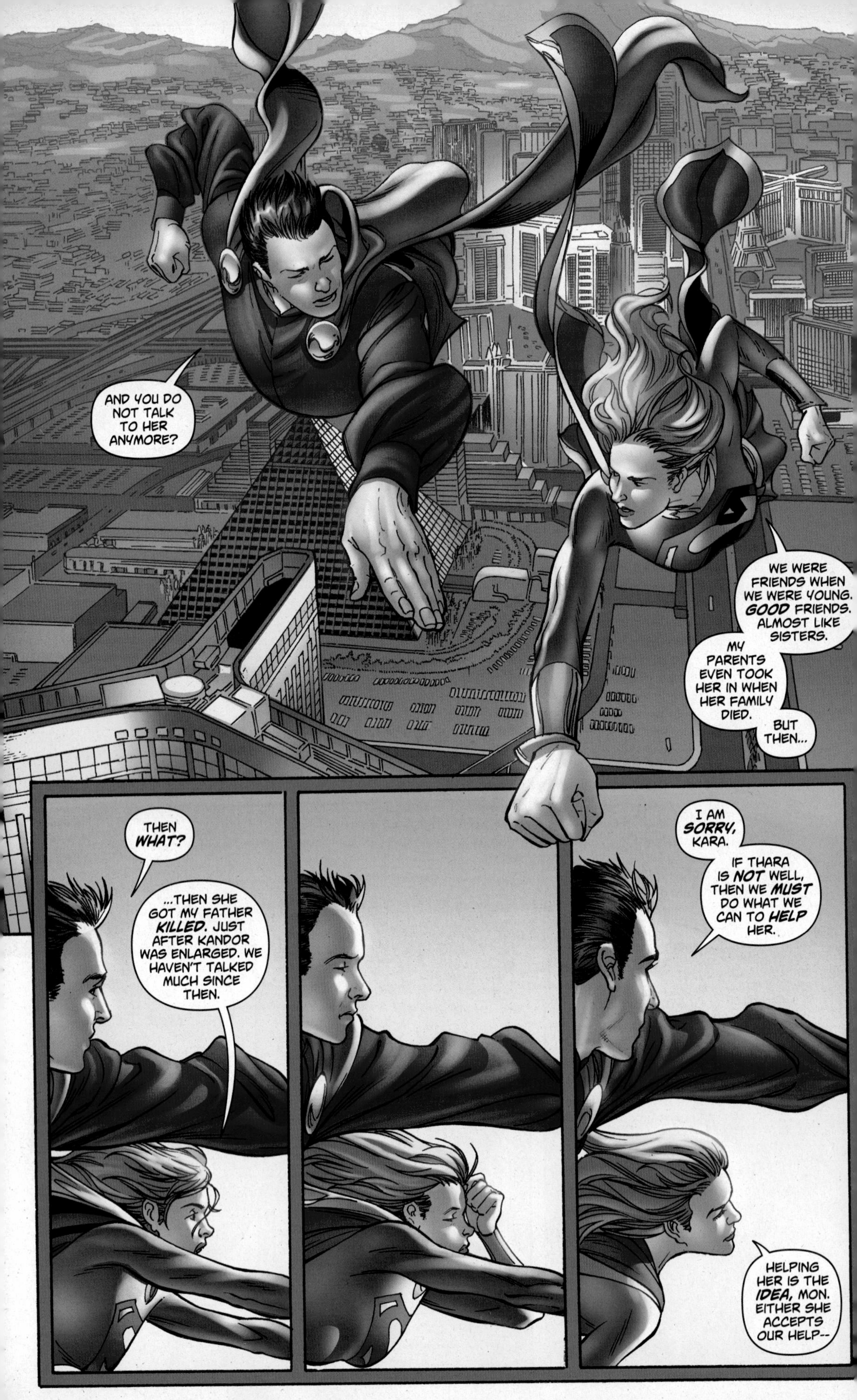
AND YOU DO NOT TALK TO HER ANYMORE?
WE WERE FRIENDS WHEN WE WERE YOUNG. GOOD FRIENDS. ALMOST LIKE SISTERS.
MY PARENTS EVEN TOOK HER IN WHEN HER FAMILY DIED.
BUT THEN...
THEN WHAT?
...THEN SHE GOT MY FATHER KILLED. JUST AFTER KANDOR WAS ENLARGED. WE HAVEN'T TALKED MUCH SINCE THEN.
I AM SORRY, KARA.
IF THARA IS NOT WELL, THEN WE MUST DO WHAT WE CAN TO HELP HER.
HELPING HER IS THE IDEA, MON. EITHER SHE ACCEPTS OUR HELP--

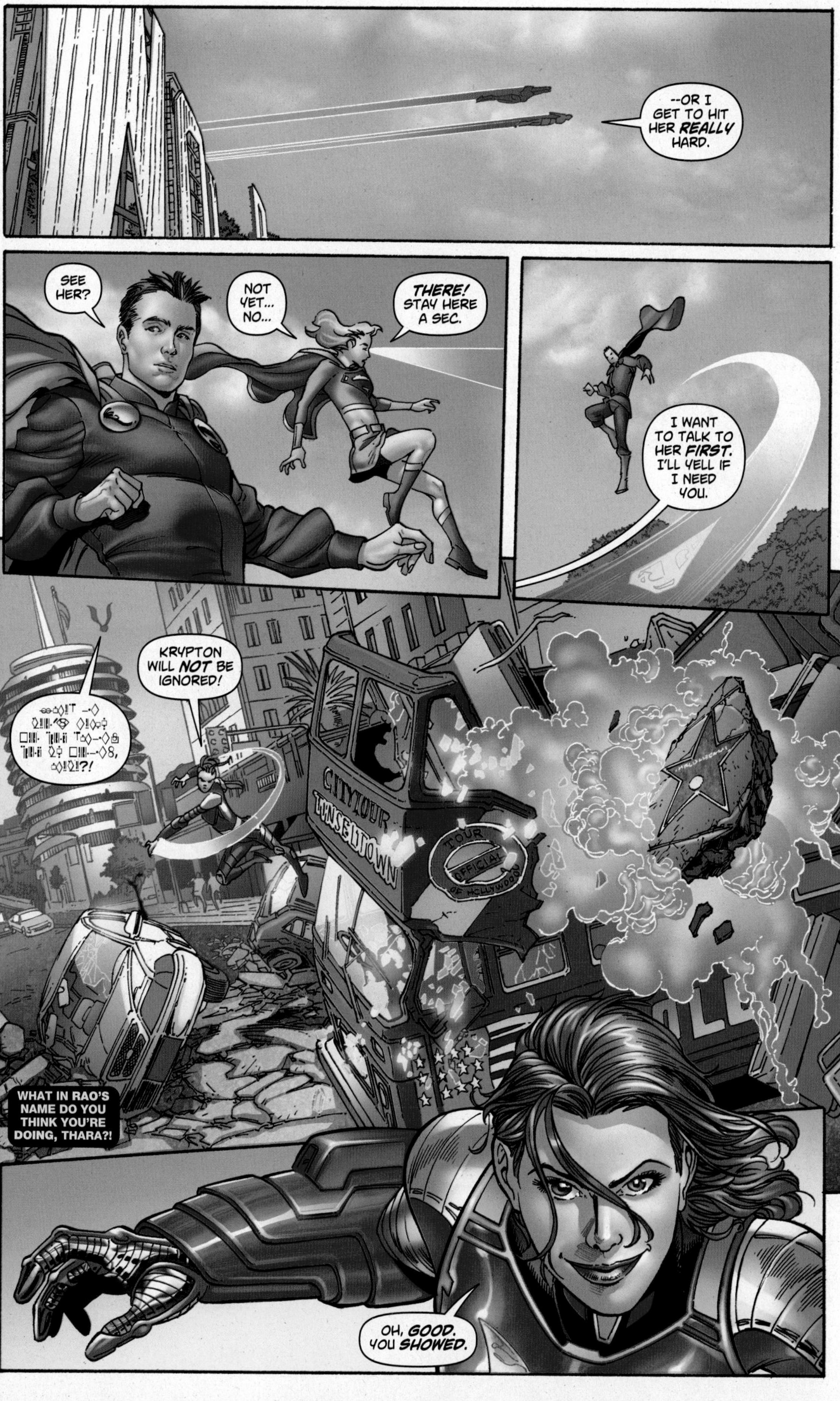
--OR I GET TO HIT HER REALLY HARD.
SEE HER?
NOT YET... NO...
THERE! STAY HERE A SEC.
I WANT TO TALK TO HER FIRST. I'LL YELL IF I NEED YOU.
KRYPTON WILL NOT BE IGNORED!
CITYTOUR
TINSELTOWN
WHAT IN RAO'S NAME DO YOU THINK YOU'RE DOING, THARA?!
OH, GOOD. YOU SHOWED.

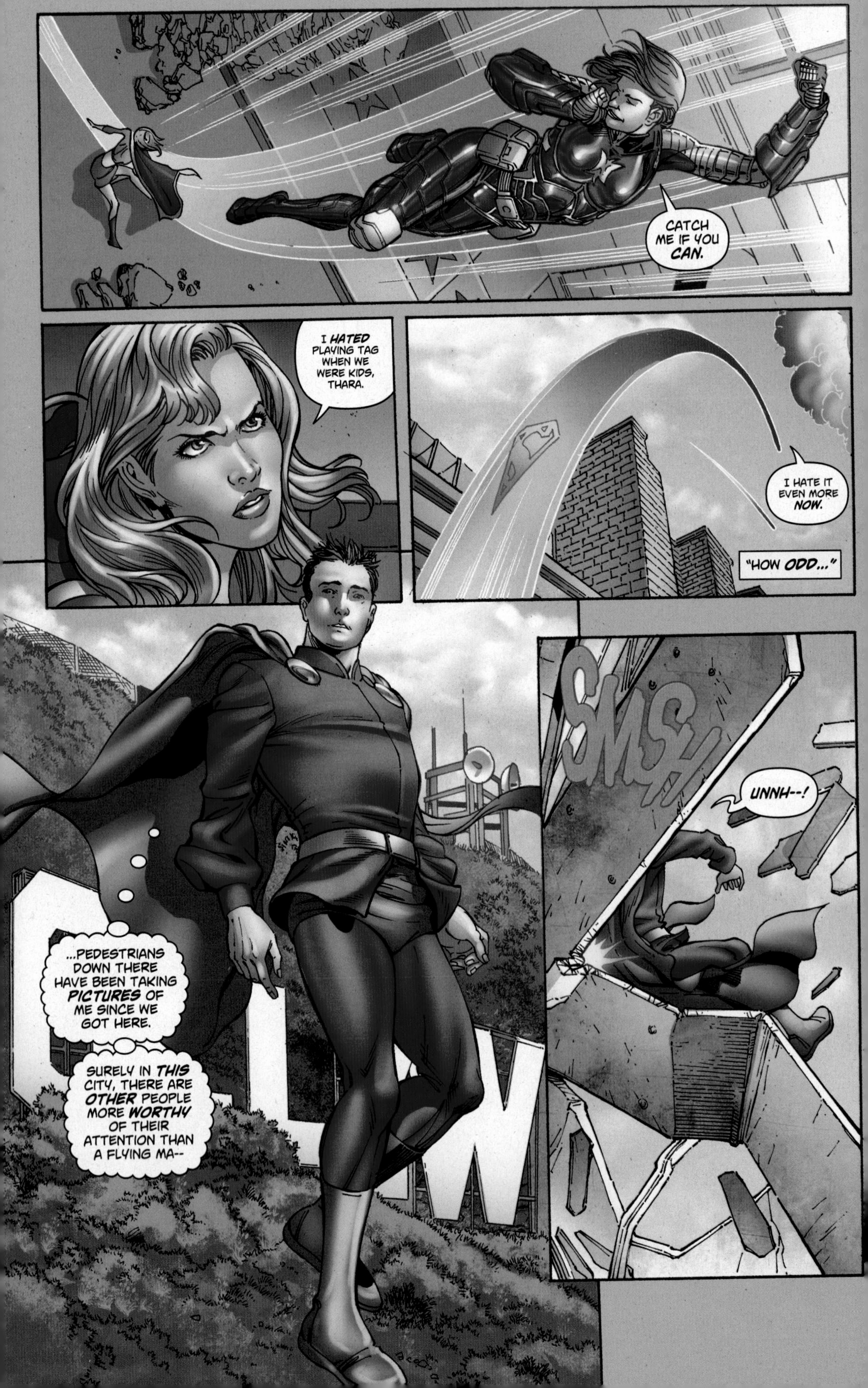

CATCH ME IF YOU CAN.
I HATED PLAYING TAG WHEN WE WERE KIDS, THARA.
I HATE IT EVEN MORE NOW.
"HOW ODD..."
...PEDESTRIANS DOWN THERE HAVE BEEN TAKING PICTURES OF ME SINCE WE GOT HERE.
SURELY IN THIS CITY, THERE ARE OTHER PEOPLE MORE WORTHY OF THEIR ATTENTION THAN A FLYING MA--
SMSH
UNNH--!

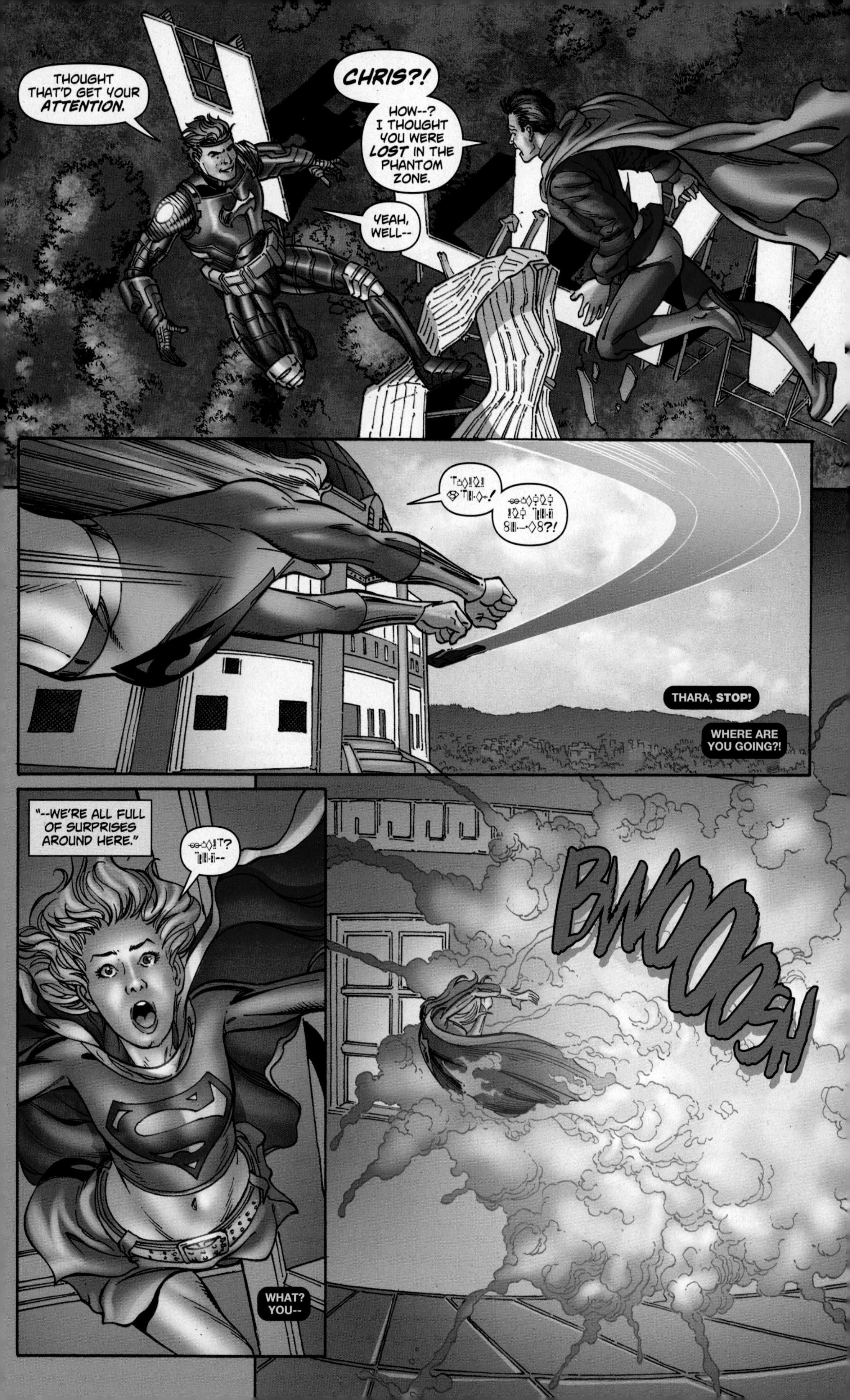
THOUGHT THAT'D GET YOUR ATTENTION.
CHRIS?!
HOW--? I THOUGHT YOU WERE LOST IN THE PHANTOM ZONE.
YEAH, WELL--
THARA, STOP!
WHERE ARE YOU GOING?!
"--WE'RE ALL FULL OF SURPRISES AROUND HERE."
WHAT? YOU--
BWOOOSH

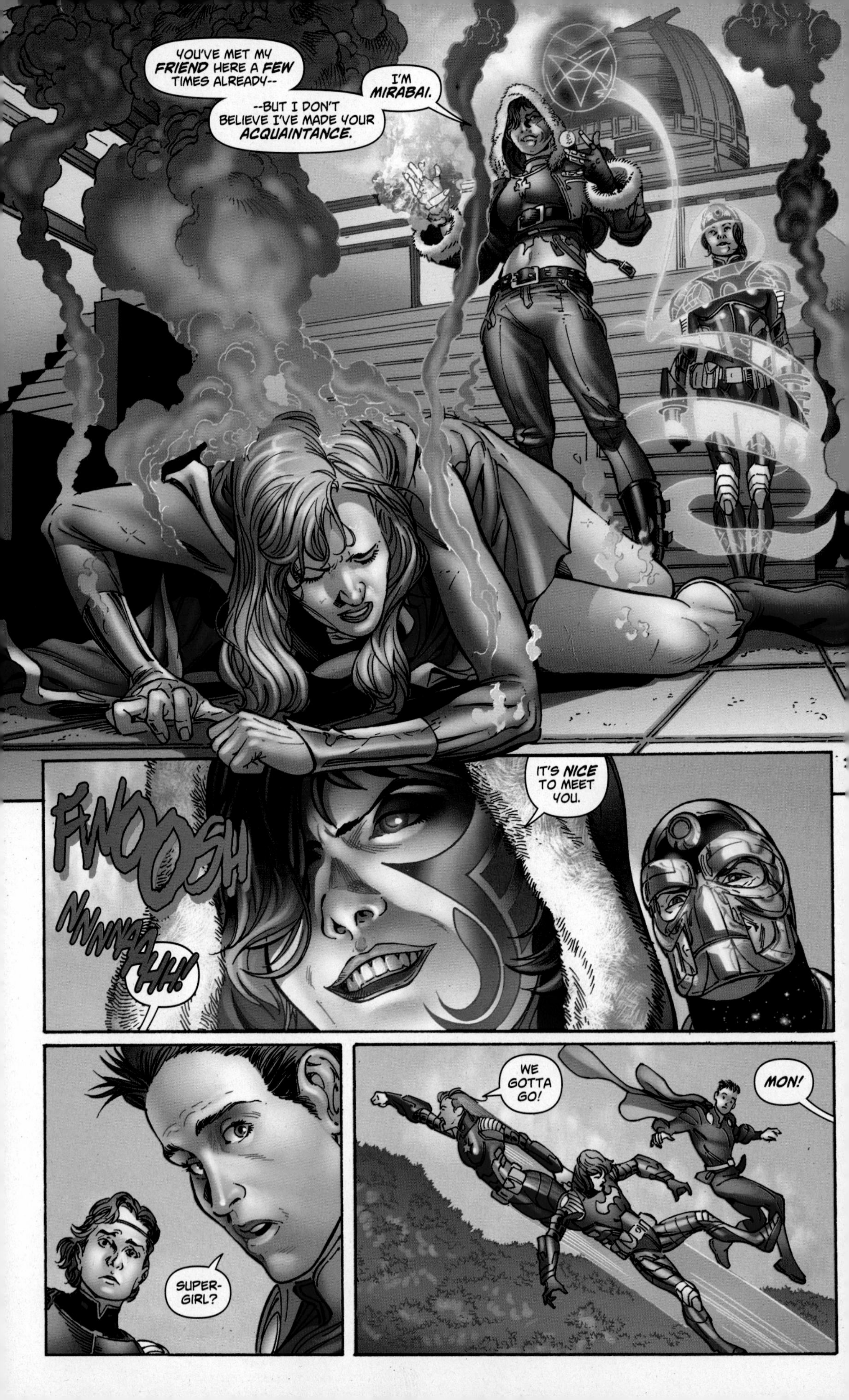
YOU'VE MET MY FRIEND HERE A FEW TIMES ALREADY--
--BUT I DON'T BELIEVE I'VE MADE YOUR ACQUAINTANCE.
I'M MIRABAI.
IT'S NICE TO MEET YOU.
FWOOSH
NNNNAAHH!
SUPER-GIRL?
WE GOTTA GO!
MON!

WE HAVE TO **STOP** THEM!

SHE **TOLD** ME WHAT THEY WERE **PLANNING!**

WHERE ARE THEY--

METROPOLIS!

"SOMETHING **BIG** IS GOING TO HAPPEN IN **METROPOLIS!**"

BZZZT BZZZT

UNKNOWN CALLER

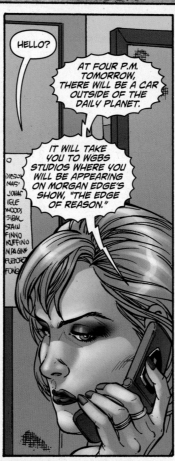

HELLO?

AT FOUR P.M. TOMORROW, THERE WILL BE A CAR OUTSIDE OF THE DAILY PLANET.

IT WILL TAKE YOU TO WGBS STUDIOS WHERE YOU WILL BE APPEARING ON MORGAN EDGE'S SHOW, "THE EDGE OF REASON."

FASTER!

"WHAT? WHO **IS** THIS?"

AND **WHY** WOULD I GO ON EDGE'S SHOW?

YOU'LL **KNOW** WHY BY THE END OF THE DAY. FOUR P.M., MS. GRANT--

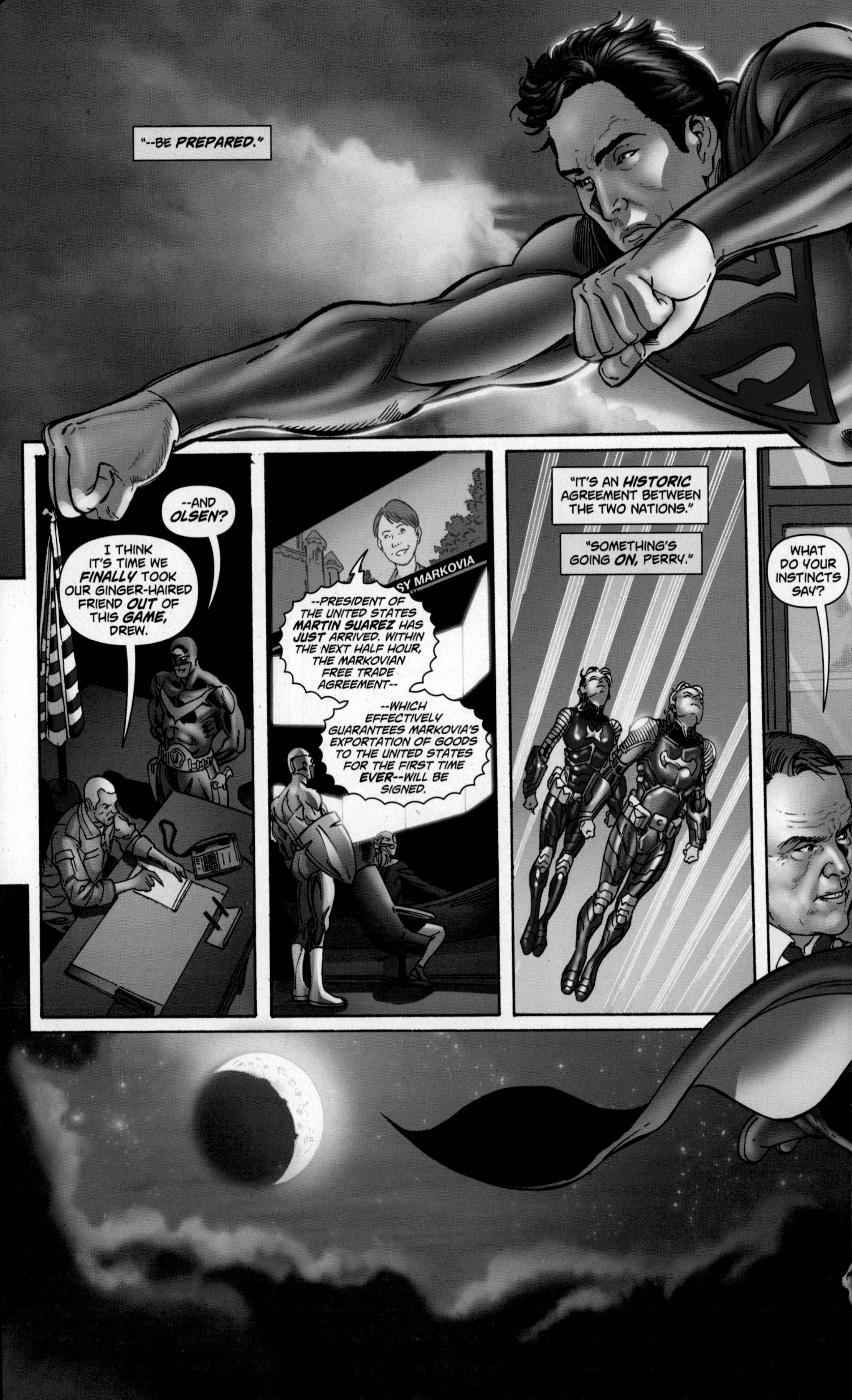
"--BE PREPARED."
--AND OLSEN?
I THINK IT'S TIME WE FINALLY TOOK OUR GINGER-HAIRED FRIEND OUT OF THIS GAME, DREW.
SY MARKOVIA
--PRESIDENT OF THE UNITED STATES MARTIN SUAREZ HAS JUST ARRIVED. WITHIN THE NEXT HALF HOUR, THE MARKOVIAN FREE TRADE AGREEMENT--
--WHICH EFFECTIVELY GUARANTEES MARKOVIA'S EXPORTATION OF GOODS TO THE UNITED STATES FOR THE FIRST TIME EVER--WILL BE SIGNED.
"IT'S AN HISTORIC AGREEMENT BETWEEN THE TWO NATIONS."
"SOMETHING'S GOING ON, PERRY."
WHAT DO YOUR INSTINCTS SAY?

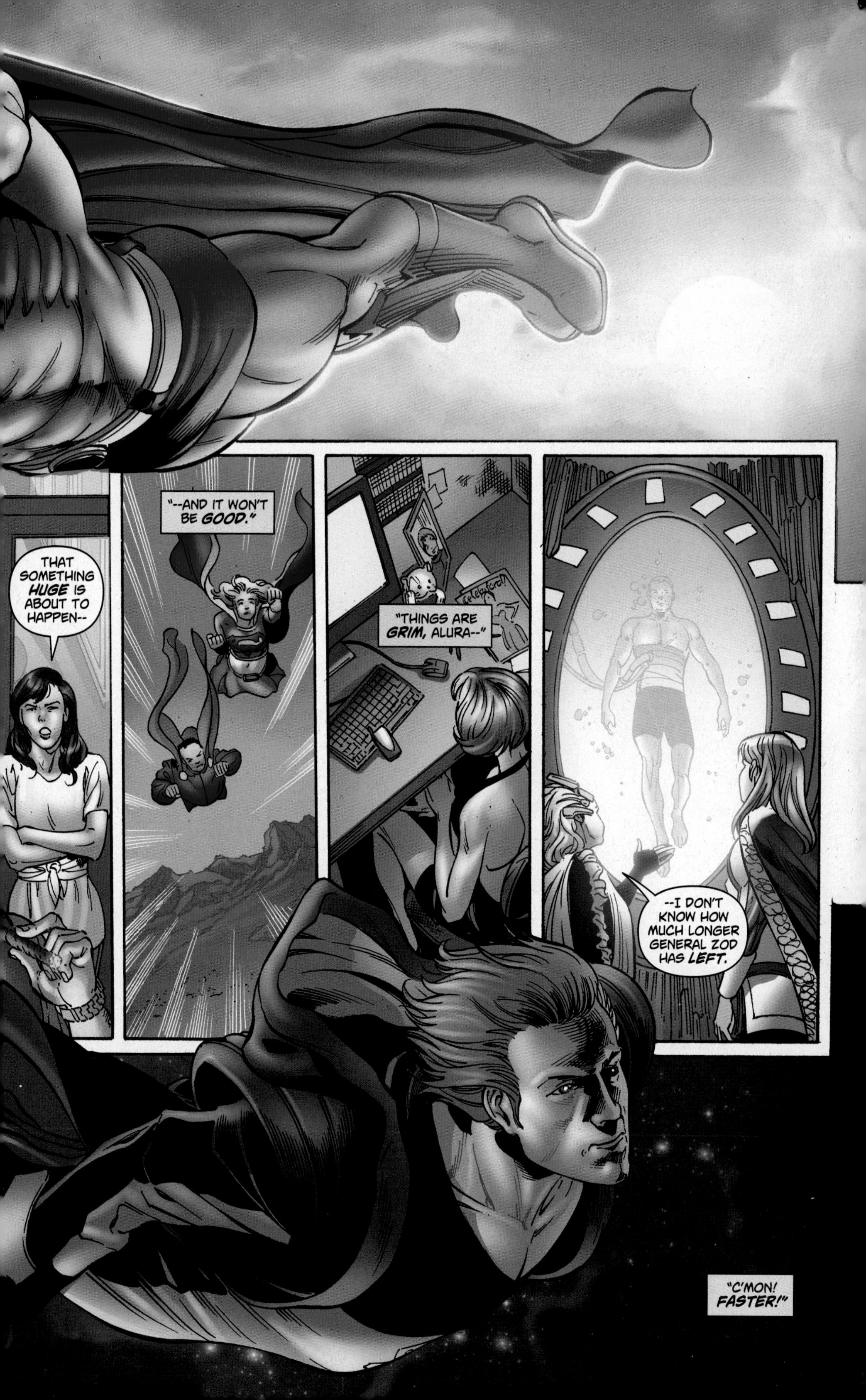

THAT SOMETHING HUGE IS ABOUT TO HAPPEN--
"--AND IT WON'T BE GOOD."
"THINGS ARE GRIM, ALURA--"
--I DON'T KNOW HOW MUCH LONGER GENERAL ZOD HAS LEFT.
"C'MON! FASTER!"

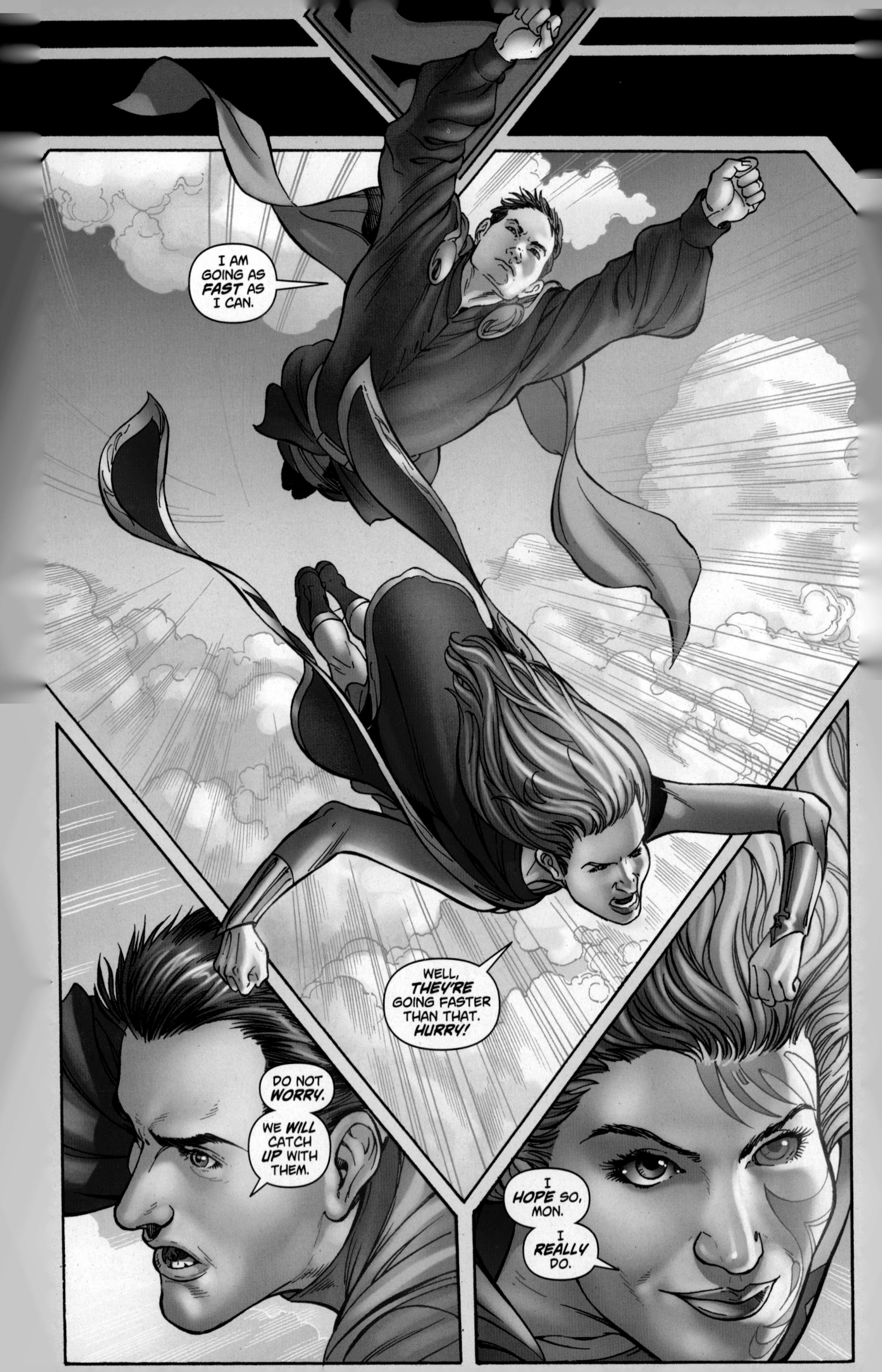
I AM GOING AS FAST AS I CAN.
WELL, THEY'RE GOING FASTER THAN THAT. HURRY!
DO NOT WORRY.
WE WILL CATCH UP WITH THEM.
I HOPE SO, MON.
I REALLY DO.

<SUPERMAN 691>
COVER ART BY **FERNANDO DAGNINO** & **RAÚL FERNANDEZ** WITH **MAZI**

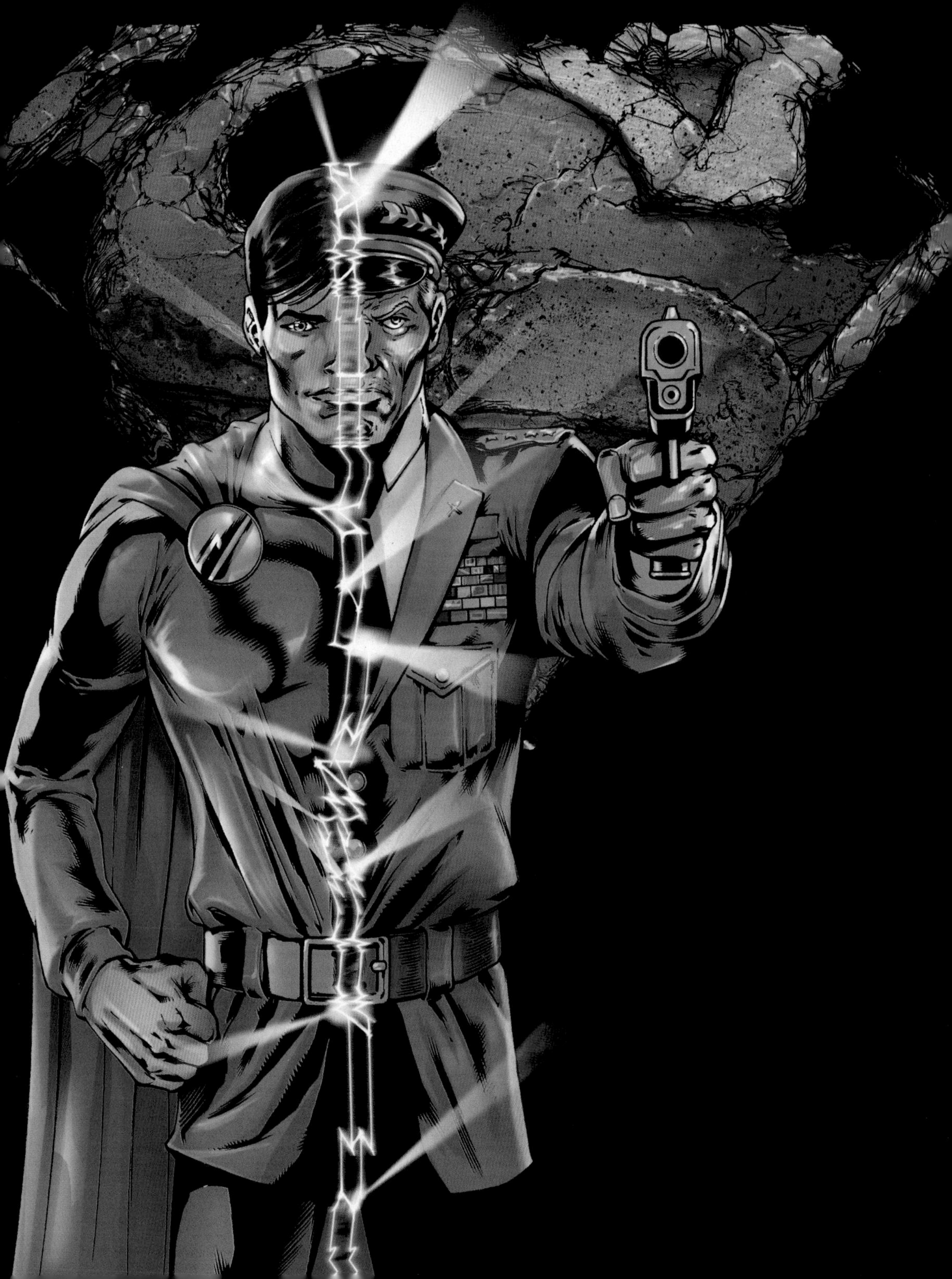

CODENAME: PATRIOT <PART FOUR>

JAMES ROBINSON - WRITER

RENATO GUEDES WITH EDUARDO PANSICA - PENCILLERS

JOSÉ WILSON MAGALHÃES WITH SANDRO RIBEIRO - INKERS

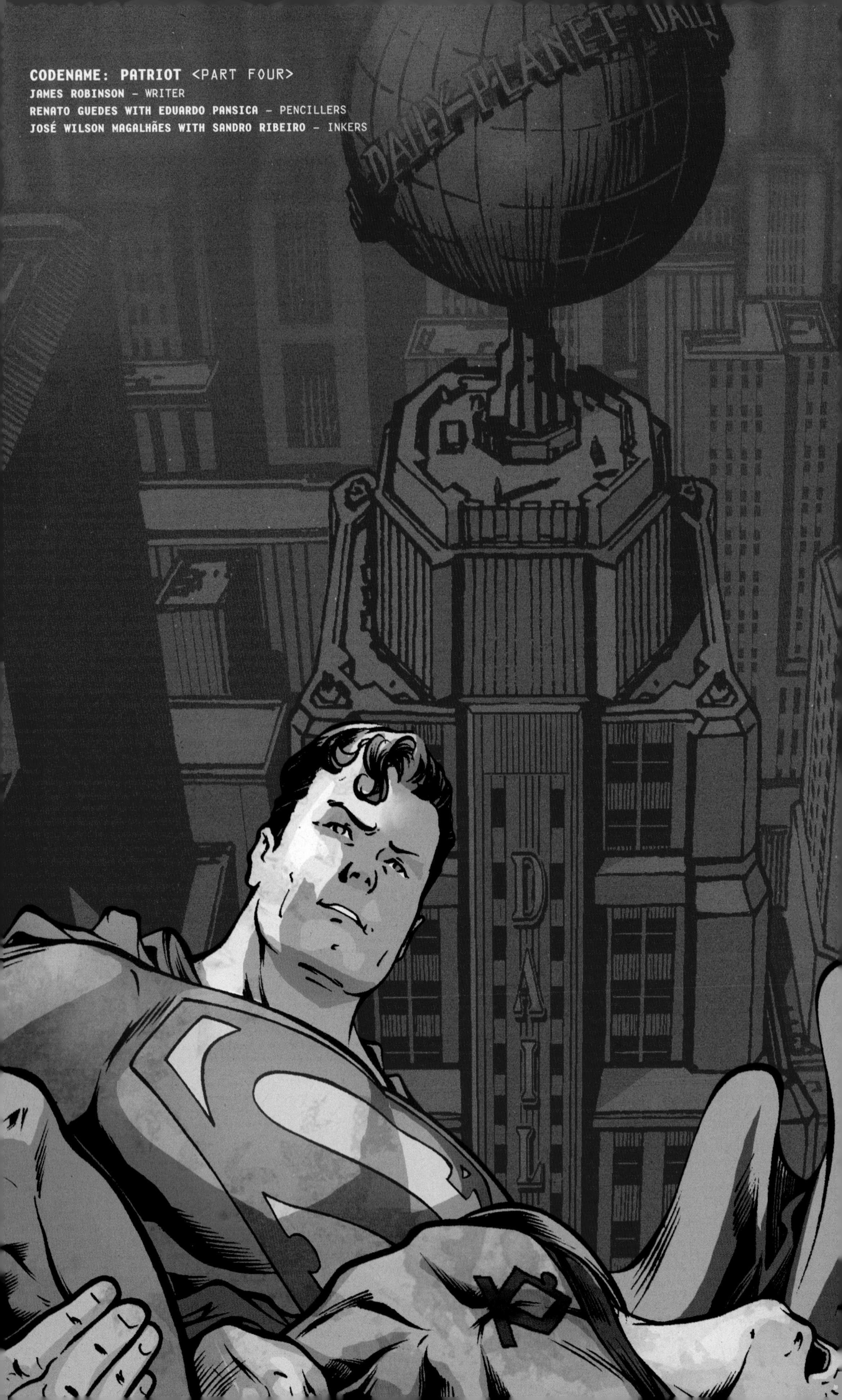
DAILY PLANET
DAIL

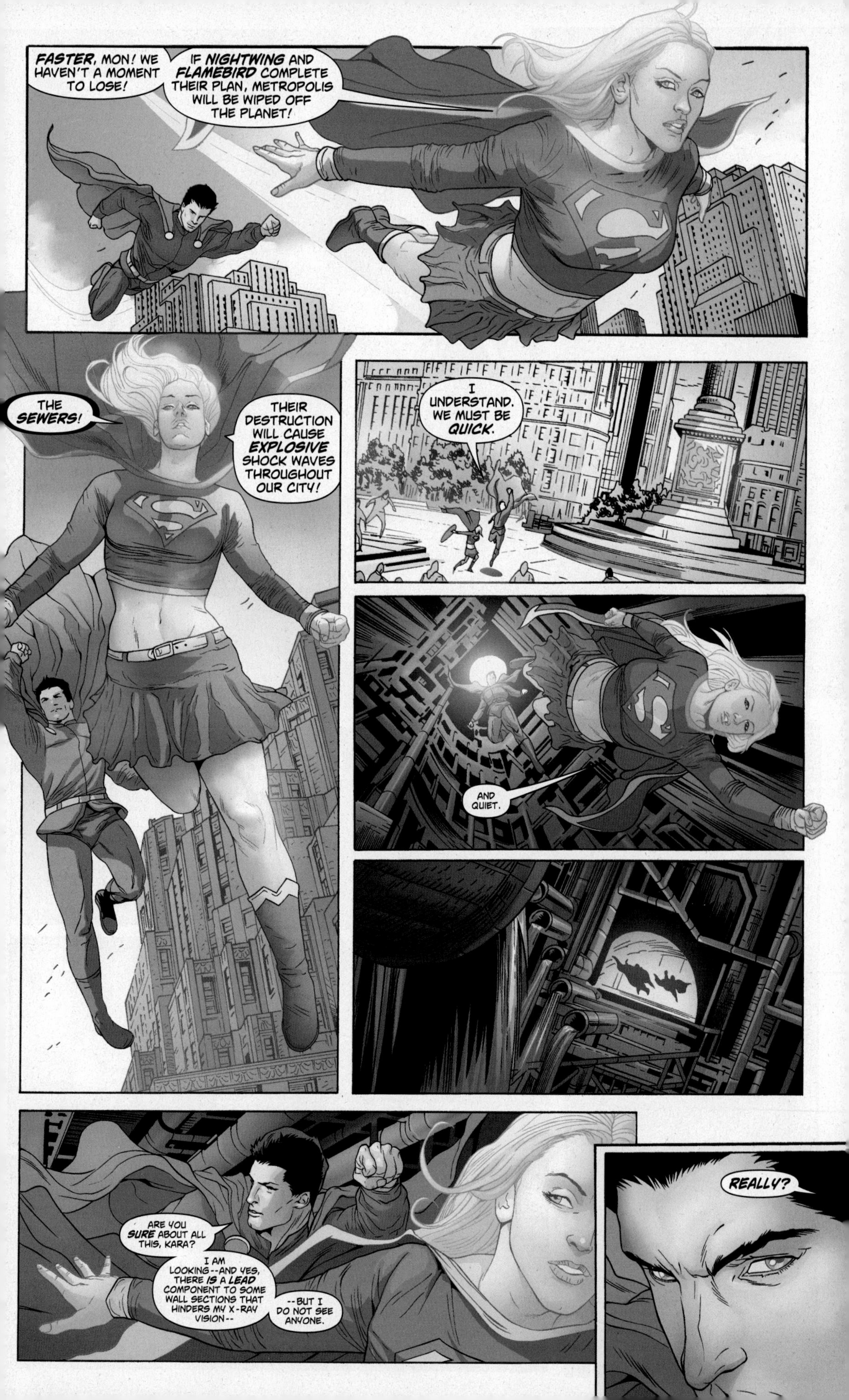
FASTER, MON! WE HAVEN'T A MOMENT TO LOSE!
IF NIGHTWING AND FLAMEBIRD COMPLETE THEIR PLAN, METROPOLIS WILL BE WIPED OFF THE PLANET!
THE SEWERS!
THEIR DESTRUCTION WILL CAUSE EXPLOSIVE SHOCK WAVES THROUGHOUT OUR CITY!
I UNDERSTAND. WE MUST BE QUICK.
AND QUIET.
ARE YOU SURE ABOUT ALL THIS, KARA?
I AM LOOKING--AND YES, THERE IS A LEAD COMPONENT TO SOME WALL SECTIONS THAT HINDERS MY X-RAY VISION--
--BUT I DO NOT SEE ANYONE.
REALLY?

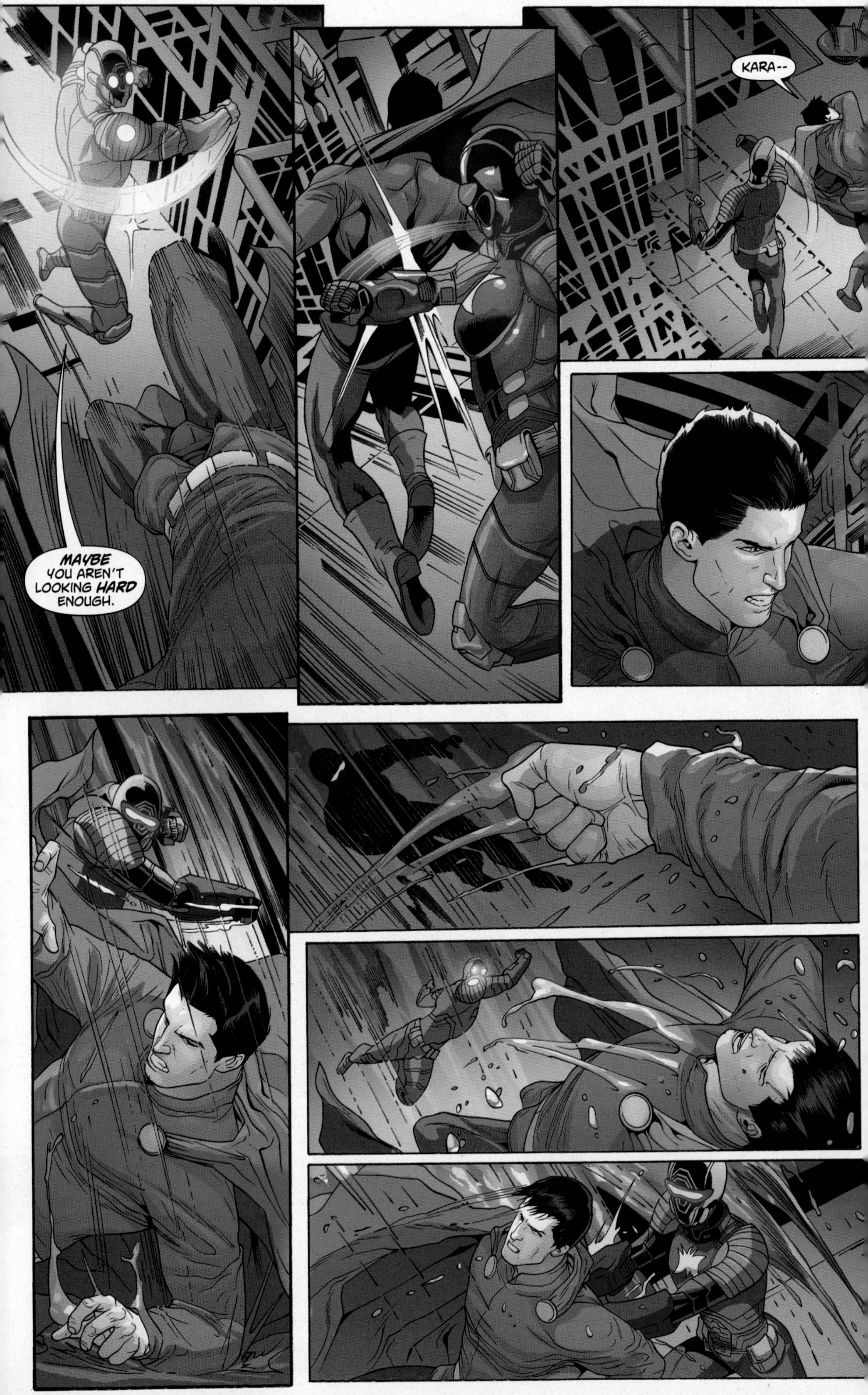
KARA--
MAYBE YOU AREN'T LOOKING HARD ENOUGH.

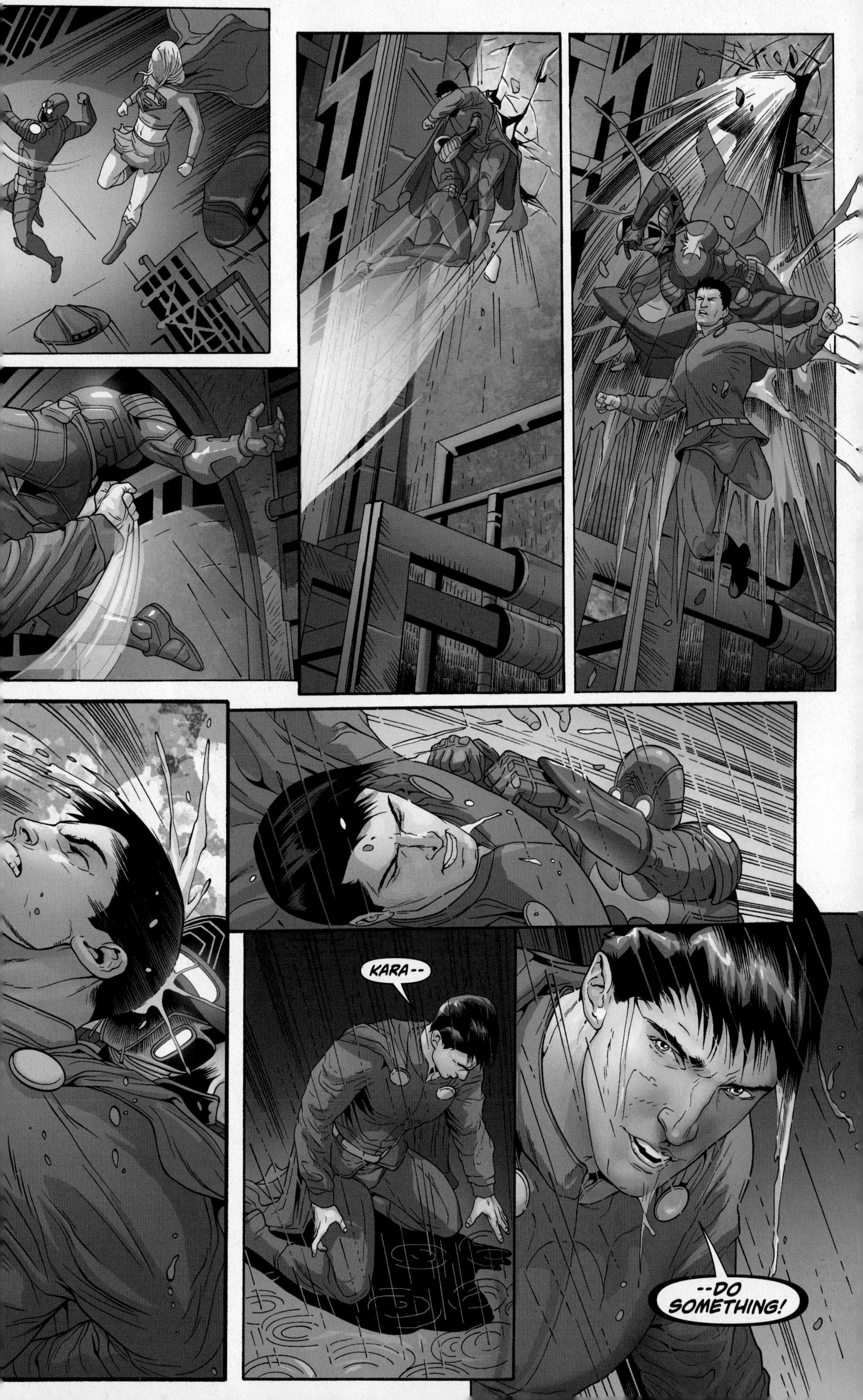
KARA--
--DO SOMETHING!

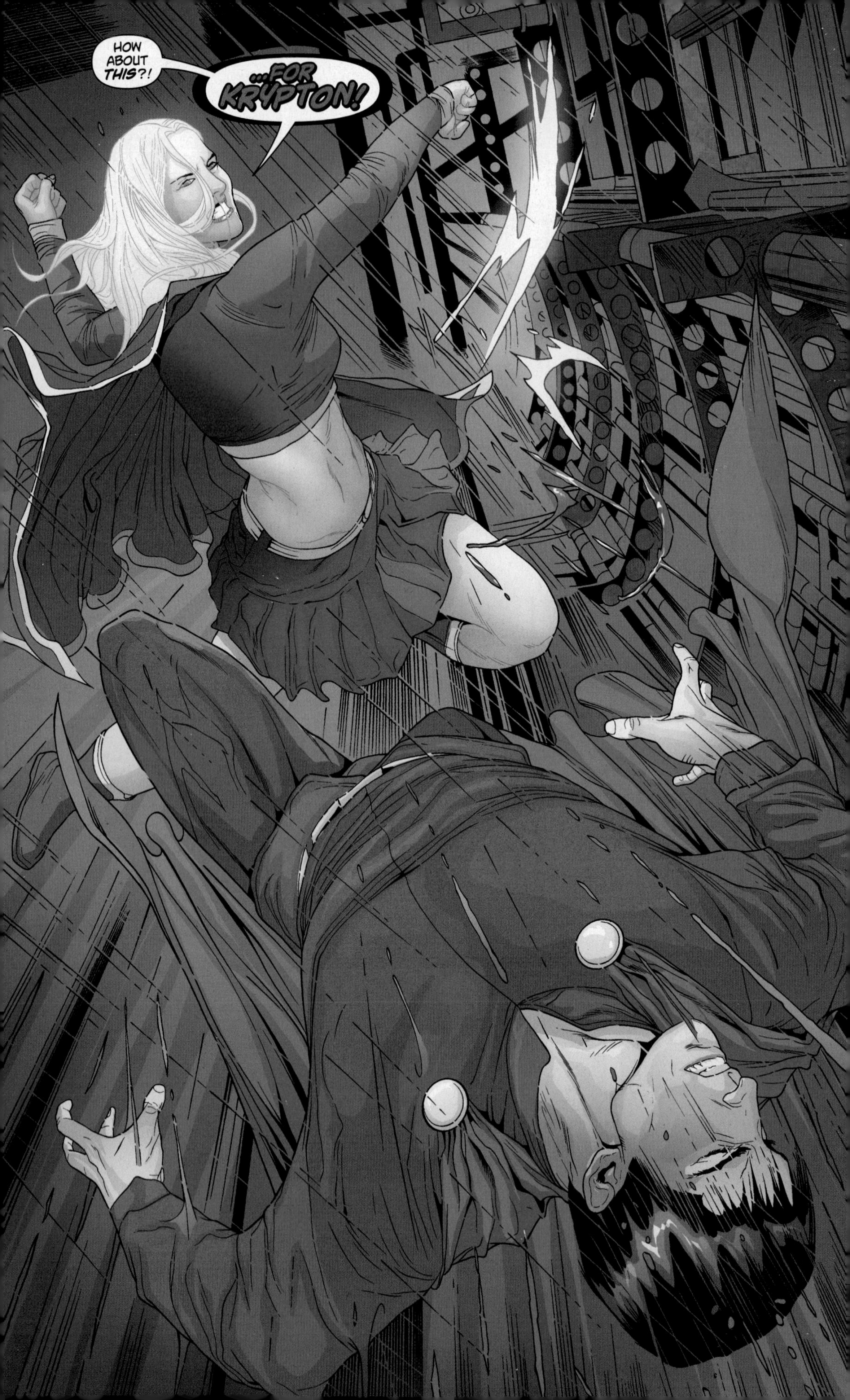
HOW ABOUT THIS?!
...FOR KRYPTON!

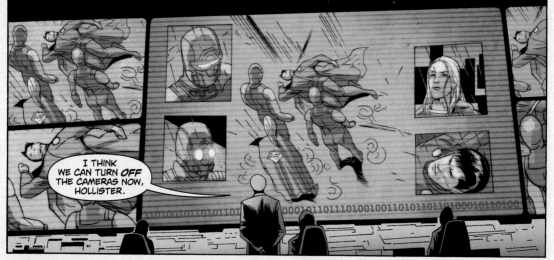

I THINK WE CAN TURN *OFF* THE CAMERAS NOW, HOLLISTER.

YES, SIR.

MOVE IN THE SUPPORT TEAM.

SUPPORT TEAM PRE-RIGGED TO FACILITATE THINGS, SIR. EXPLOSIVES ALREADY IN PLACE.

OH? ON *WHOSE* ORDER?

ER, MINE, SIR.

EXCELLENT, HOLLISTER. I DO LIKE A SOLDIER WHO, WHILE OBEYING ORDERS, CAN *ALSO* THINK FOR HIMSELF.

SO WE'RE READY TO GO?

ONCE OUR A-TEAM GETS OUT OF THERE WITH THEIR CAPTIVE, WE CAN PLANT OUR *SUBSTITUTIONS* AND MAKE THINGS HOT FOR METROPOLIS IN MINUTES.

THEN BY ALL MEANS, *LIGHT* THE OVEN.

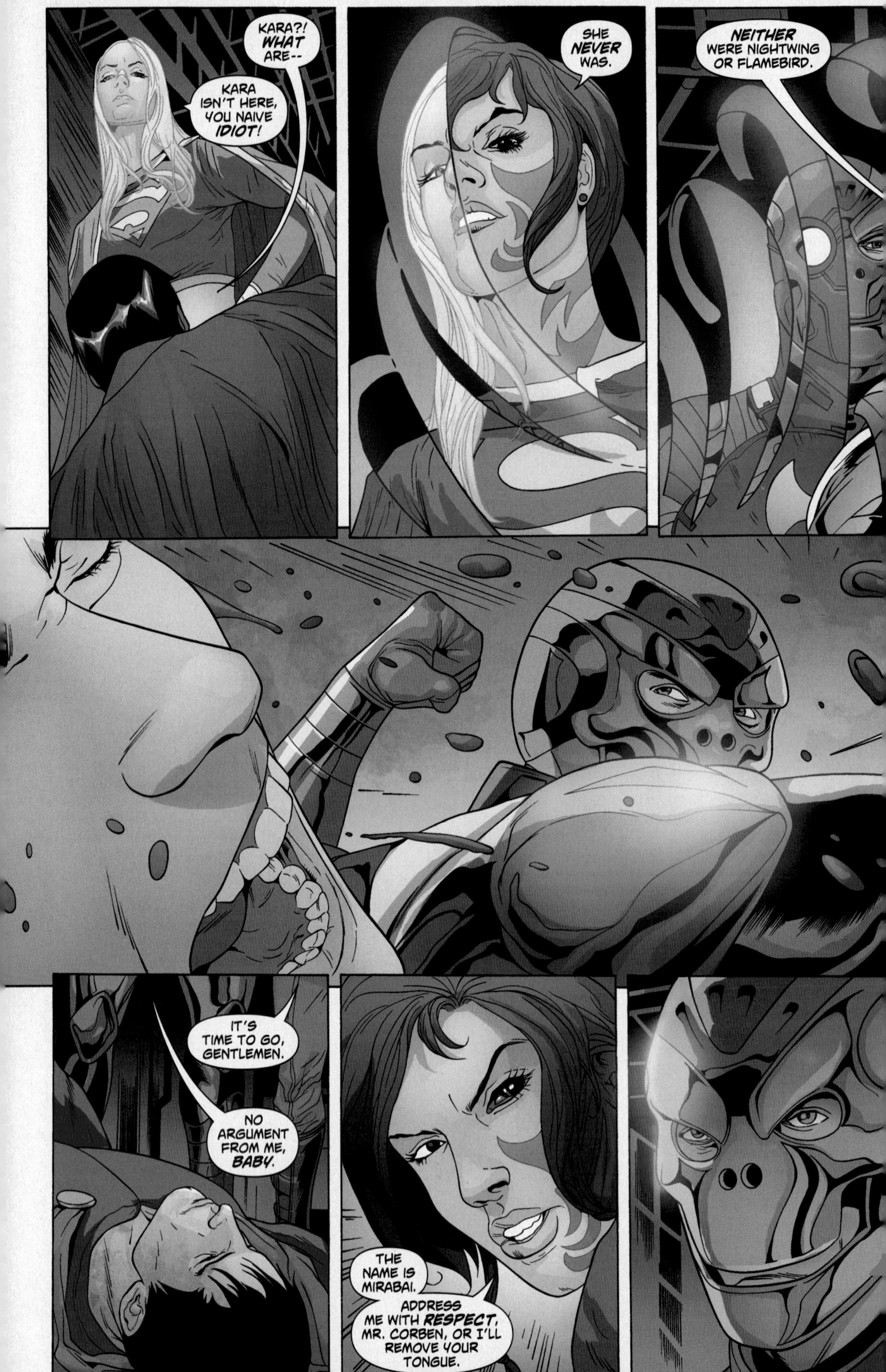
KARA?! WHAT ARE--
KARA ISN'T HERE, YOU NAIVE IDIOT!
SHE NEVER WAS.
NEITHER WERE NIGHTWING OR FLAMEBIRD.
IT'S TIME TO GO, GENTLEMEN.
NO ARGUMENT FROM ME, BABY.
THE NAME IS MIRABAI.
ADDRESS ME WITH RESPECT, MR. CORBEN, OR I'LL REMOVE YOUR TONGUE.

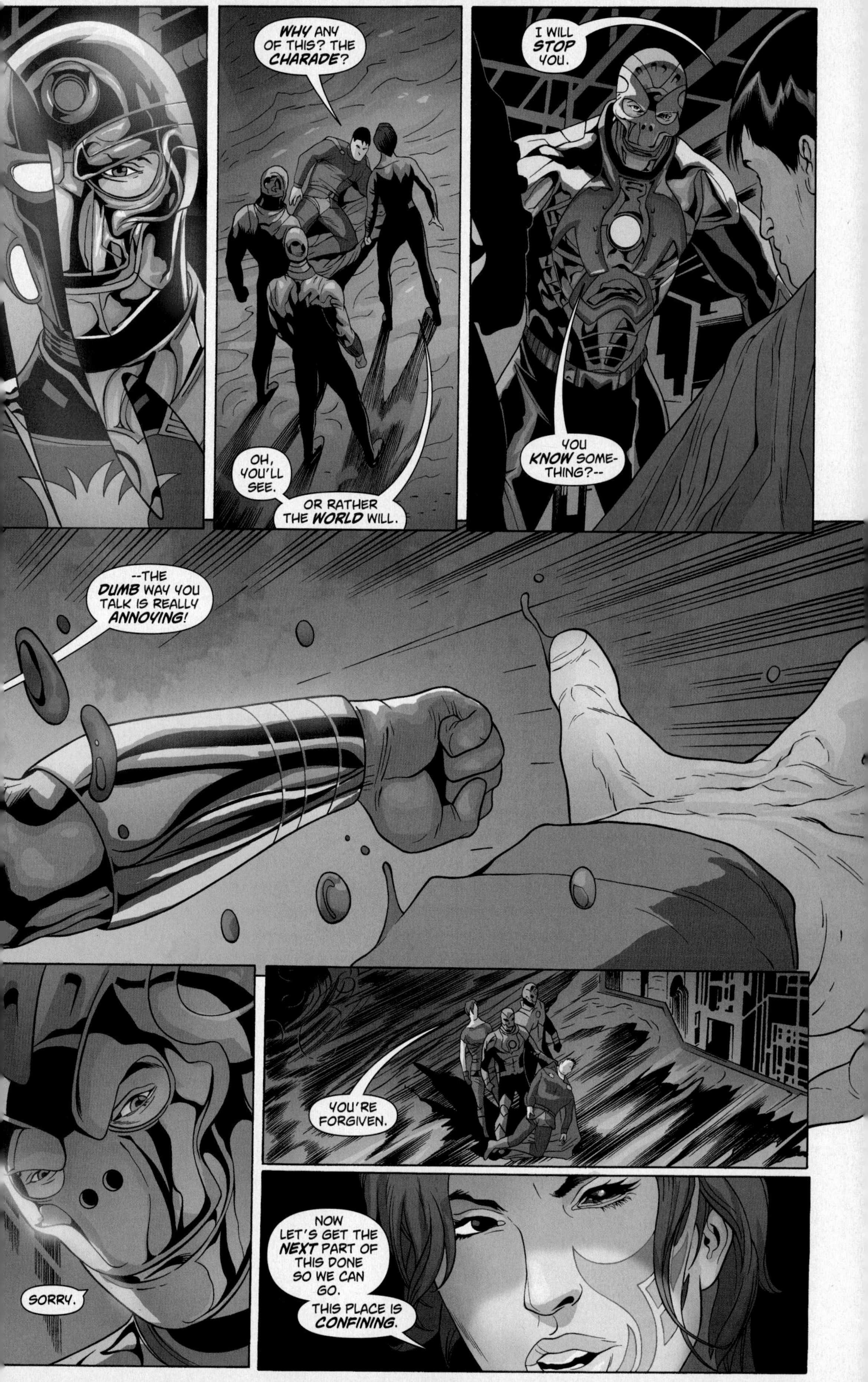
WHY ANY OF THIS? THE CHARADE?
OH, YOU'LL SEE.
OR RATHER THE WORLD WILL.
I WILL STOP YOU.
YOU KNOW SOME-THING?--
--THE DUMB WAY YOU TALK IS REALLY ANNOYING!
SORRY.
YOU'RE FORGIVEN.
NOW LET'S GET THE NEXT PART OF THIS DONE SO WE CAN GO.
THIS PLACE IS CONFINING.

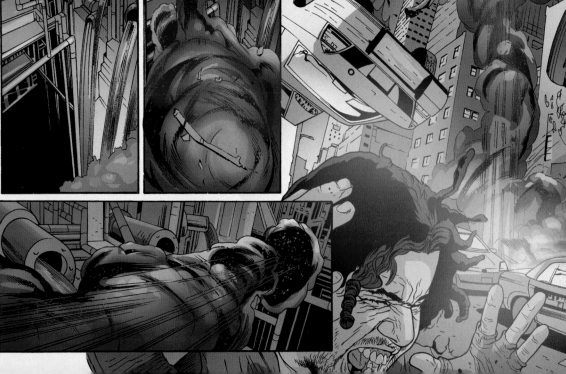

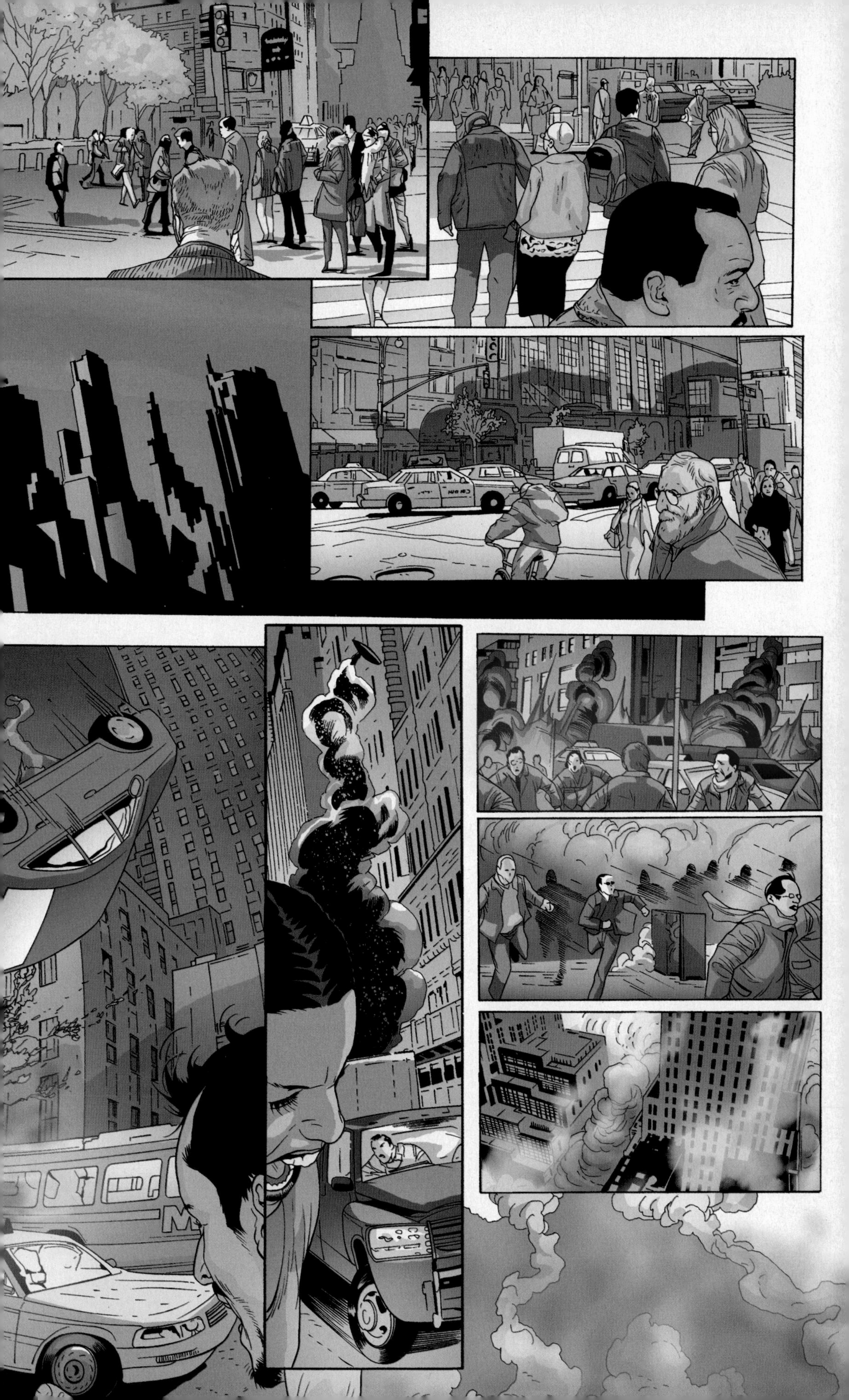

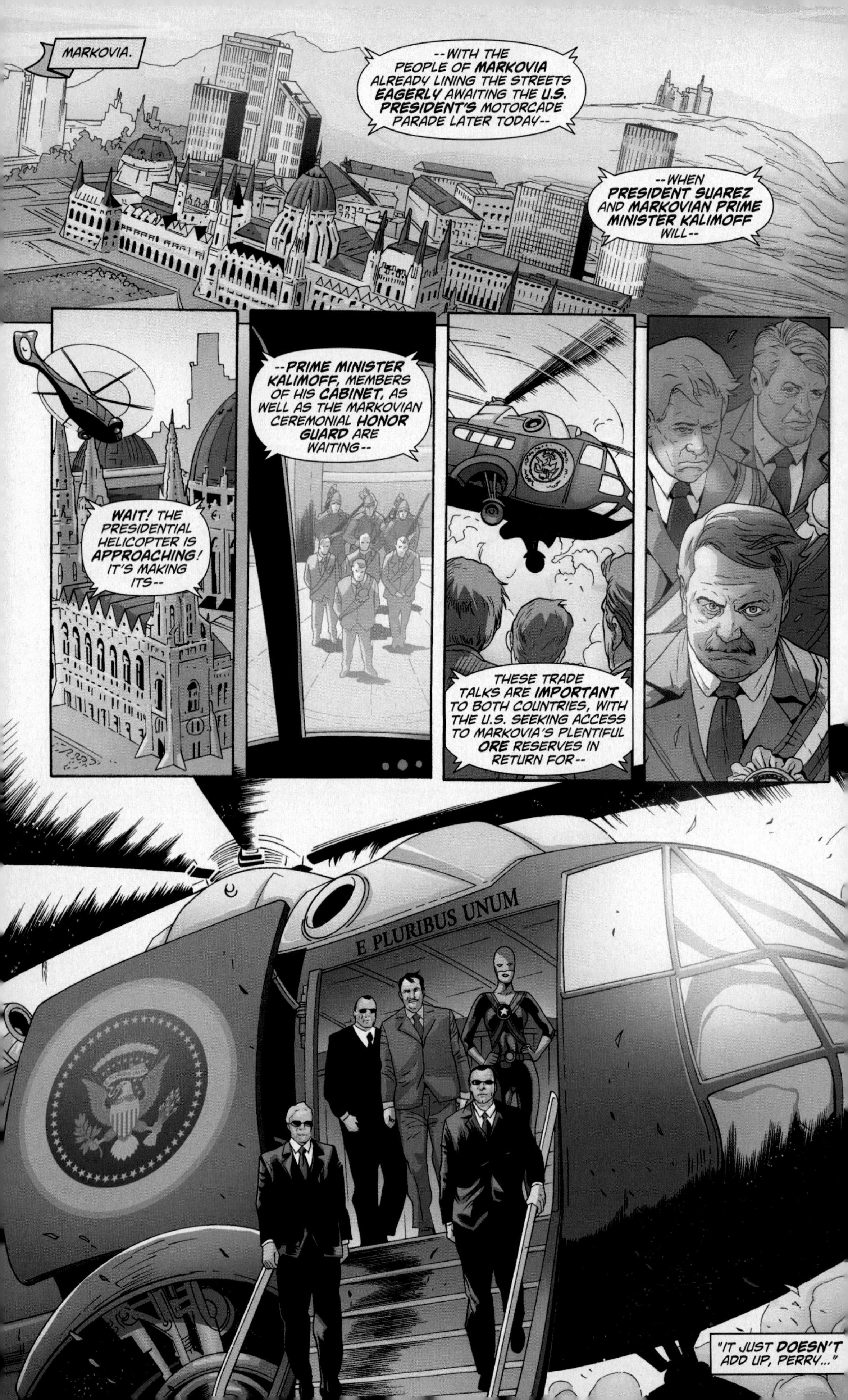
MARKOVIA.
--WITH THE PEOPLE OF MARKOVIA ALREADY LINING THE STREETS EAGERLY AWAITING THE U.S. PRESIDENT'S MOTORCADE PARADE LATER TODAY--
--WHEN PRESIDENT SUAREZ AND MARKOVIAN PRIME MINISTER KALIMOFF WILL--
WAIT! THE PRESIDENTIAL HELICOPTER IS APPROACHING! IT'S MAKING ITS--
--PRIME MINISTER KALIMOFF, MEMBERS OF HIS CABINET, AS WELL AS THE MARKOVIAN CEREMONIAL HONOR GUARD ARE WAITING--
THESE TRADE TALKS ARE IMPORTANT TO BOTH COUNTRIES, WITH THE U.S. SEEKING ACCESS TO MARKOVIA'S PLENTIFUL ORE RESERVES IN RETURN FOR--
E PLURIBUS UNUM
"IT JUST DOESN'T ADD UP, PERRY..."

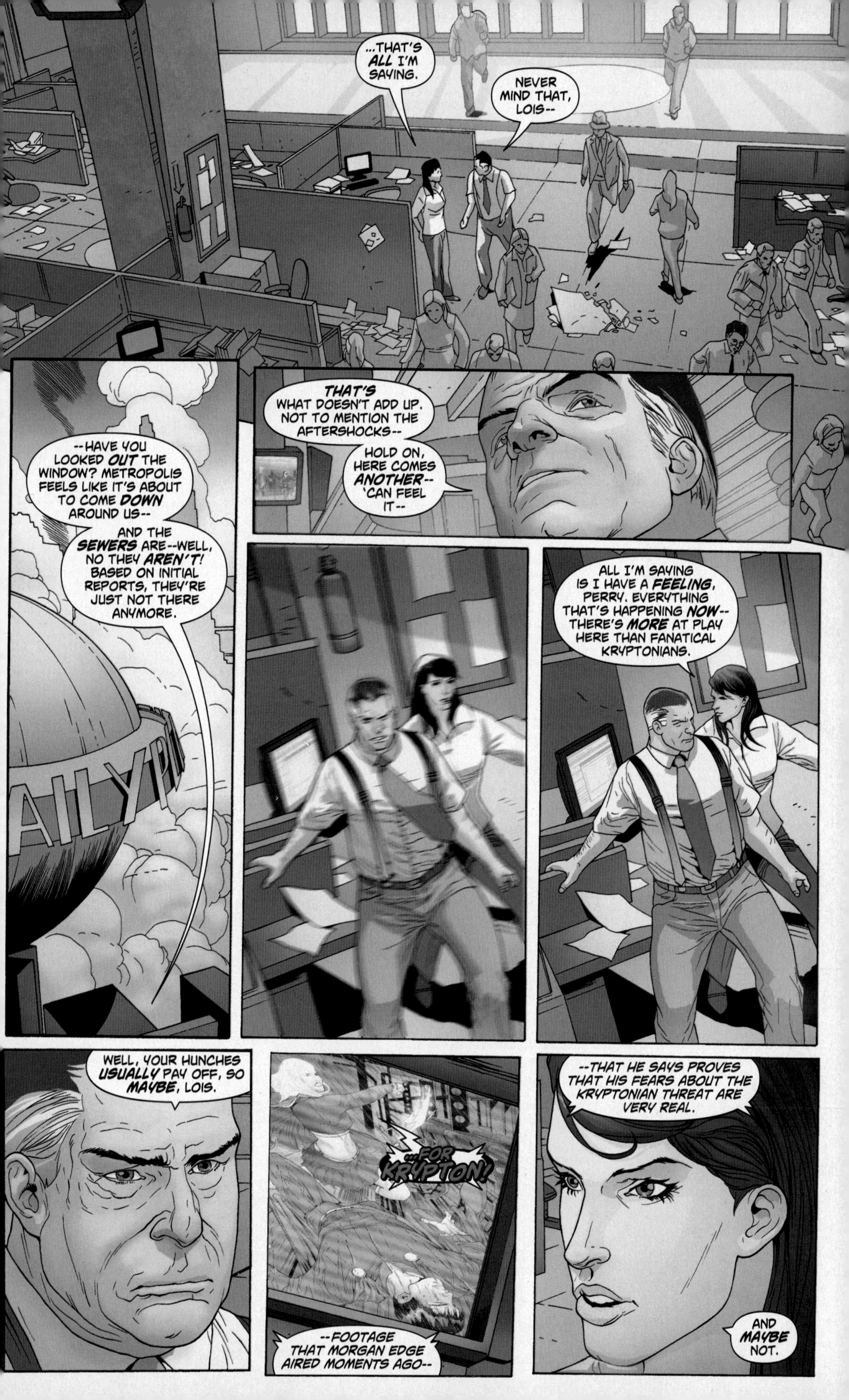
...THAT'S ALL I'M SAYING.
NEVER MIND THAT, LOIS--
--HAVE YOU LOOKED OUT THE WINDOW? METROPOLIS FEELS LIKE IT'S ABOUT TO COME DOWN AROUND US--
AND THE SEWERS ARE--WELL, NO THEY AREN'T! BASED ON INITIAL REPORTS, THEY'RE JUST NOT THERE ANYMORE.
AILY P
THAT'S WHAT DOESN'T ADD UP. NOT TO MENTION THE AFTERSHOCKS--
HOLD ON, HERE COMES ANOTHER-- 'CAN FEEL IT--
ALL I'M SAYING IS I HAVE A FEELING, PERRY. EVERYTHING THAT'S HAPPENING NOW-- THERE'S MORE AT PLAY HERE THAN FANATICAL KRYPTONIANS.
WELL, YOUR HUNCHES USUALLY PAY OFF, SO MAYBE, LOIS.
...FOR KRYPTON!
--FOOTAGE THAT MORGAN EDGE AIRED MOMENTS AGO--
--THAT HE SAYS PROVES THAT HIS FEARS ABOUT THE KRYPTONIAN THREAT ARE VERY REAL.
AND MAYBE NOT.

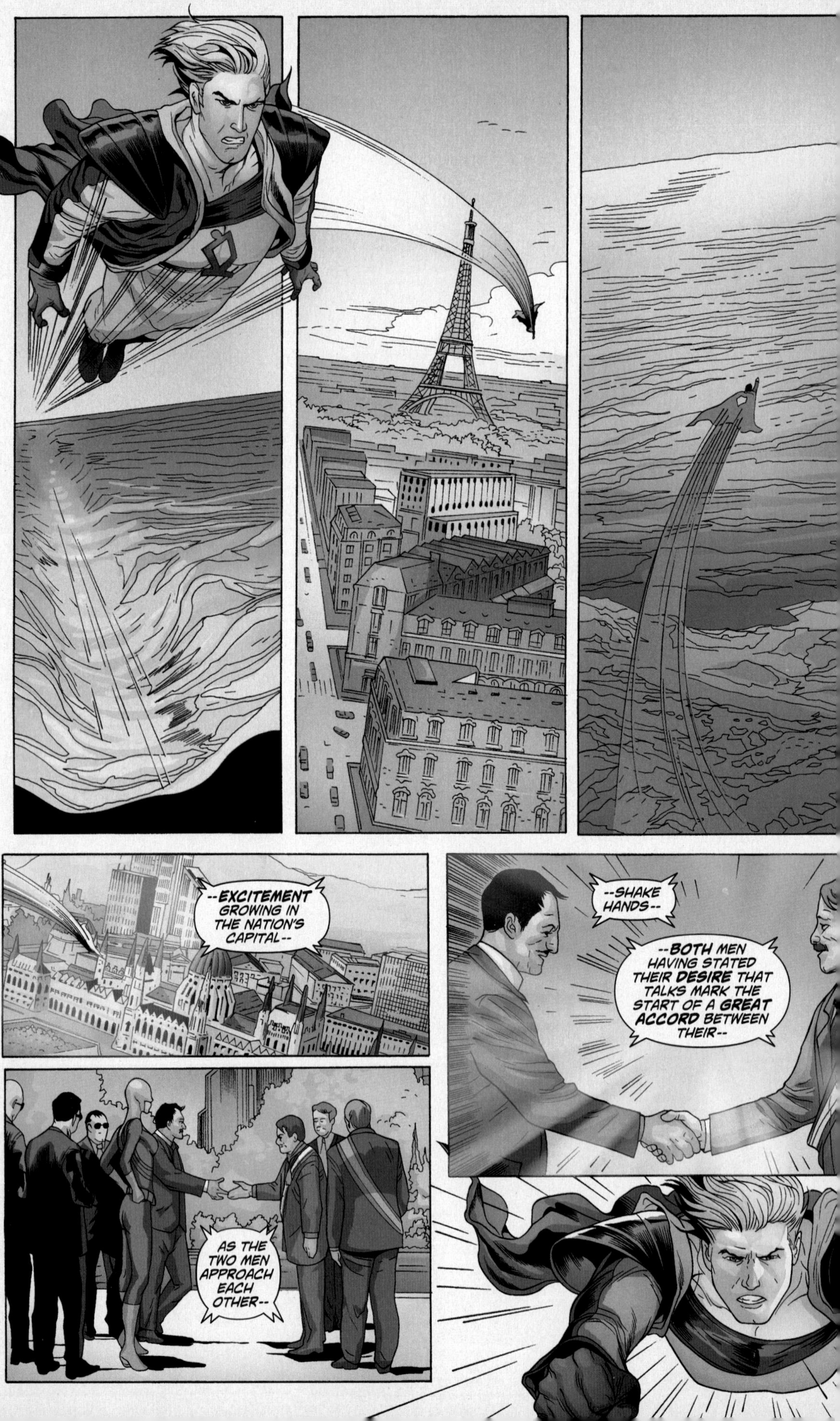
--EXCITEMENT GROWING IN THE NATION'S CAPITAL--
--SHAKE HANDS--
--BOTH MEN HAVING STATED THEIR DESIRE THAT TALKS MARK THE START OF A GREAT ACCORD BETWEEN THEIR--
AS THE TWO MEN APPROACH EACH OTHER--

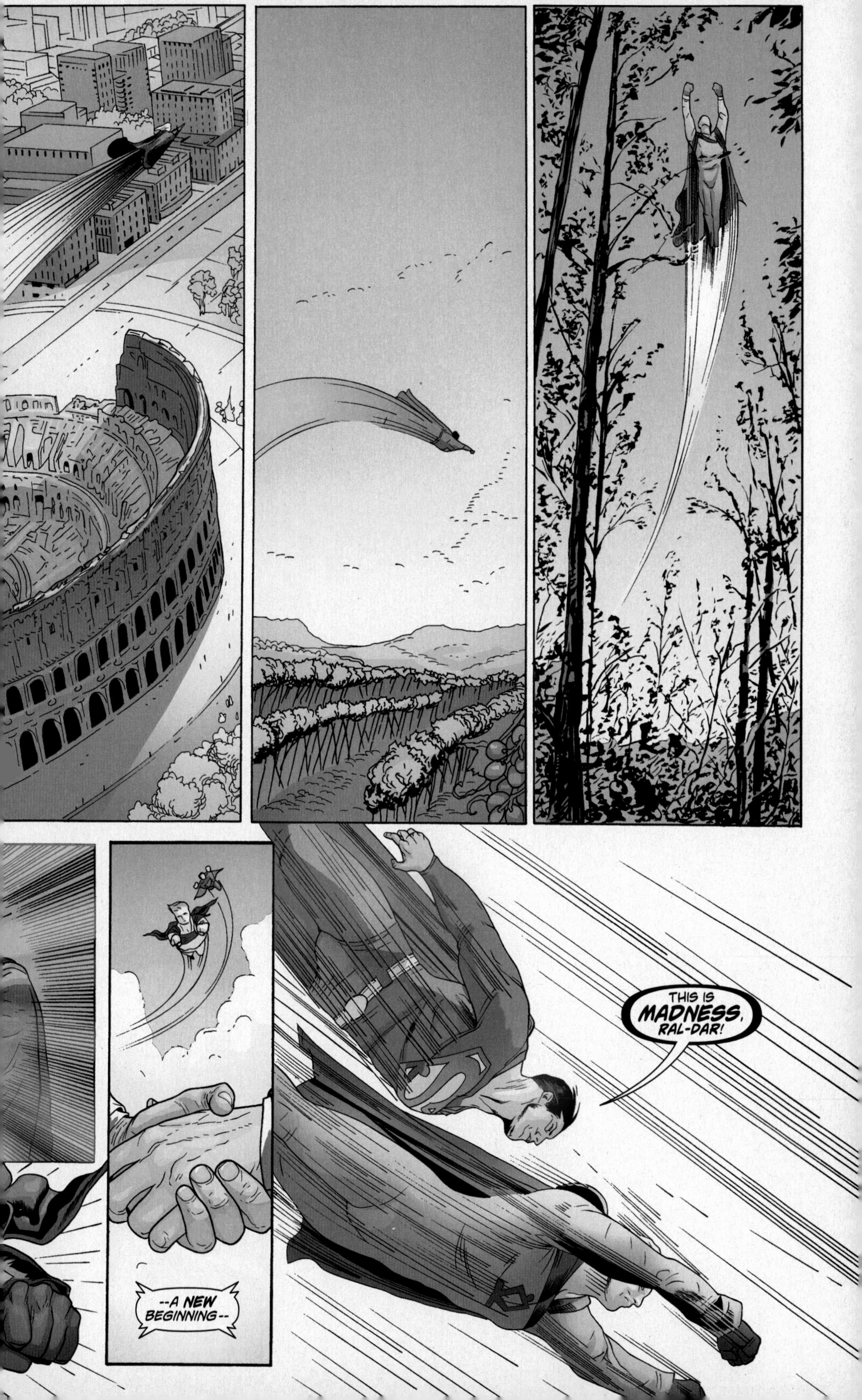
THIS IS MADNESS, RAL-DAR!
--A NEW BEGINNING--

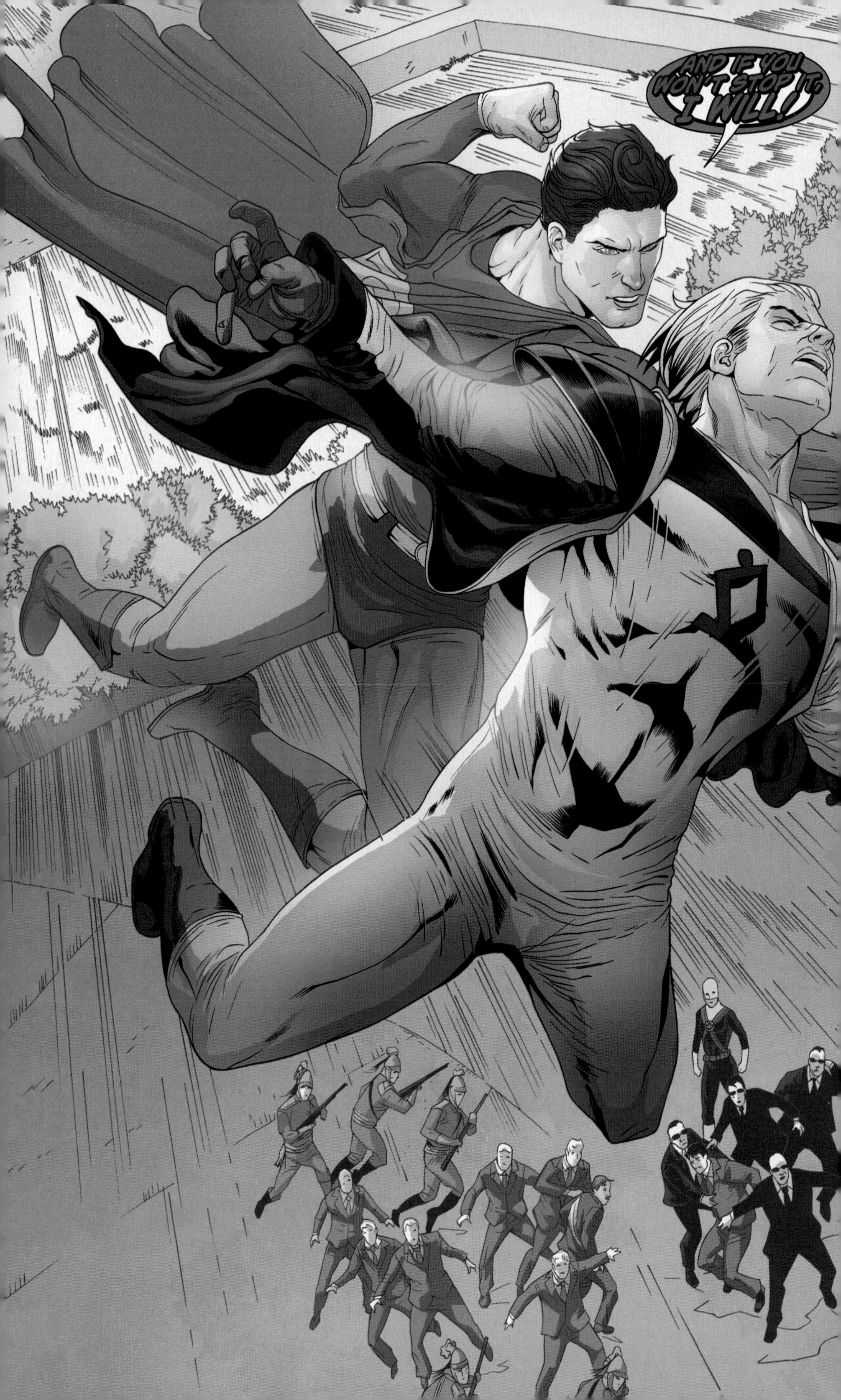
AND IF YOU WON'T STOP IT, I WILL!

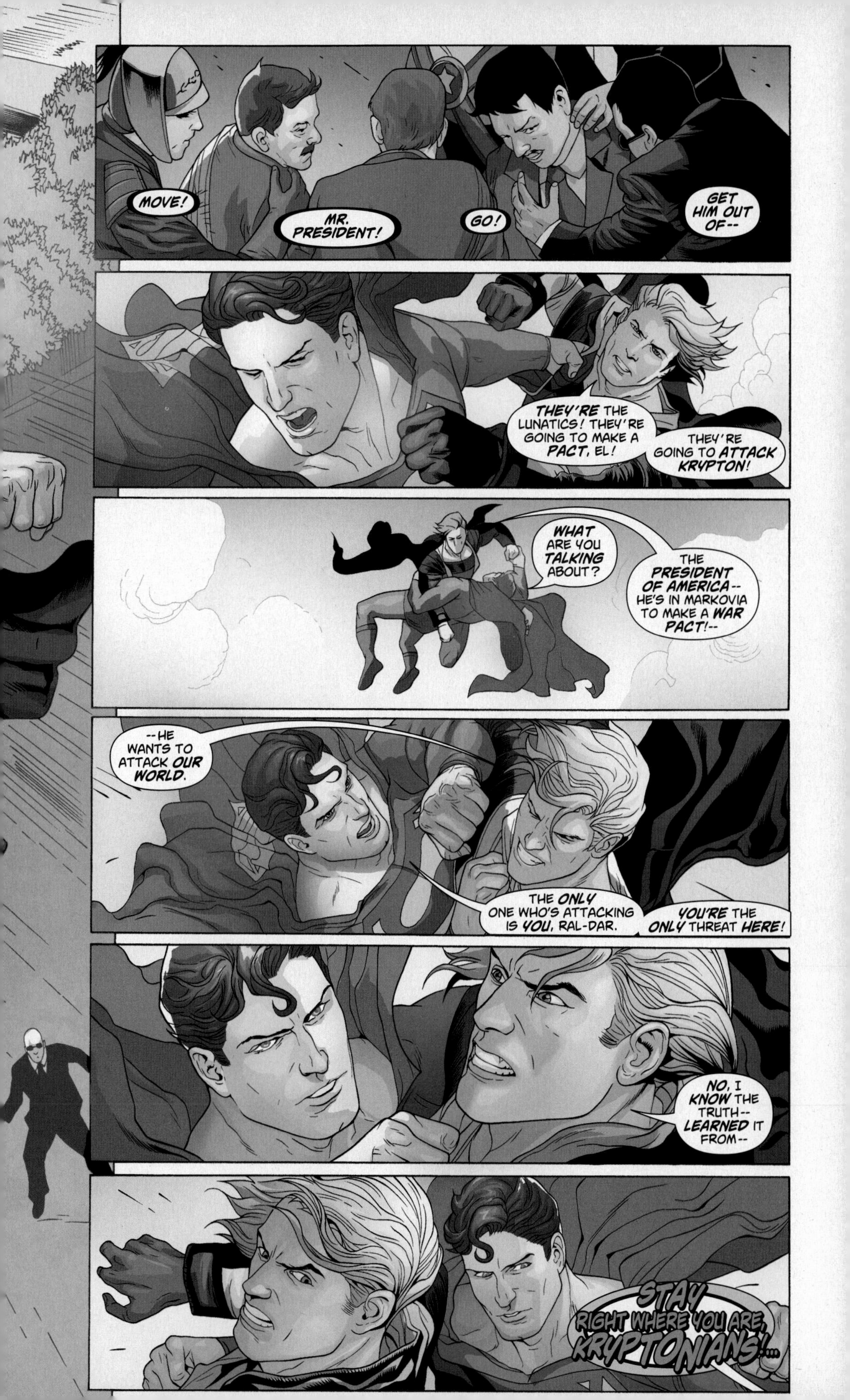
MOVE!
MR. PRESIDENT!
GO!
GET HIM OUT OF--
THEY'RE THE LUNATICS! THEY'RE GOING TO MAKE A PACT, EL!
THEY'RE GOING TO ATTACK KRYPTON!
WHAT ARE YOU TALKING ABOUT?
THE PRESIDENT OF AMERICA-- HE'S IN MARKOVIA TO MAKE A WAR PACT!--
--HE WANTS TO ATTACK OUR WORLD.
THE ONLY ONE WHO'S ATTACKING IS YOU, RAL-DAR.
YOU'RE THE ONLY THREAT HERE!
NO, I KNOW THE TRUTH-- LEARNED IT FROM--
STAY RIGHT WHERE YOU ARE, KRYPTONIANS!...

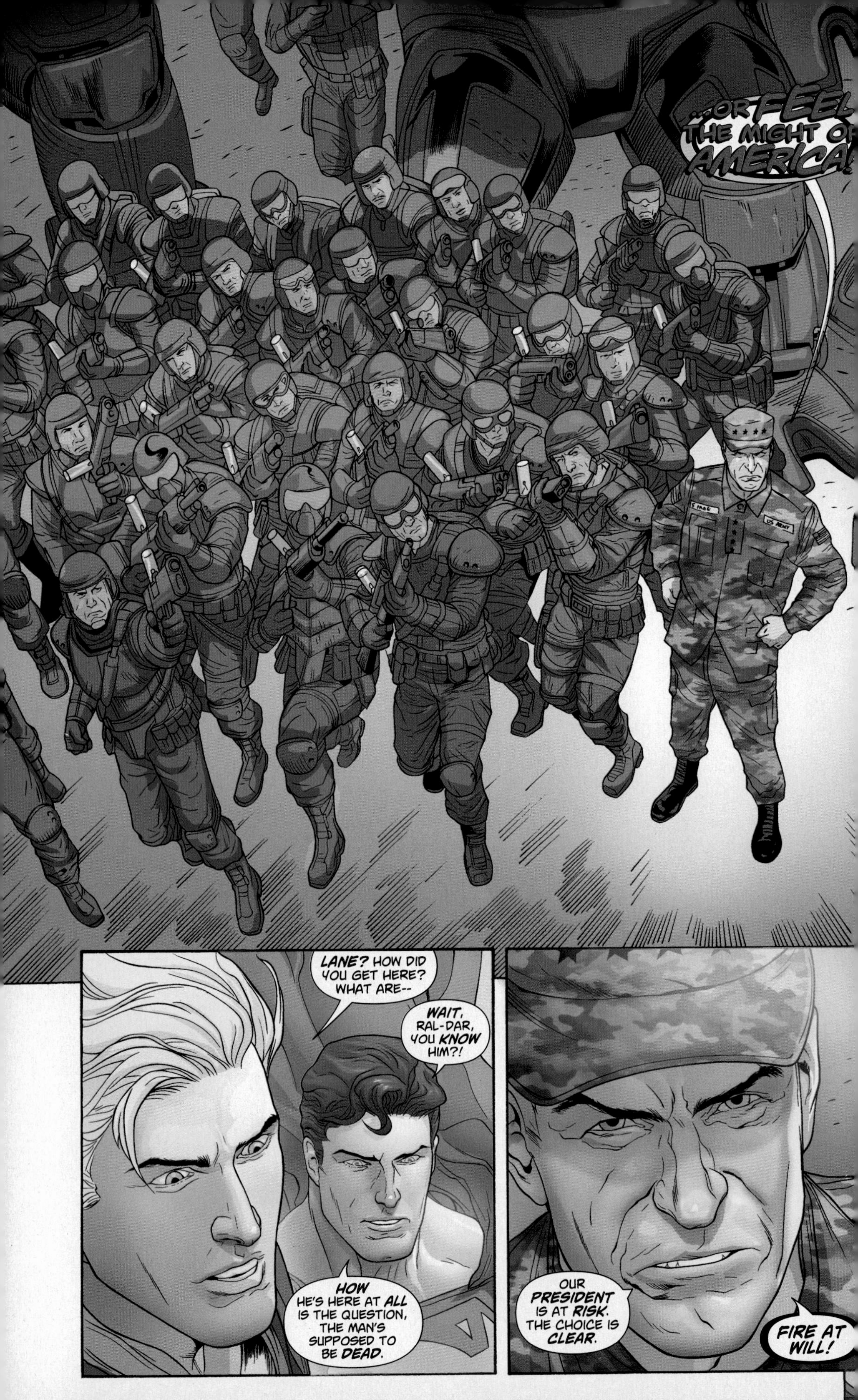
...OR FEEL THE MIGHT OF AMERICA!
LANE? HOW DID YOU GET HERE? WHAT ARE--
WAIT, RAL-DAR, YOU KNOW HIM?!
HOW HE'S HERE AT ALL IS THE QUESTION, THE MAN'S SUPPOSED TO BE DEAD.
OUR PRESIDENT IS AT RISK. THE CHOICE IS CLEAR.
FIRE AT WILL!

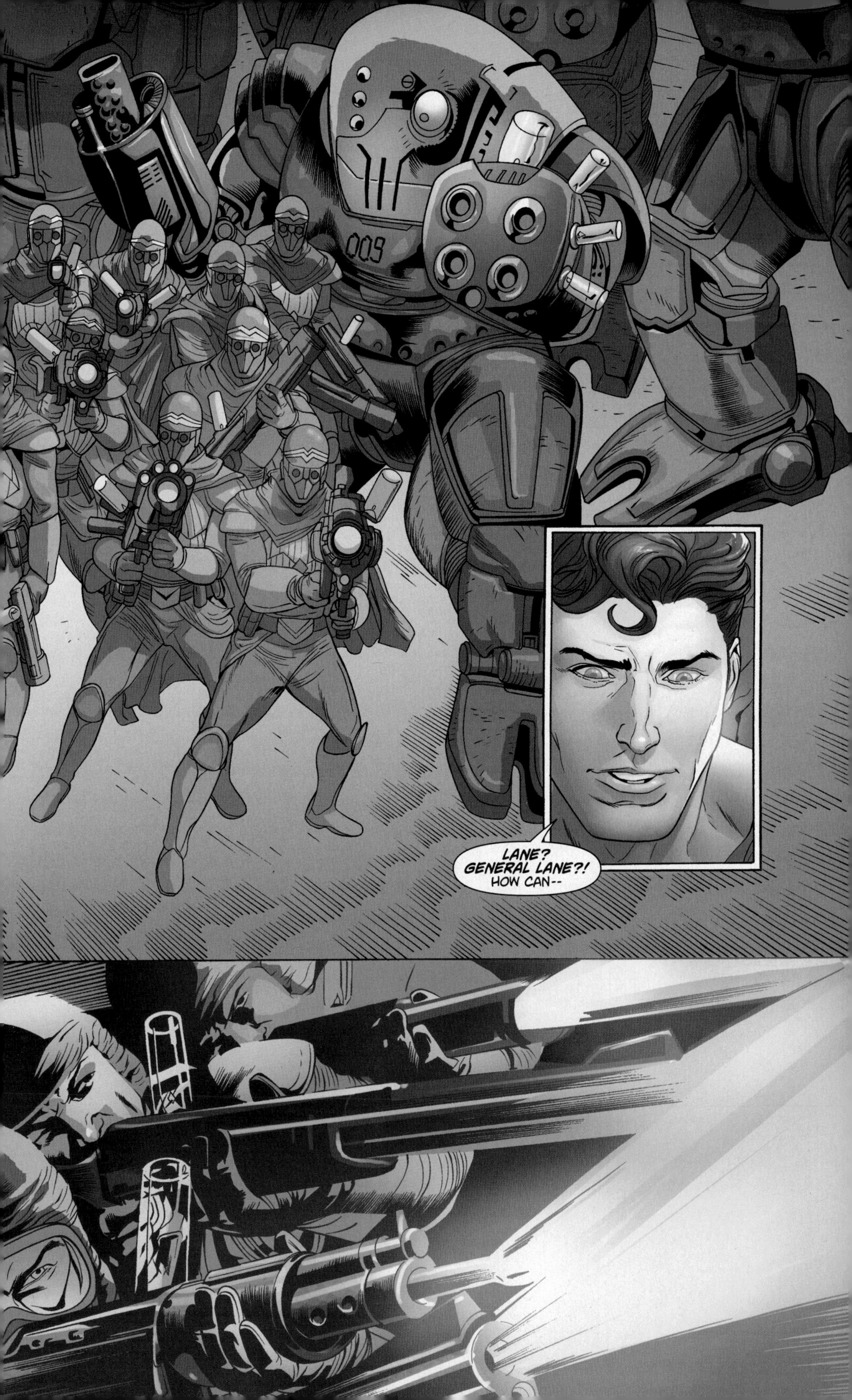
LANE? GENERAL LANE?! HOW CAN--

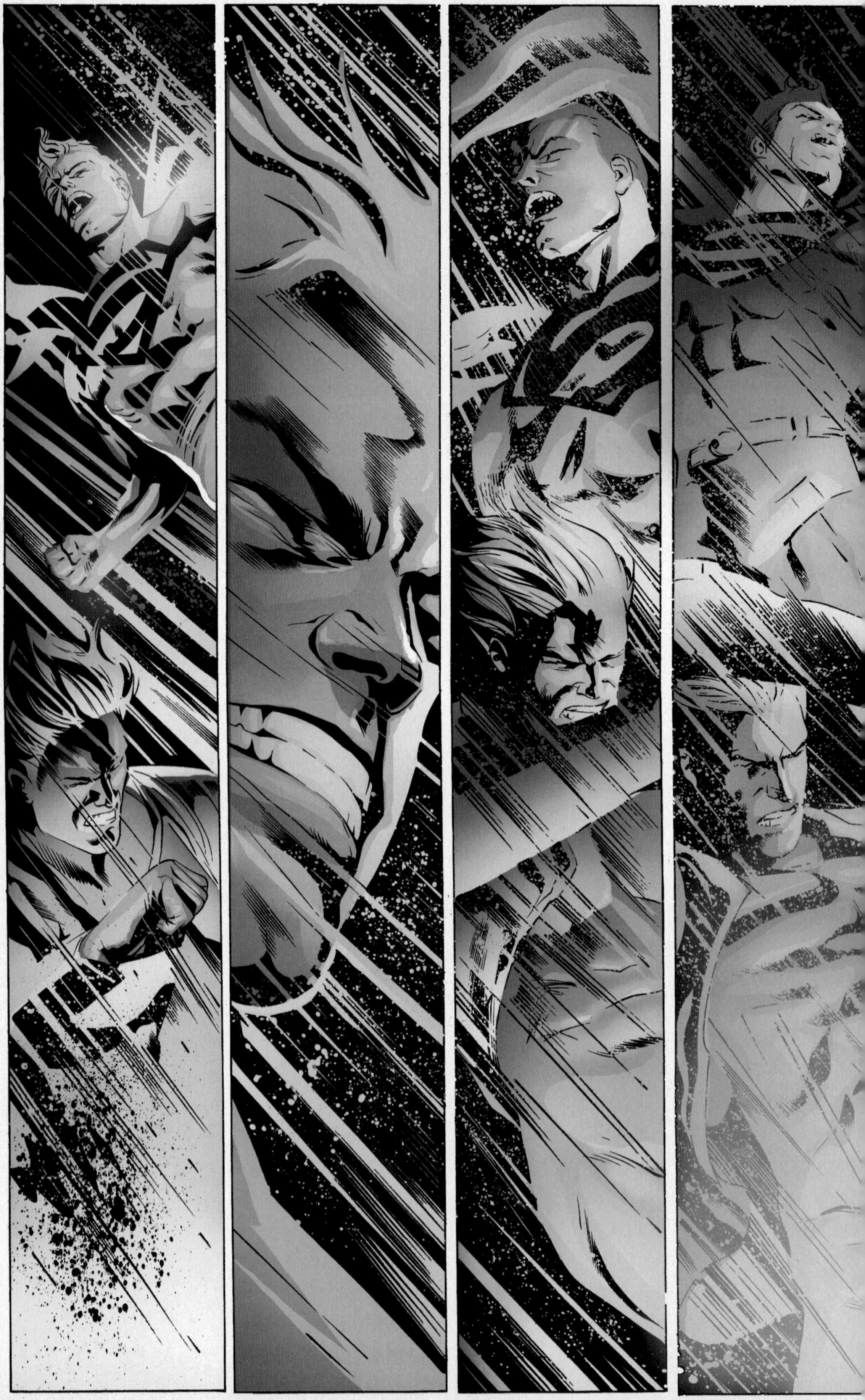

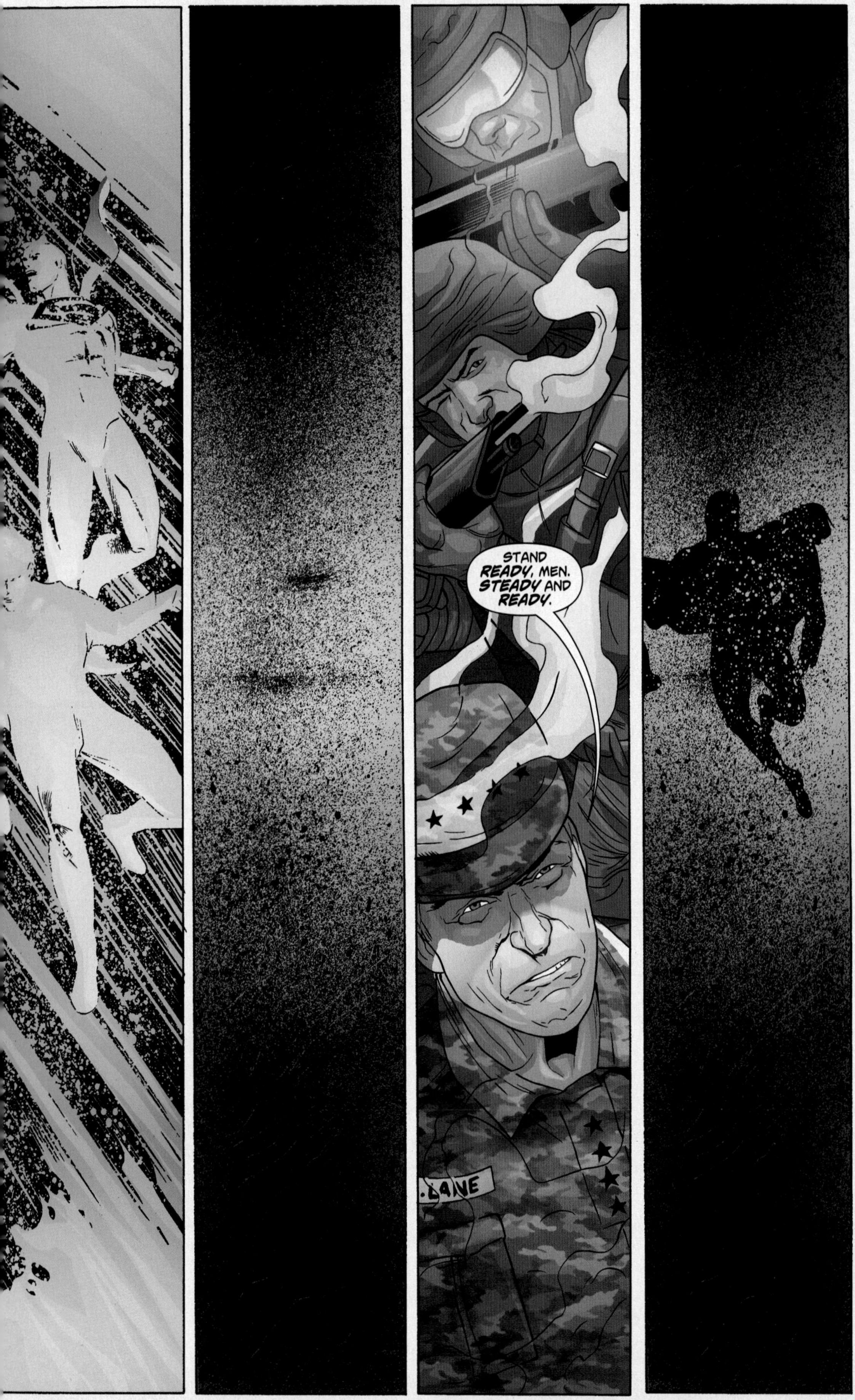
STAND READY, MEN. STEADY AND READY.
LANE

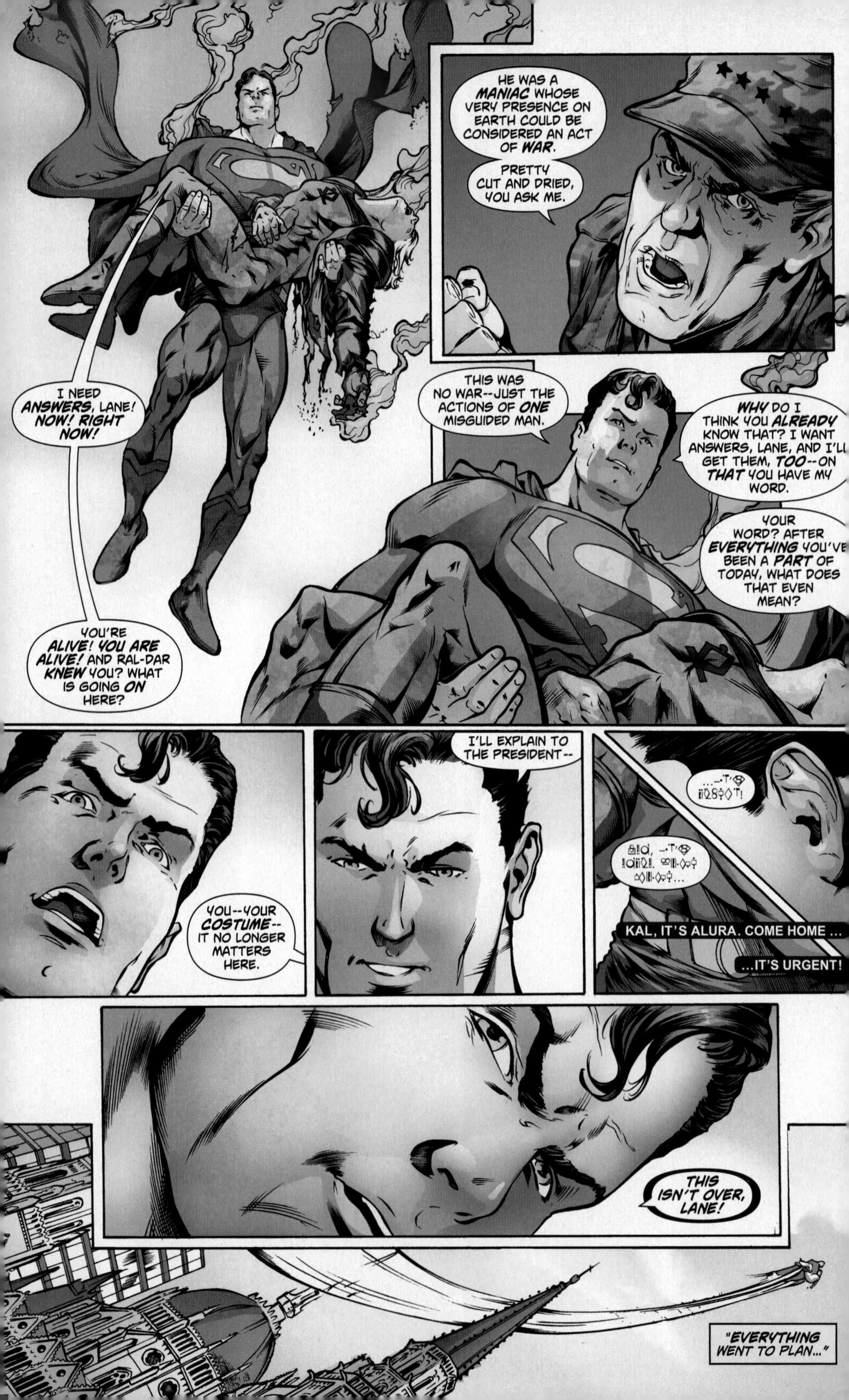
HE WAS A MANIAC WHOSE VERY PRESENCE ON EARTH COULD BE CONSIDERED AN ACT OF WAR.
PRETTY CUT AND DRIED, YOU ASK ME.
THIS WAS NO WAR--JUST THE ACTIONS OF ONE MISGUIDED MAN.
WHY DO I THINK YOU ALREADY KNOW THAT? I WANT ANSWERS, LANE, AND I'LL GET THEM, TOO--ON THAT YOU HAVE MY WORD.
YOUR WORD? AFTER EVERYTHING YOU'VE BEEN A PART OF TODAY, WHAT DOES THAT EVEN MEAN?
I NEED ANSWERS, LANE! NOW! RIGHT NOW!
YOU'RE ALIVE! YOU ARE ALIVE! AND RAL-DAR KNEW YOU? WHAT IS GOING ON HERE?
YOU--YOUR COSTUME--IT NO LONGER MATTERS HERE.
I'LL EXPLAIN TO THE PRESIDENT--
KAL, IT'S ALURA. COME HOME ...
...IT'S URGENT!
THIS ISN'T OVER, LANE!
"EVERYTHING WENT TO PLAN..."

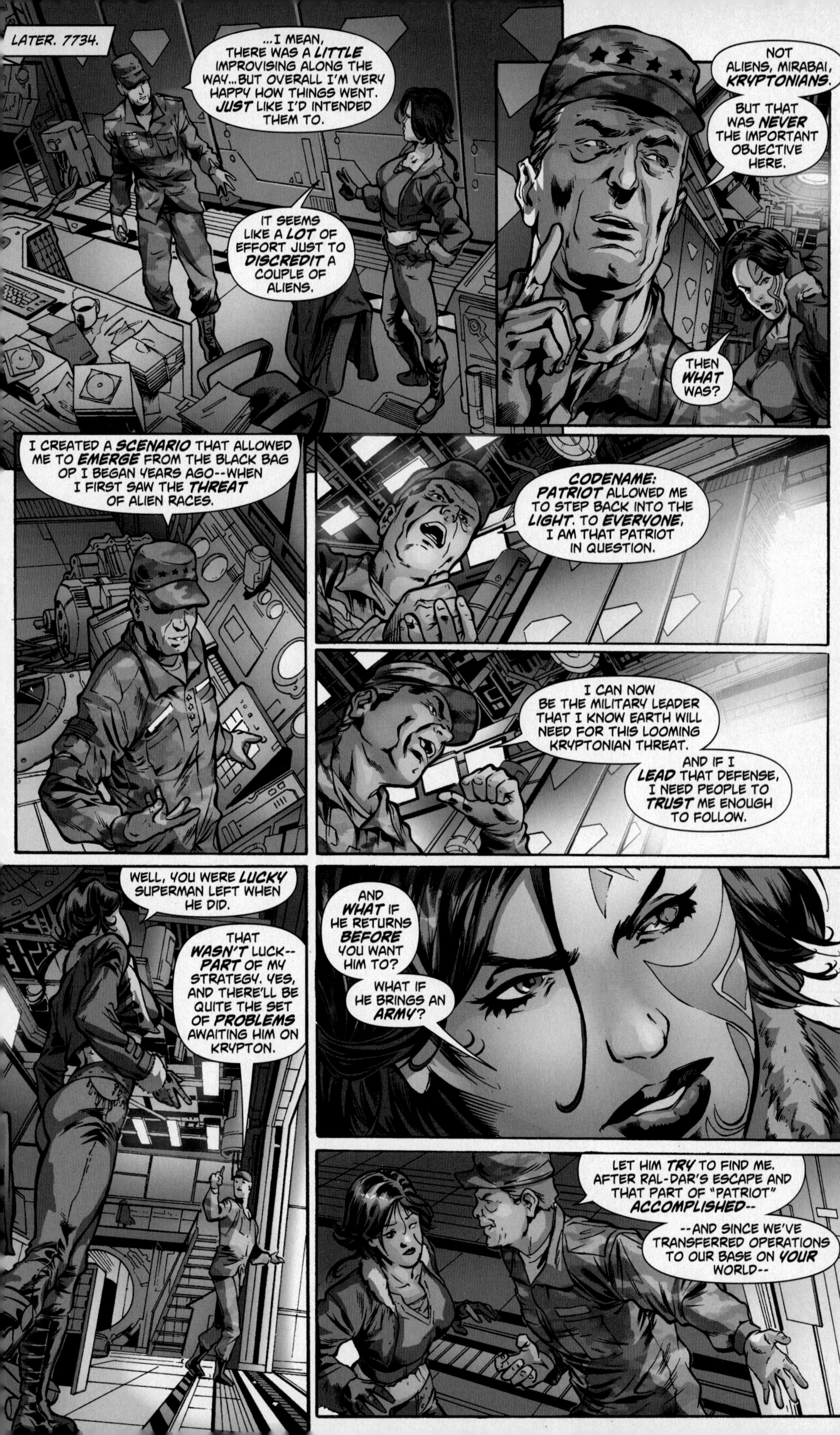
LATER. 7734.
...I MEAN, THERE WAS A LITTLE IMPROVISING ALONG THE WAY...BUT OVERALL I'M VERY HAPPY HOW THINGS WENT. JUST LIKE I'D INTENDED THEM TO.
IT SEEMS LIKE A LOT OF EFFORT JUST TO DISCREDIT A COUPLE OF ALIENS.
NOT ALIENS, MIRABAI, KRYPTONIANS.
BUT THAT WAS NEVER THE IMPORTANT OBJECTIVE HERE.
THEN WHAT WAS?
I CREATED A SCENARIO THAT ALLOWED ME TO EMERGE FROM THE BLACK BAG OP I BEGAN YEARS AGO--WHEN I FIRST SAW THE THREAT OF ALIEN RACES.
CODENAME: PATRIOT ALLOWED ME TO STEP BACK INTO THE LIGHT. TO EVERYONE, I AM THAT PATRIOT IN QUESTION.
I CAN NOW BE THE MILITARY LEADER THAT I KNOW EARTH WILL NEED FOR THIS LOOMING KRYPTONIAN THREAT.
AND IF I LEAD THAT DEFENSE, I NEED PEOPLE TO TRUST ME ENOUGH TO FOLLOW.
WELL, YOU WERE LUCKY SUPERMAN LEFT WHEN HE DID.
THAT WASN'T LUCK-- PART OF MY STRATEGY. YES, AND THERE'LL BE QUITE THE SET OF PROBLEMS AWAITING HIM ON KRYPTON.
AND WHAT IF HE RETURNS BEFORE YOU WANT HIM TO?
WHAT IF HE BRINGS AN ARMY?
LET HIM TRY TO FIND ME. AFTER RAL-DAR'S ESCAPE AND THAT PART OF "PATRIOT" ACCOMPLISHED--
--AND SINCE WE'VE TRANSFERRED OPERATIONS TO OUR BASE ON YOUR WORLD--

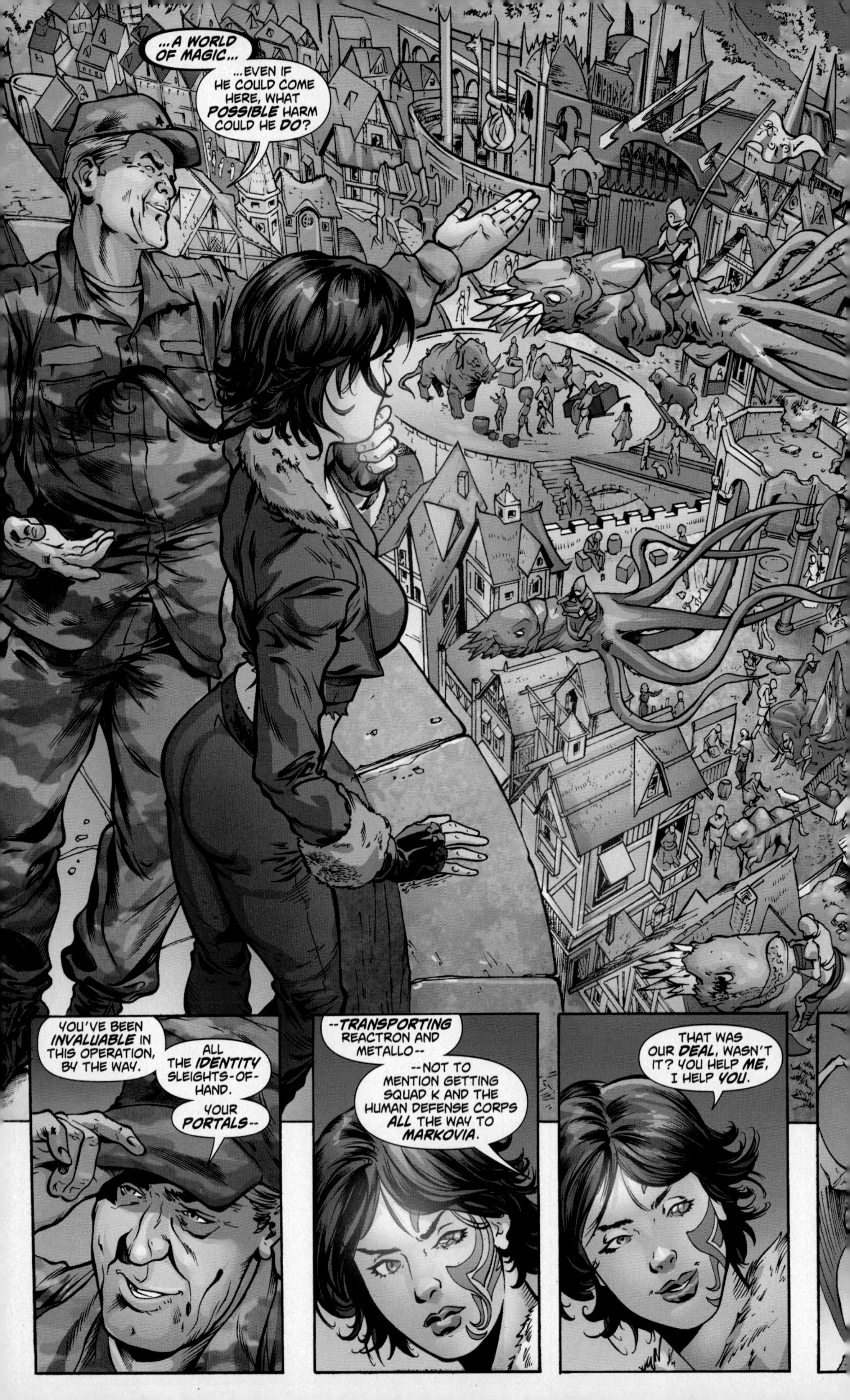
...A WORLD OF MAGIC...
...EVEN IF HE COULD COME HERE, WHAT POSSIBLE HARM COULD HE DO?
YOU'VE BEEN INVALUABLE IN THIS OPERATION, BY THE WAY.
ALL THE IDENTITY SLEIGHTS-OF-HAND.
YOUR PORTALS--
--TRANSPORTING REACTRON AND METALLO--
--NOT TO MENTION GETTING SQUAD K AND THE HUMAN DEFENSE CORPS ALL THE WAY TO MARKOVIA.
THAT WAS OUR DEAL, WASN'T IT? YOU HELP ME, I HELP YOU.

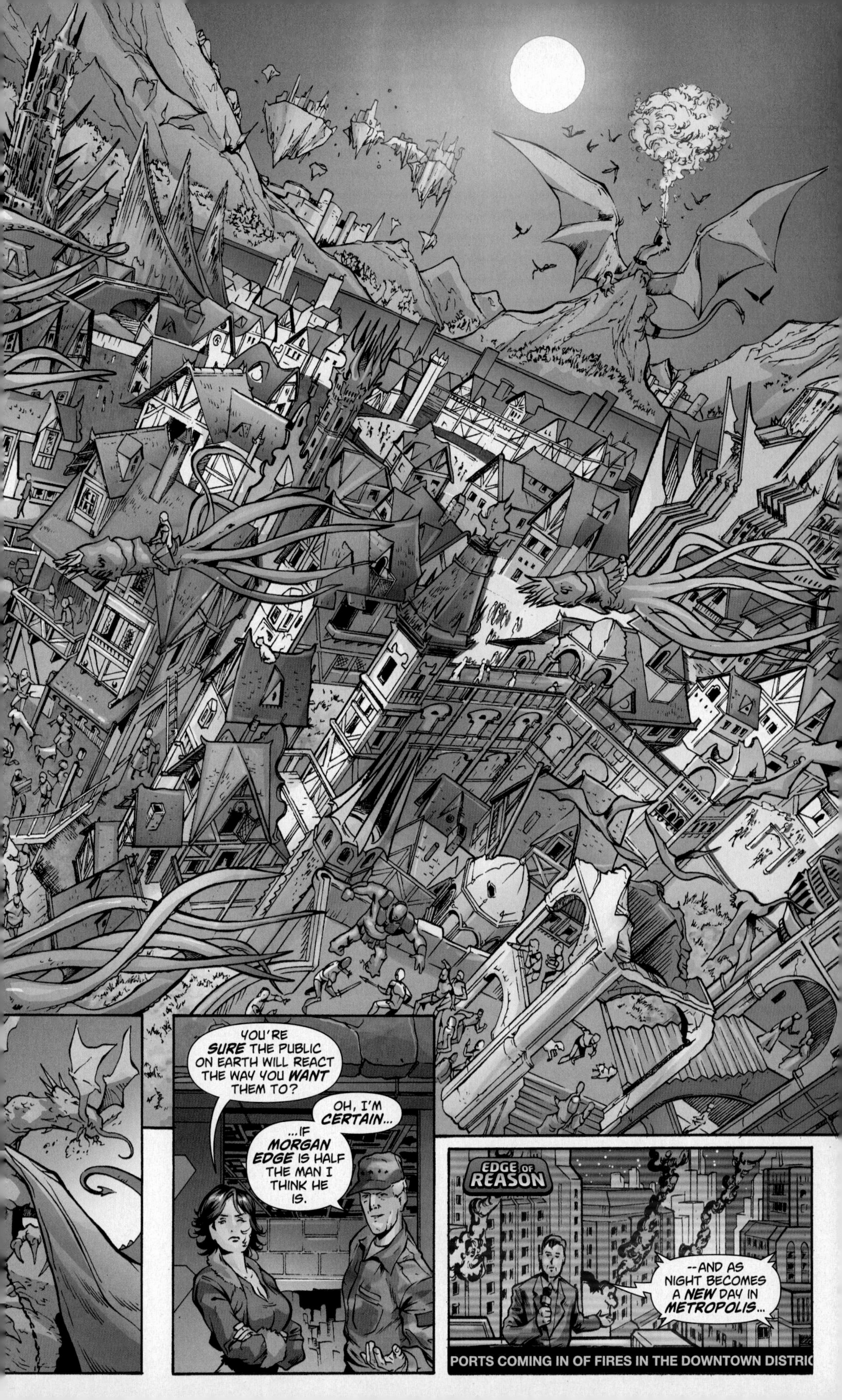
YOU'RE SURE THE PUBLIC ON EARTH WILL REACT THE WAY YOU WANT THEM TO?
OH, I'M CERTAIN...
...IF MORGAN EDGE IS HALF THE MAN I THINK HE IS.
EDGE OF REASON
--AND AS NIGHT BECOMES A NEW DAY IN METROPOLIS...
PORTS COMING IN OF FIRES IN THE DOWNTOWN DISTRIC

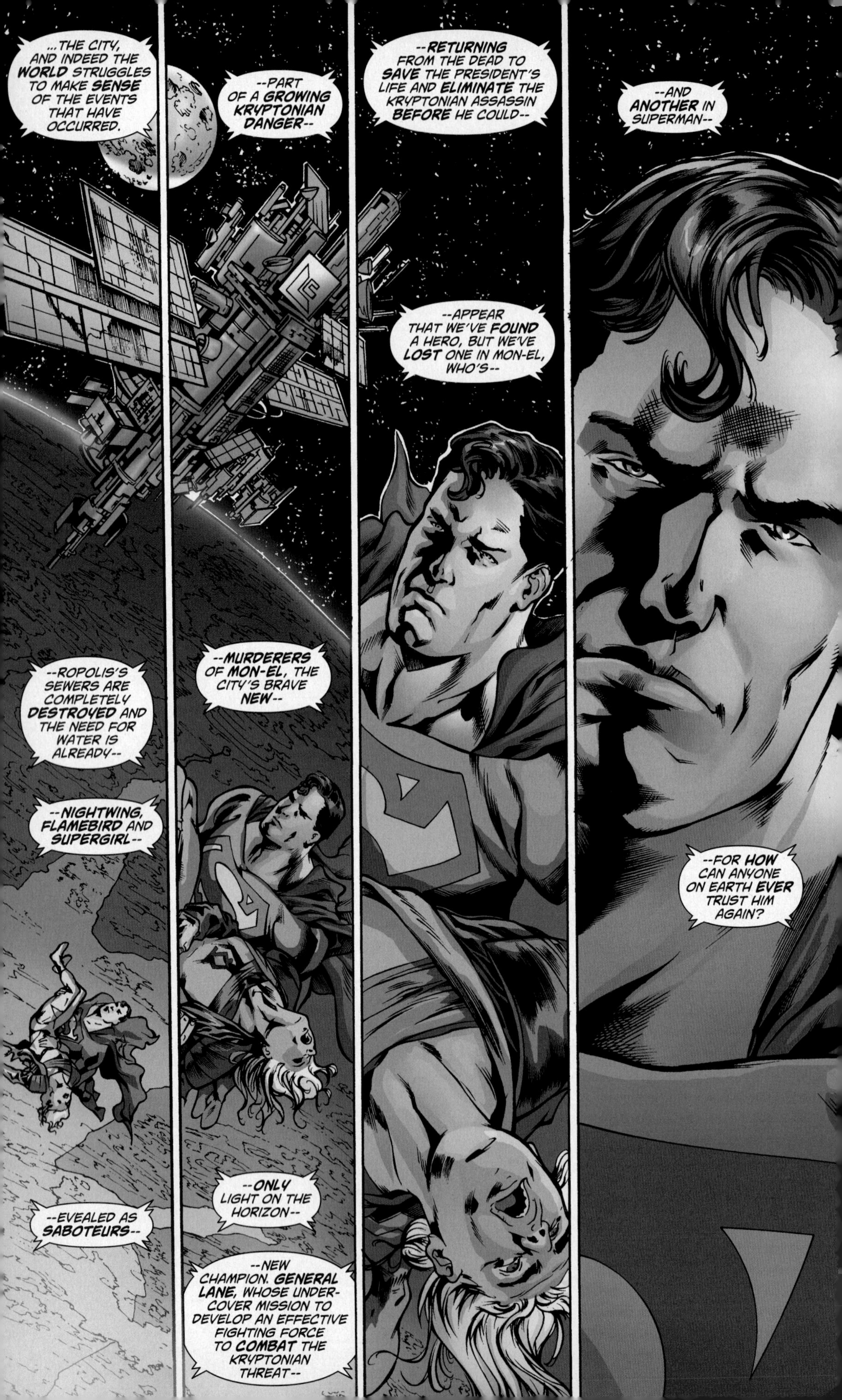
...THE CITY, AND INDEED THE WORLD STRUGGLES TO MAKE SENSE OF THE EVENTS THAT HAVE OCCURRED.
--PART OF A GROWING KRYPTONIAN DANGER--
--RETURNING FROM THE DEAD TO SAVE THE PRESIDENT'S LIFE AND ELIMINATE THE KRYPTONIAN ASSASSIN BEFORE HE COULD--
--AND ANOTHER IN SUPERMAN--
--APPEAR THAT WE'VE FOUND A HERO, BUT WE'VE LOST ONE IN MON-EL, WHO'S--
--ROPOLIS'S SEWERS ARE COMPLETELY DESTROYED AND THE NEED FOR WATER IS ALREADY--
--MURDERERS OF MON-EL, THE CITY'S BRAVE NEW--
--NIGHTWING, FLAMEBIRD AND SUPERGIRL--
--FOR HOW CAN ANYONE ON EARTH EVER TRUST HIM AGAIN?
--EVEALED AS SABOTEURS--
--ONLY LIGHT ON THE HORIZON--
--NEW CHAMPION. GENERAL LANE, WHOSE UNDER-COVER MISSION TO DEVELOP AN EFFECTIVE FIGHTING FORCE TO COMBAT THE KRYPTONIAN THREAT--

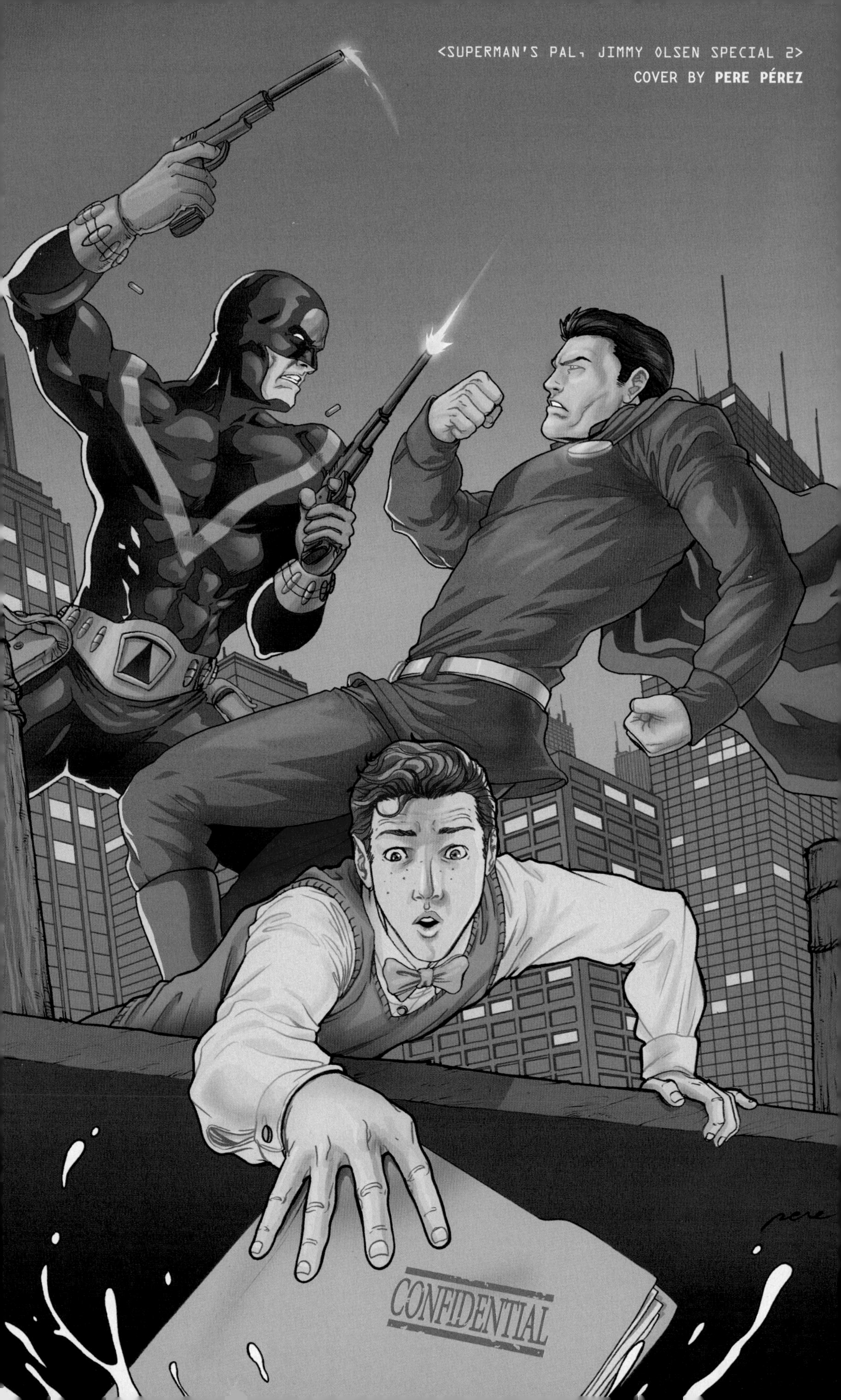
pere
CONFIDENTIAL

<SUPERMAN'S PAL, JIMMY OLSEN SPECIAL 2>
COVER BY **PERE PÉREZ**

CODENAME: PATRIOT <EPILOGUE>

JAMES ROBINSON – WRITER

BERNARD CHANG – ARTIST

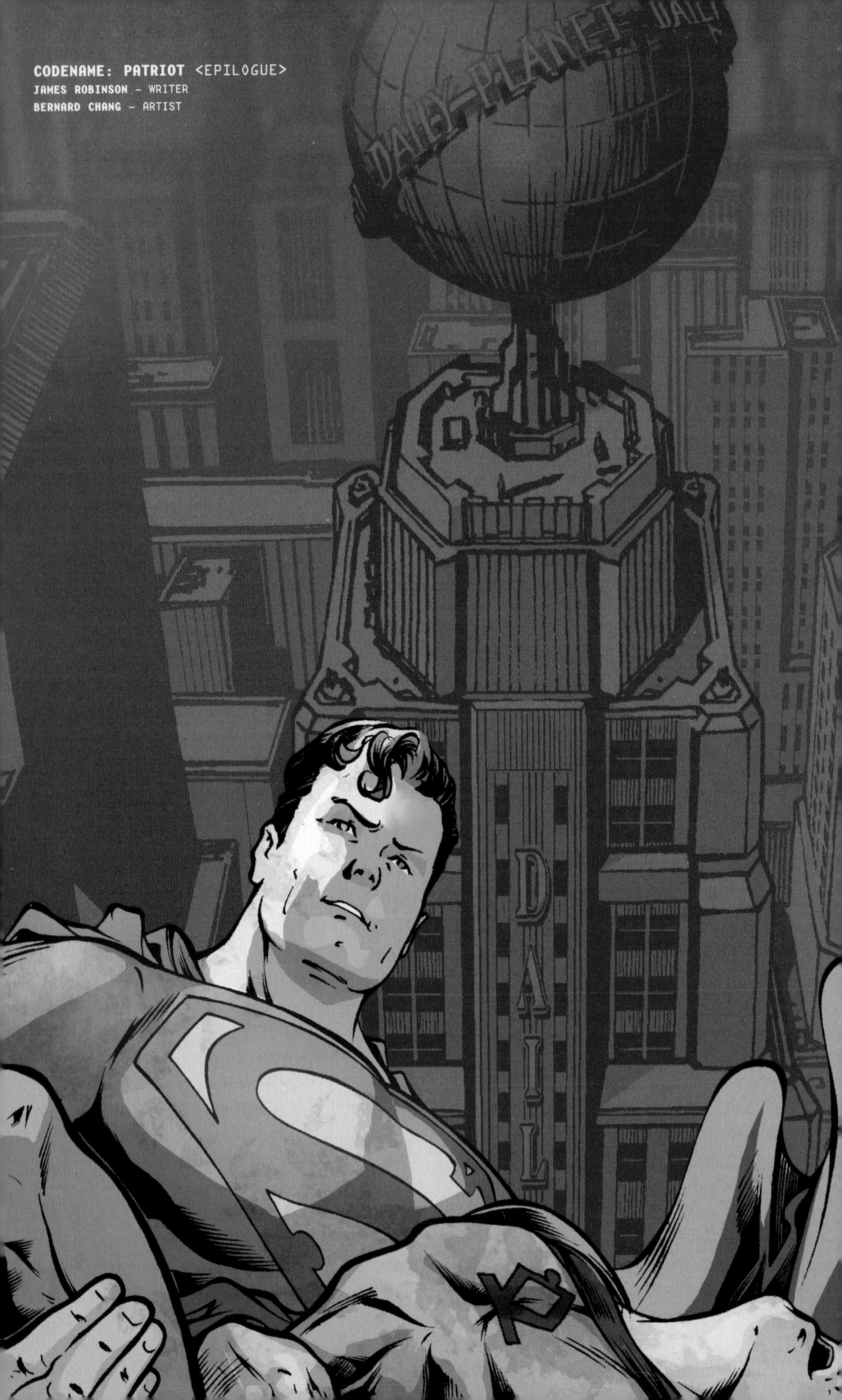
DAILY PLANET

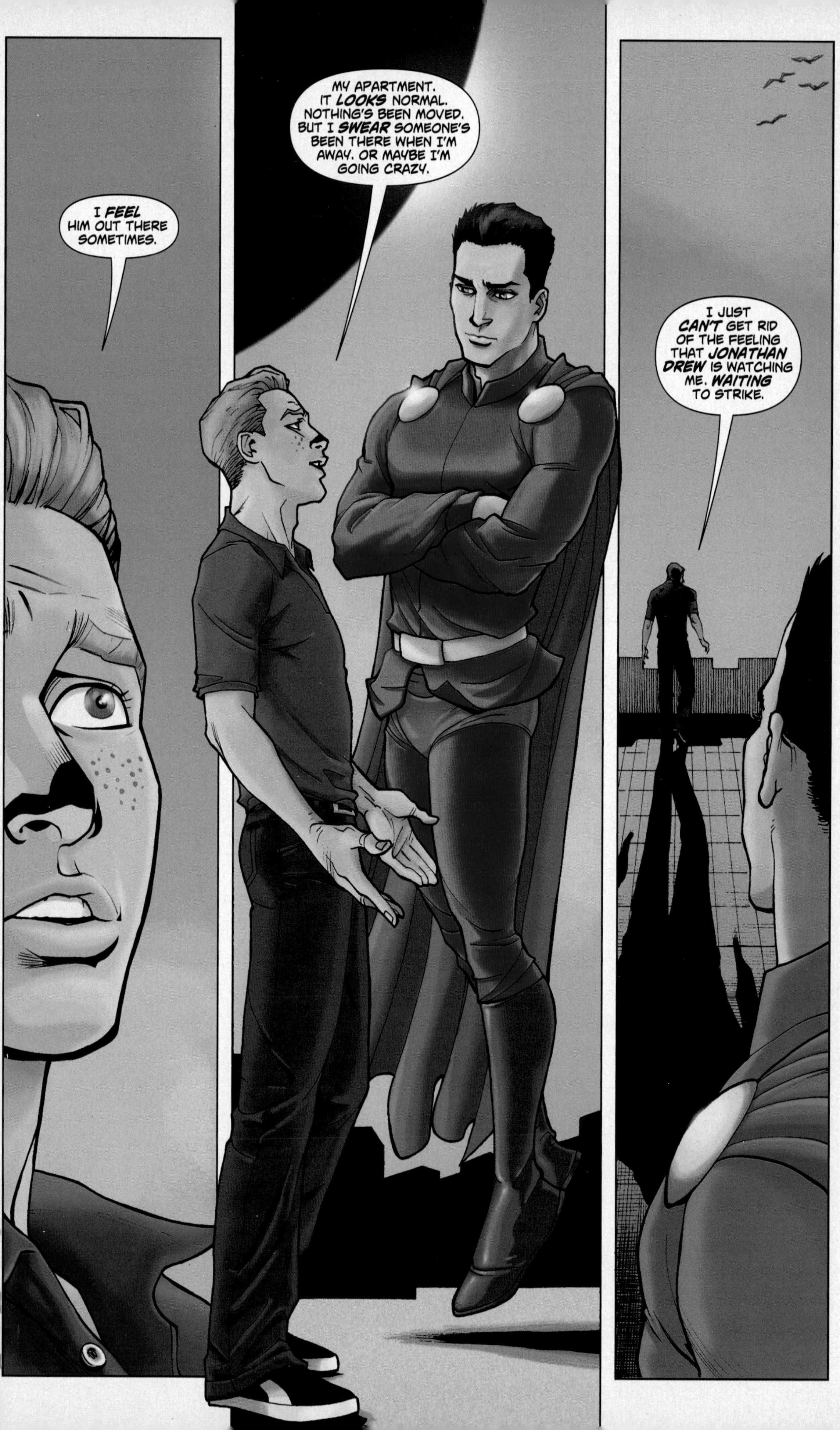
I FEEL HIM OUT THERE SOMETIMES.
MY APARTMENT. IT LOOKS NORMAL. NOTHING'S BEEN MOVED. BUT I SWEAR SOMEONE'S BEEN THERE WHEN I'M AWAY. OR MAYBE I'M GOING CRAZY.
I JUST CAN'T GET RID OF THE FEELING THAT JONATHAN DREW IS WATCHING ME. WAITING TO STRIKE.

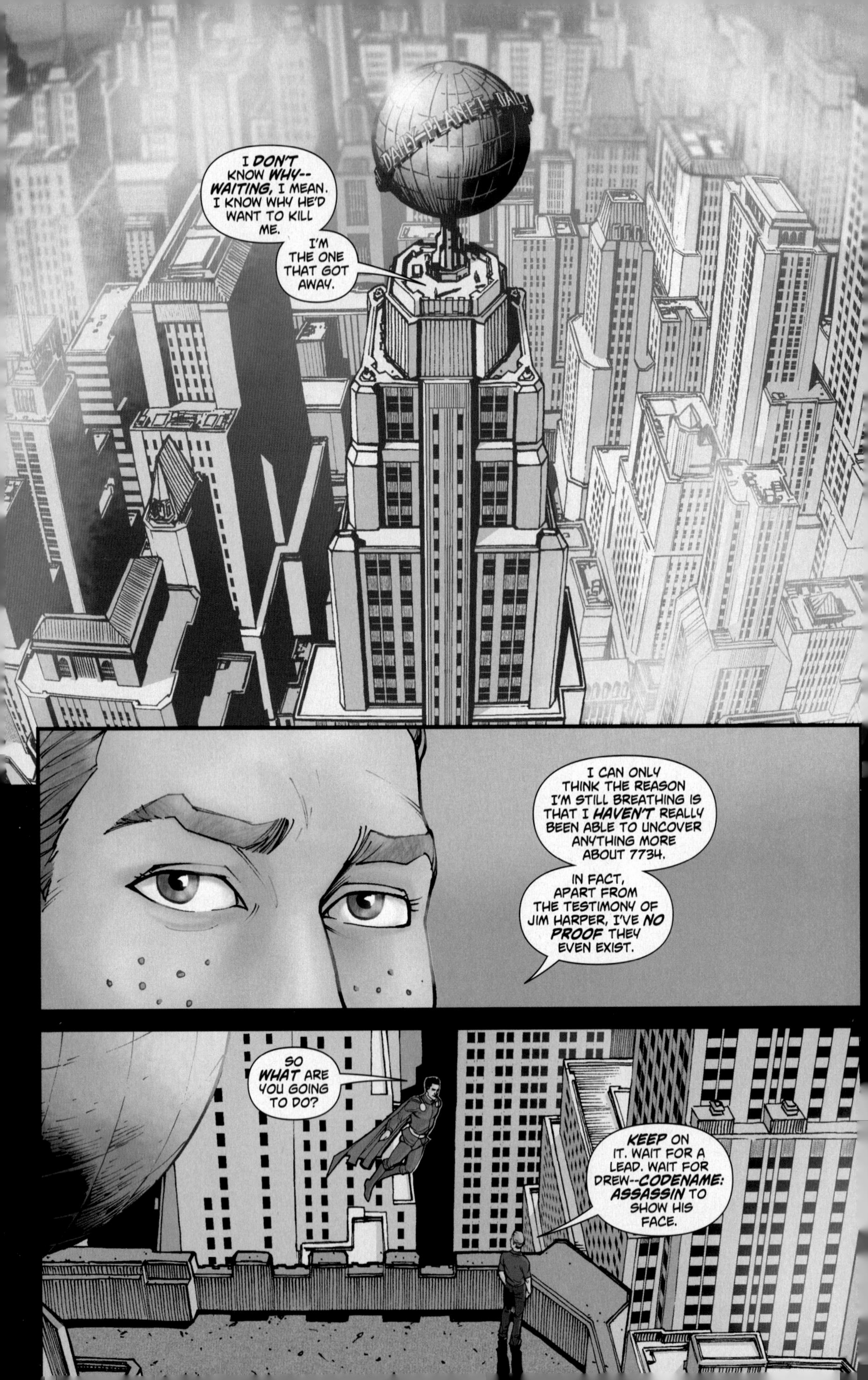

DAILY PLANET
I DON'T KNOW WHY-- WAITING, I MEAN. I KNOW WHY HE'D WANT TO KILL ME.
I'M THE ONE THAT GOT AWAY.
I CAN ONLY THINK THE REASON I'M STILL BREATHING IS THAT I HAVEN'T REALLY BEEN ABLE TO UNCOVER ANYTHING MORE ABOUT 7734.
IN FACT, APART FROM THE TESTIMONY OF JIM HARPER, I'VE NO PROOF THEY EVEN EXIST.
SO WHAT ARE YOU GOING TO DO?
KEEP ON IT. WAIT FOR A LEAD. WAIT FOR DREW--CODENAME: ASSASSIN TO SHOW HIS FACE.

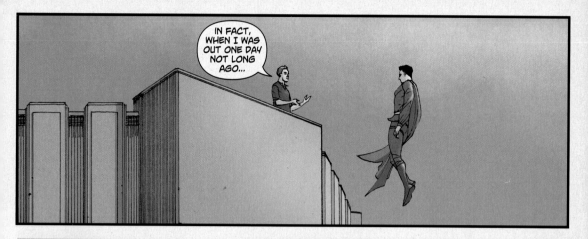

IN FACT, WHEN I WAS OUT ONE DAY NOT LONG AGO...

"...I THINK HE DID."

"OR IT WAS MAYBE JUST A TRICK OF THE SUN."

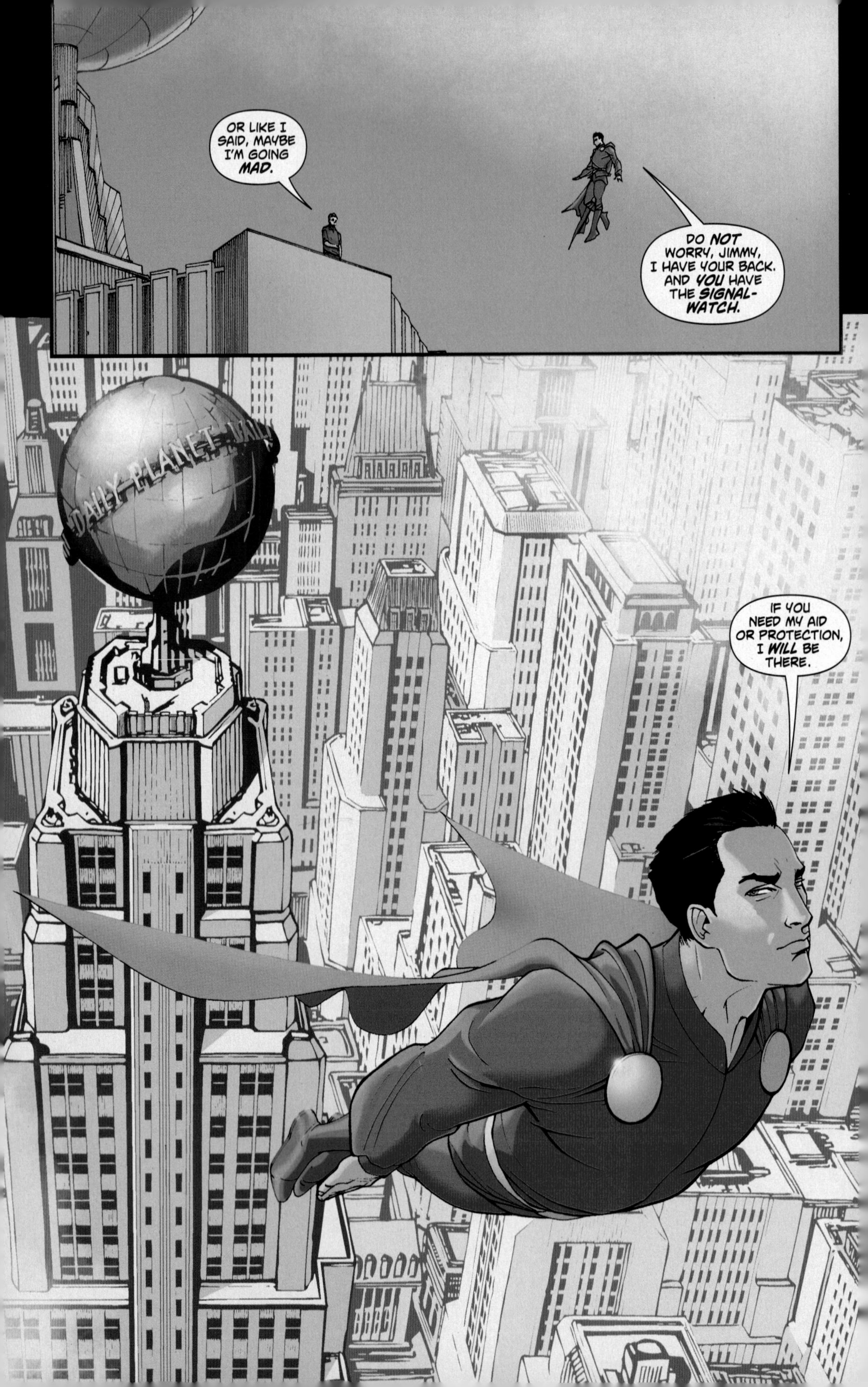
OR LIKE I SAID, MAYBE I'M GOING MAD.
DO NOT WORRY, JIMMY, I HAVE YOUR BACK. AND YOU HAVE THE SIGNAL-WATCH.
DAILY PLANET
IF YOU NEED MY AID OR PROTECTION, I WILL BE THERE.

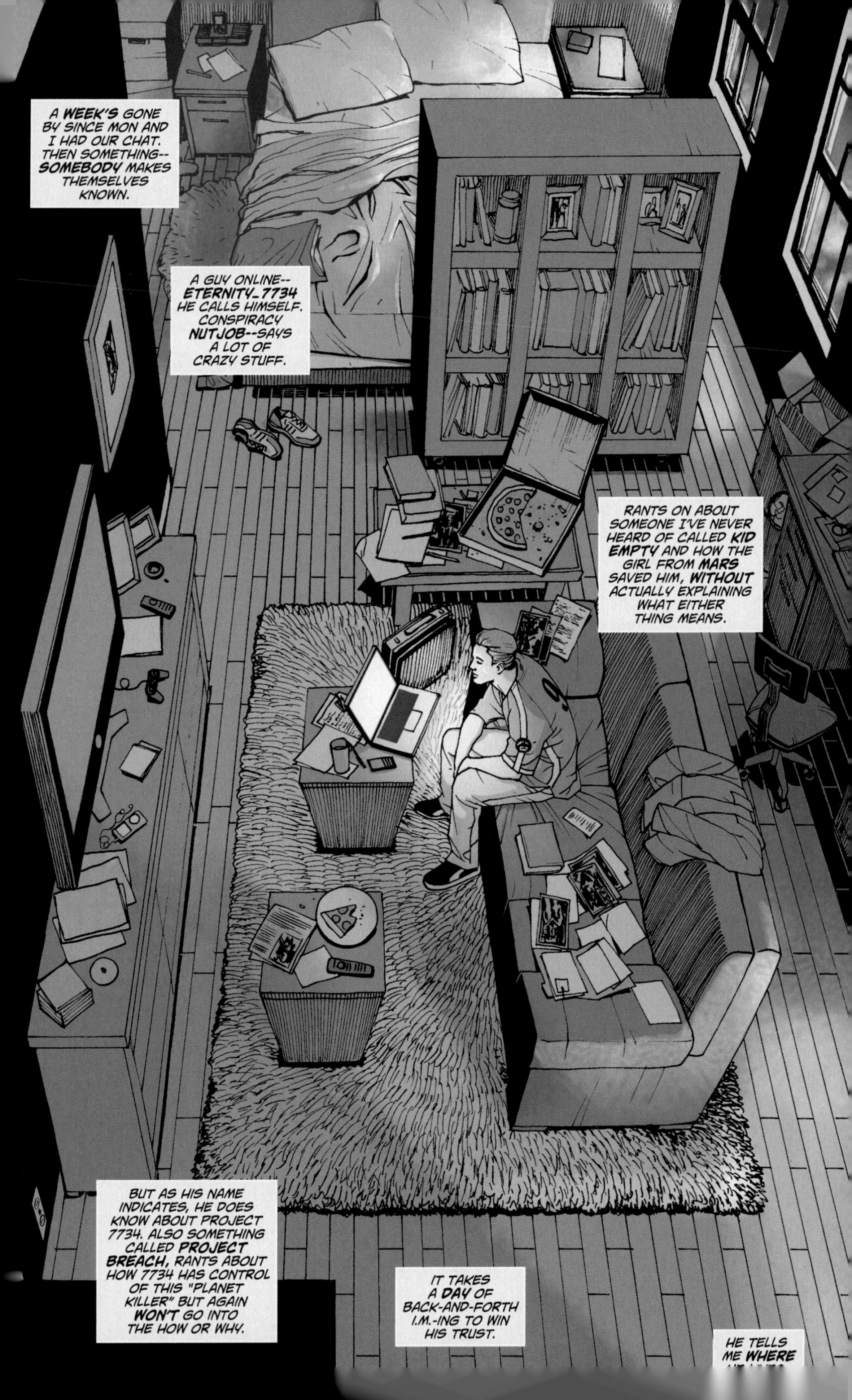
A WEEK'S GONE BY SINCE MON AND I HAD OUR CHAT. THEN SOMETHING-- SOMEBODY MAKES THEMSELVES KNOWN.
A GUY ONLINE-- ETERNITY_7734 HE CALLS HIMSELF. CONSPIRACY NUTJOB--SAYS A LOT OF CRAZY STUFF.
RANTS ON ABOUT SOMEONE I'VE NEVER HEARD OF CALLED KID EMPTY AND HOW THE GIRL FROM MARS SAVED HIM, WITHOUT ACTUALLY EXPLAINING WHAT EITHER THING MEANS.
BUT AS HIS NAME INDICATES, HE DOES KNOW ABOUT PROJECT 7734. ALSO SOMETHING CALLED PROJECT BREACH, RANTS ABOUT HOW 7734 HAS CONTROL OF THIS "PLANET KILLER" BUT AGAIN WON'T GO INTO THE HOW OR WHY.
IT TAKES A DAY OF BACK-AND-FORTH I.M.-ING TO WIN HIS TRUST.
HE TELLS ME WHERE

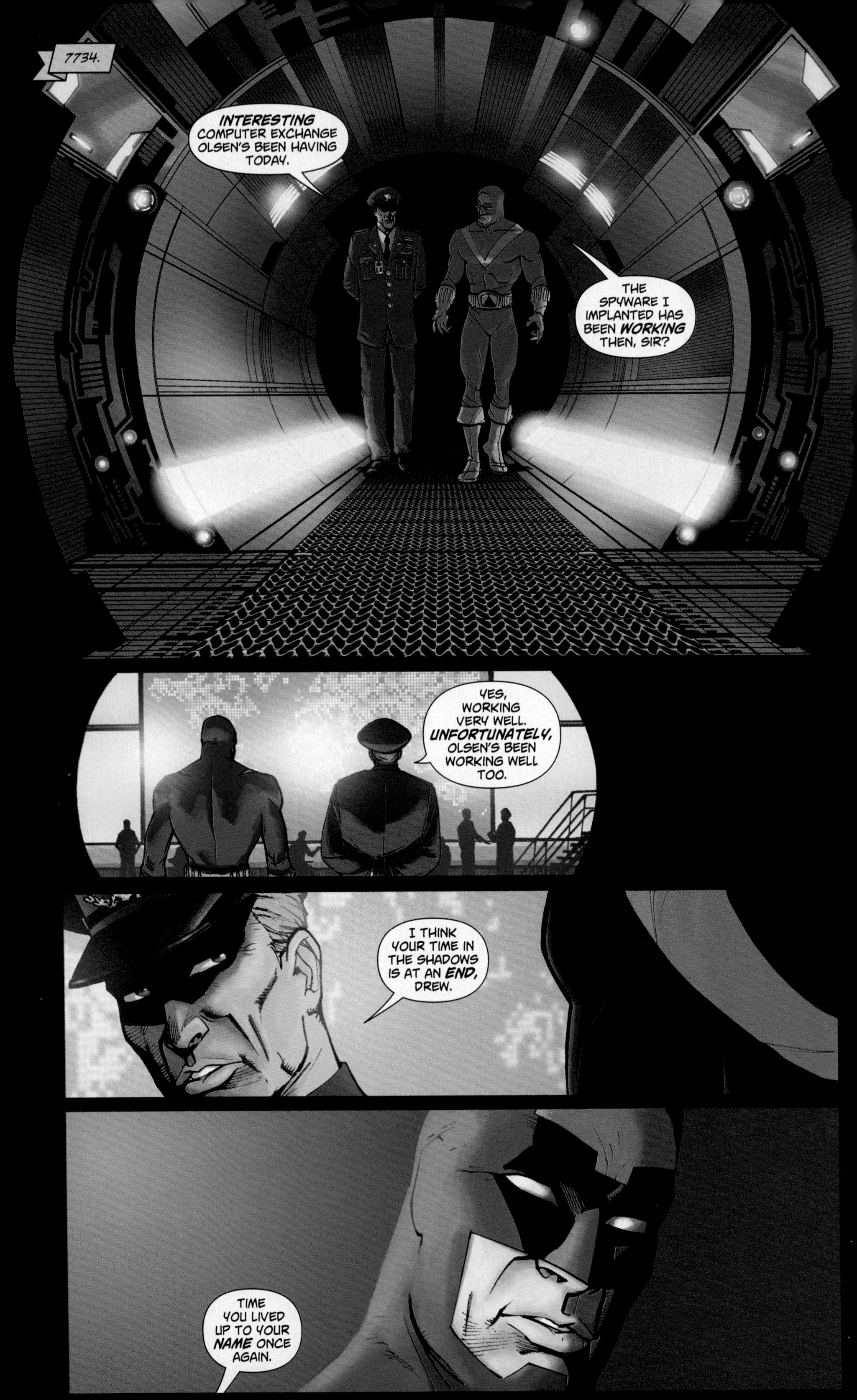
7734.
INTERESTING COMPUTER EXCHANGE OLSEN'S BEEN HAVING TODAY.
THE SPYWARE I IMPLANTED HAS BEEN WORKING THEN, SIR?
YES, WORKING VERY WELL. UNFORTUNATELY, OLSEN'S BEEN WORKING WELL TOO.
I THINK YOUR TIME IN THE SHADOWS IS AT AN END, DREW.
TIME YOU LIVED UP TO YOUR NAME ONCE AGAIN.

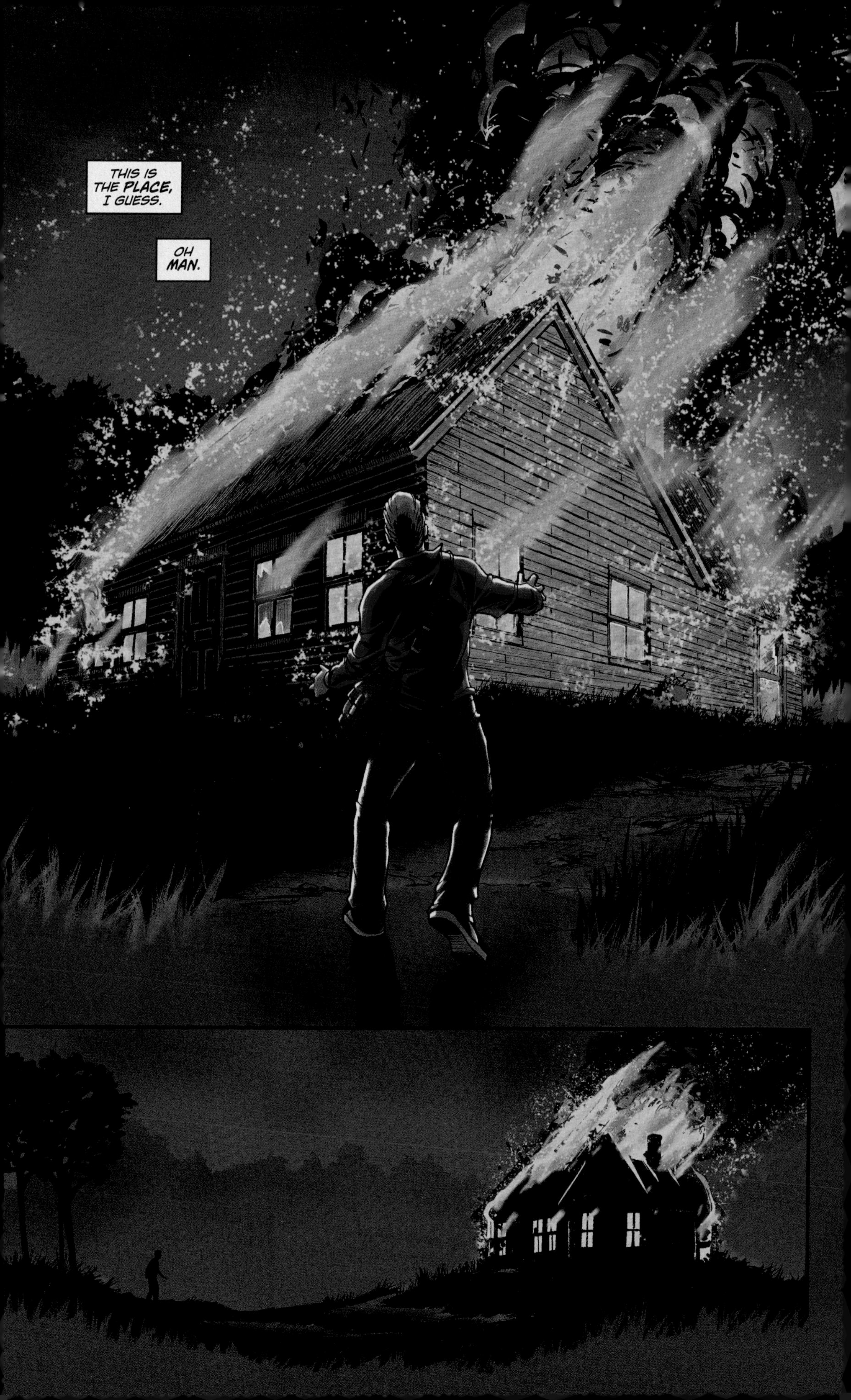
THIS IS THE PLACE, I GUESS.
OH MAN.

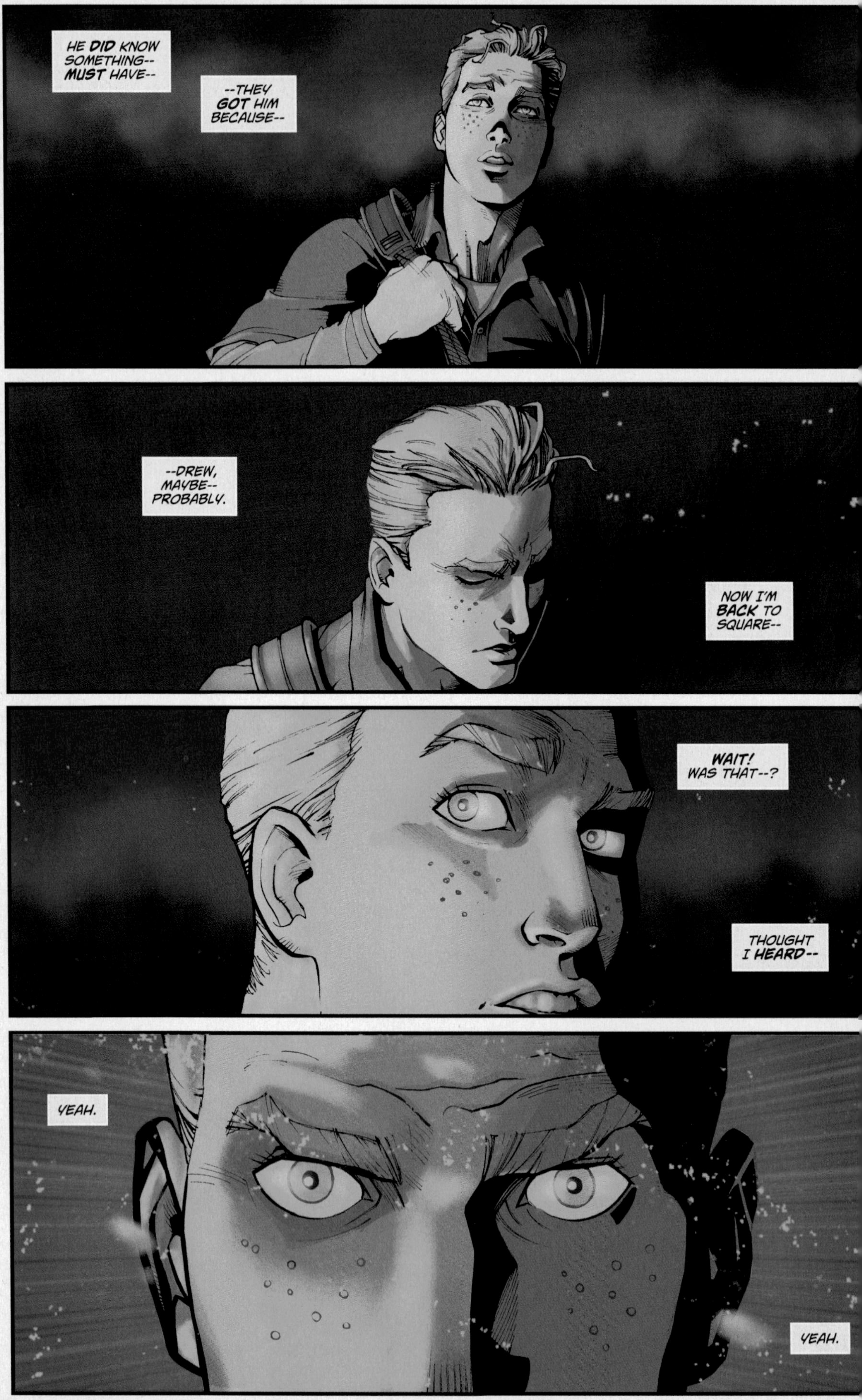
HE DID KNOW SOMETHING-- MUST HAVE--
--THEY GOT HIM BECAUSE--
--DREW, MAYBE-- PROBABLY.
NOW I'M BACK TO SQUARE--
WAIT! WAS THAT--?
THOUGHT I HEARD--
YEAH.
YEAH.

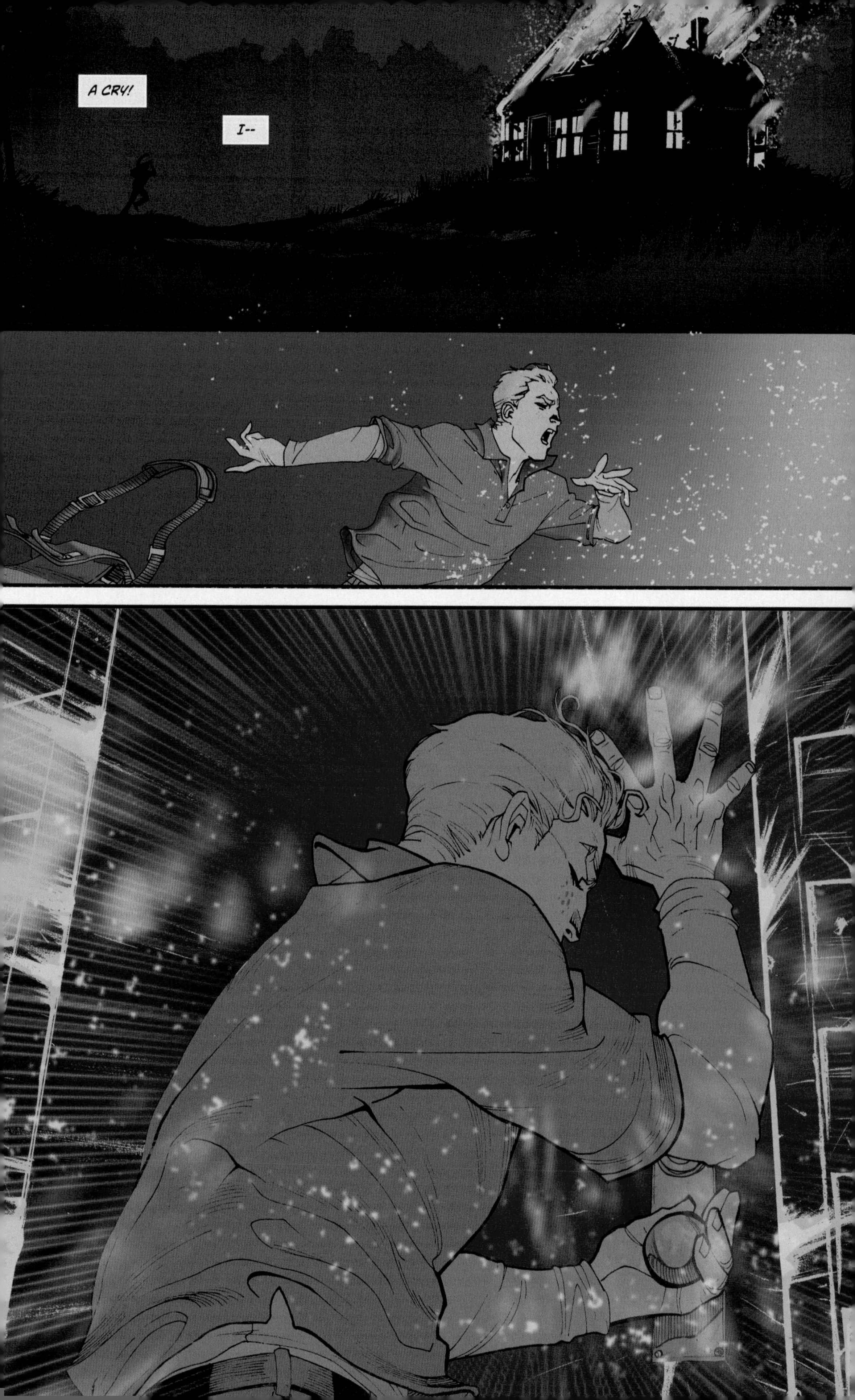
A CRY!
I--

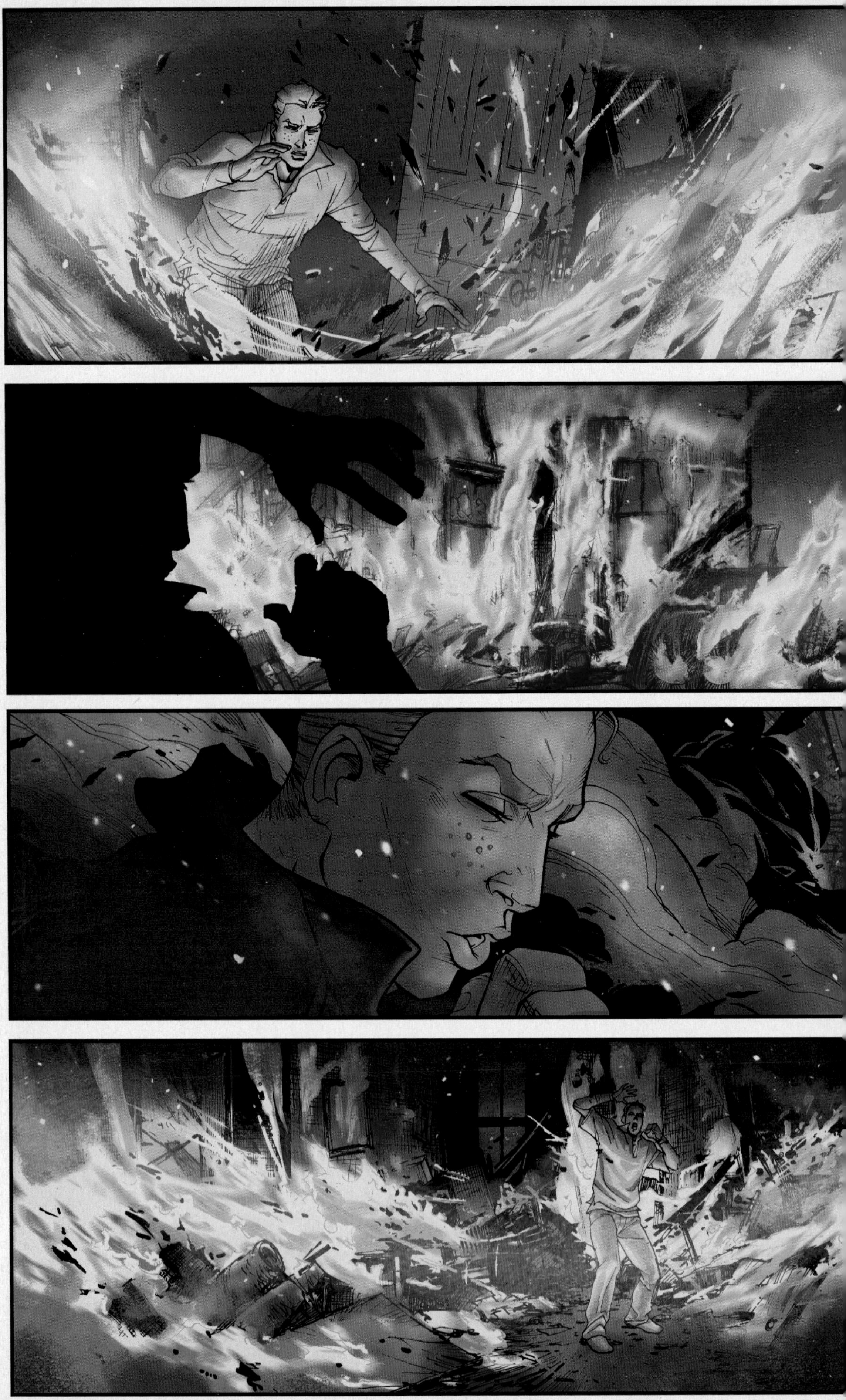

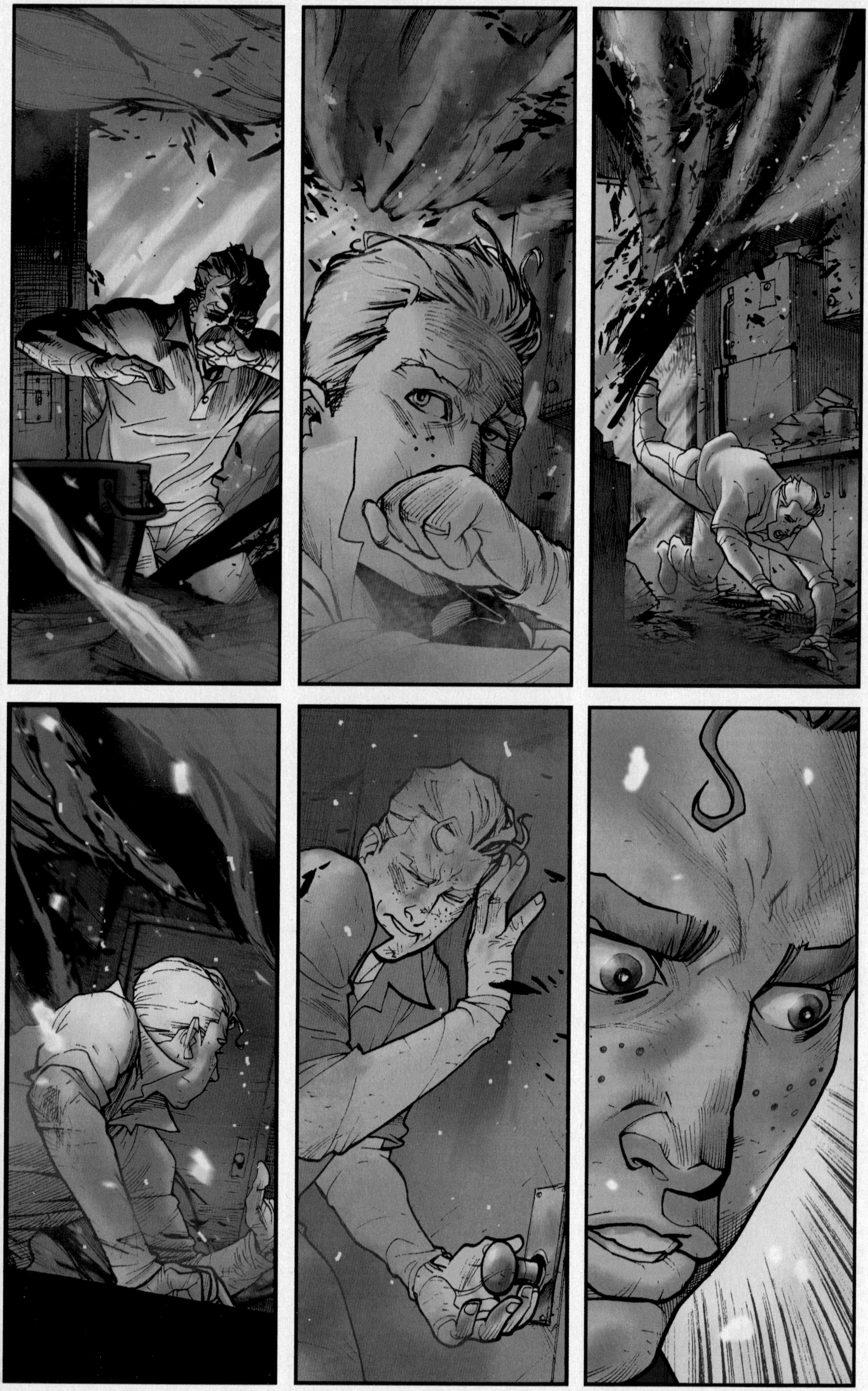

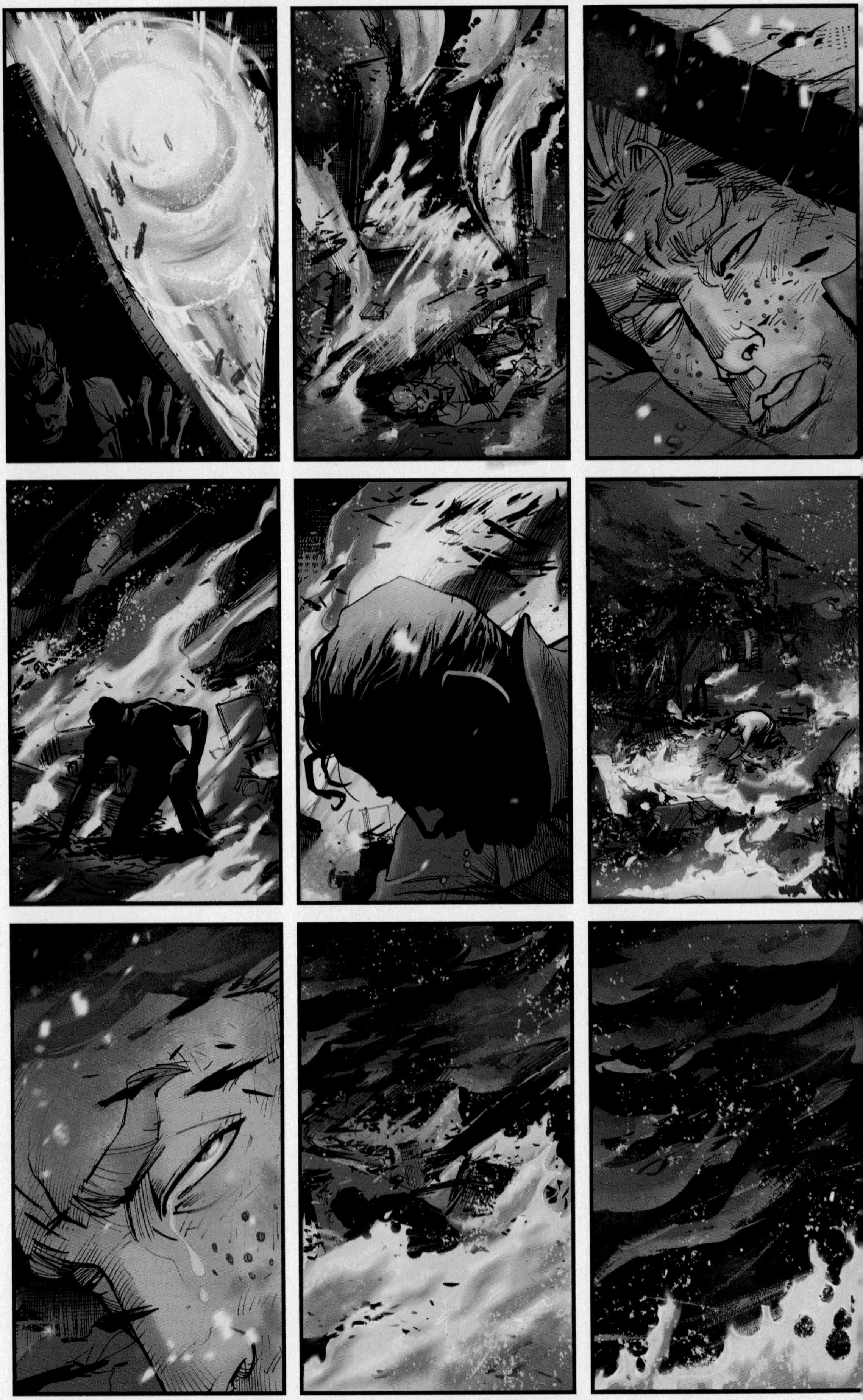

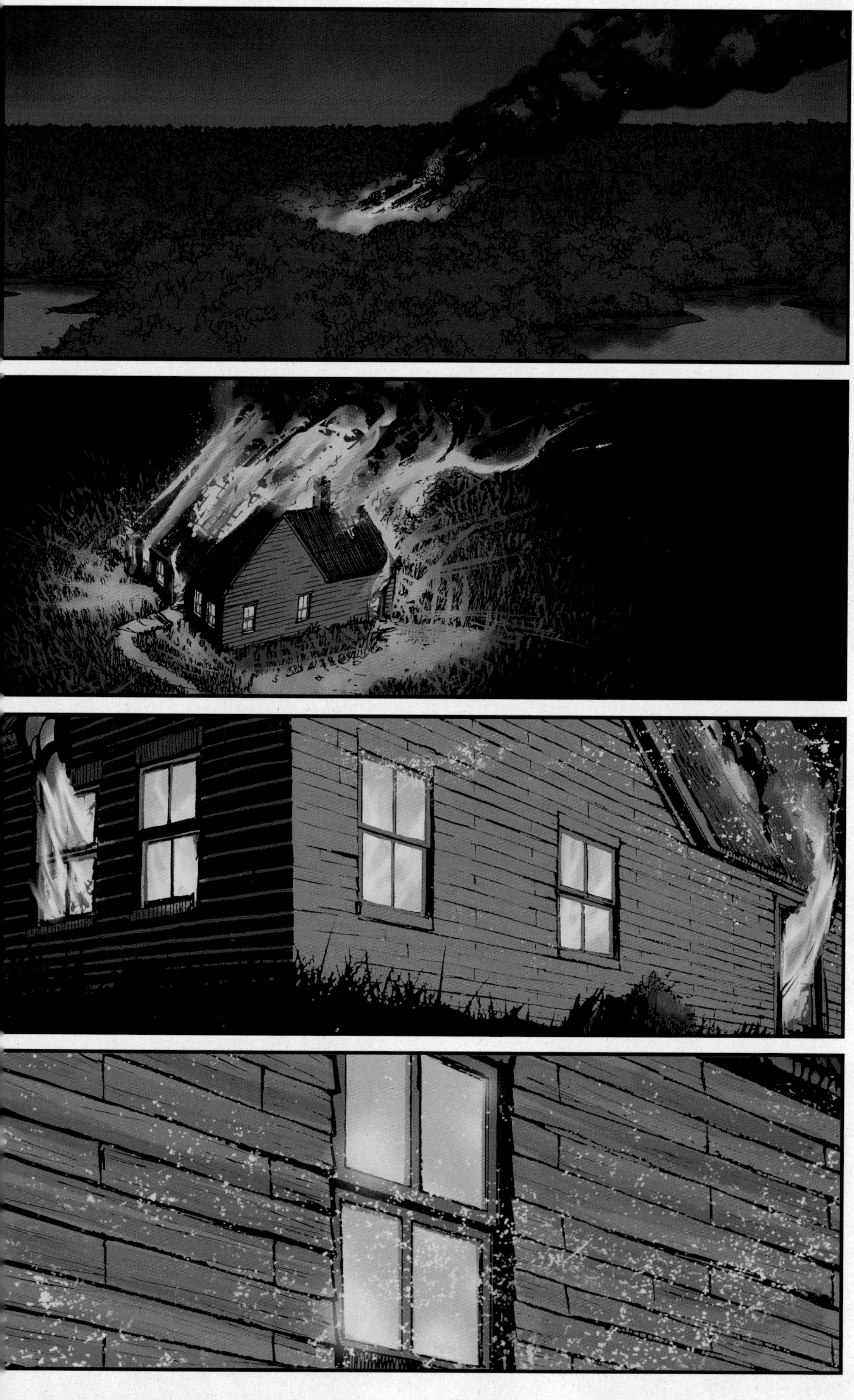

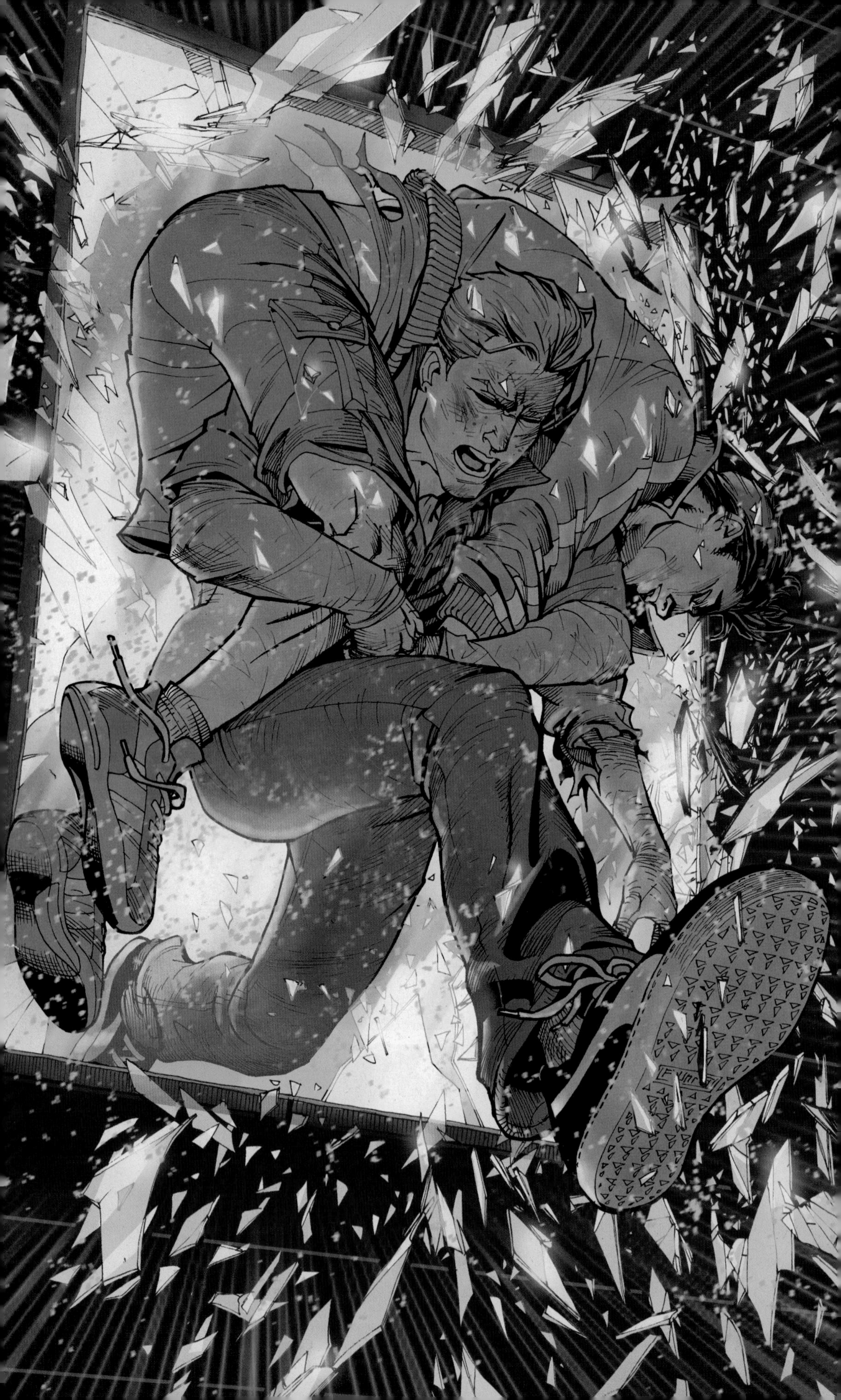

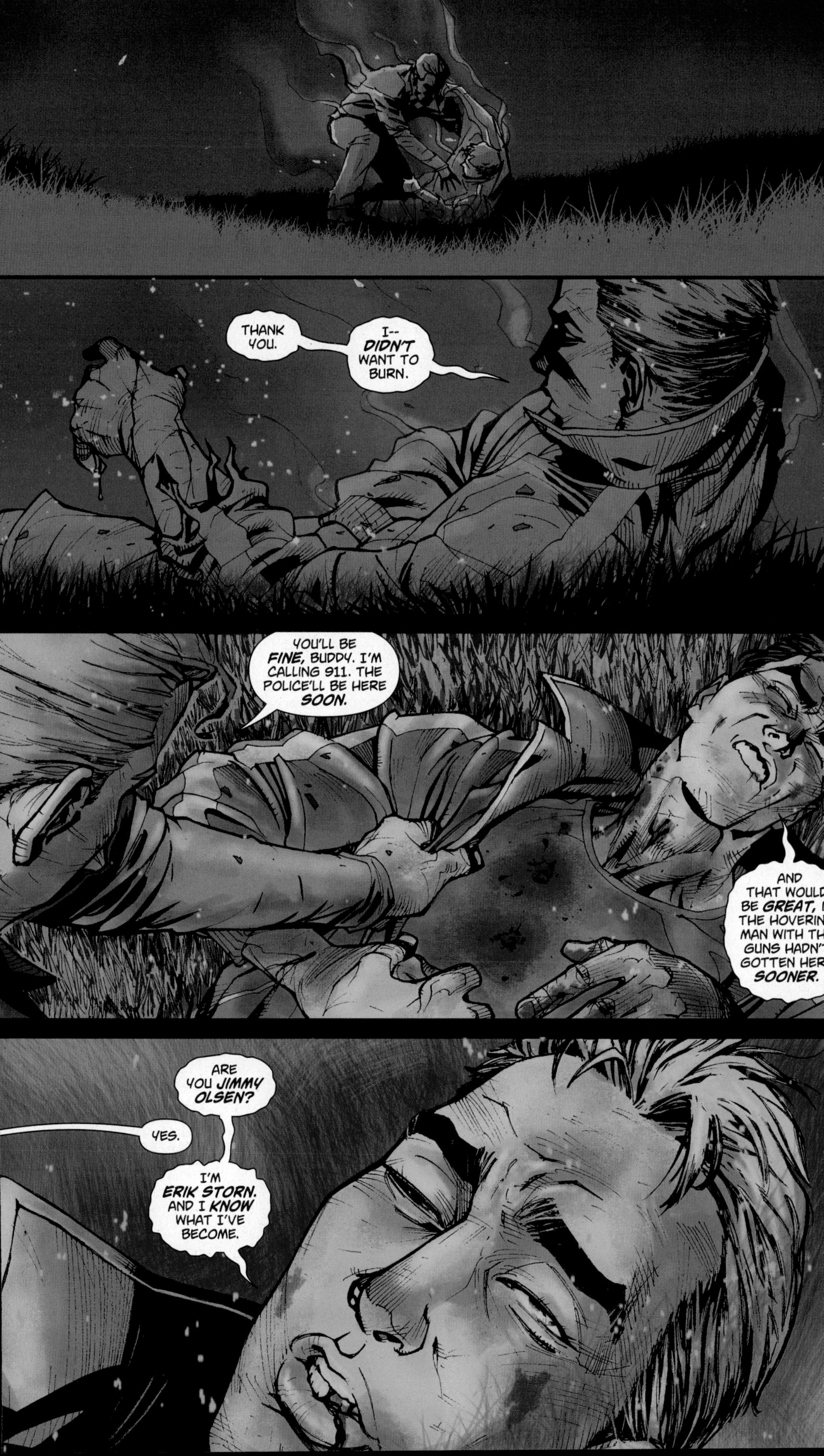
THANK YOU.
I-- DIDN'T WANT TO BURN.
YOU'LL BE FINE, BUDDY. I'M CALLING 911. THE POLICE'LL BE HERE SOON.
AND THAT WOULD BE GREAT, THE HOVERIN MAN WITH TH GUNS HADN' GOTTEN HER SOONER.
ARE YOU JIMMY OLSEN?
YES.
I'M ERIK STORN. AND I KNOW WHAT I'VE BECOME.

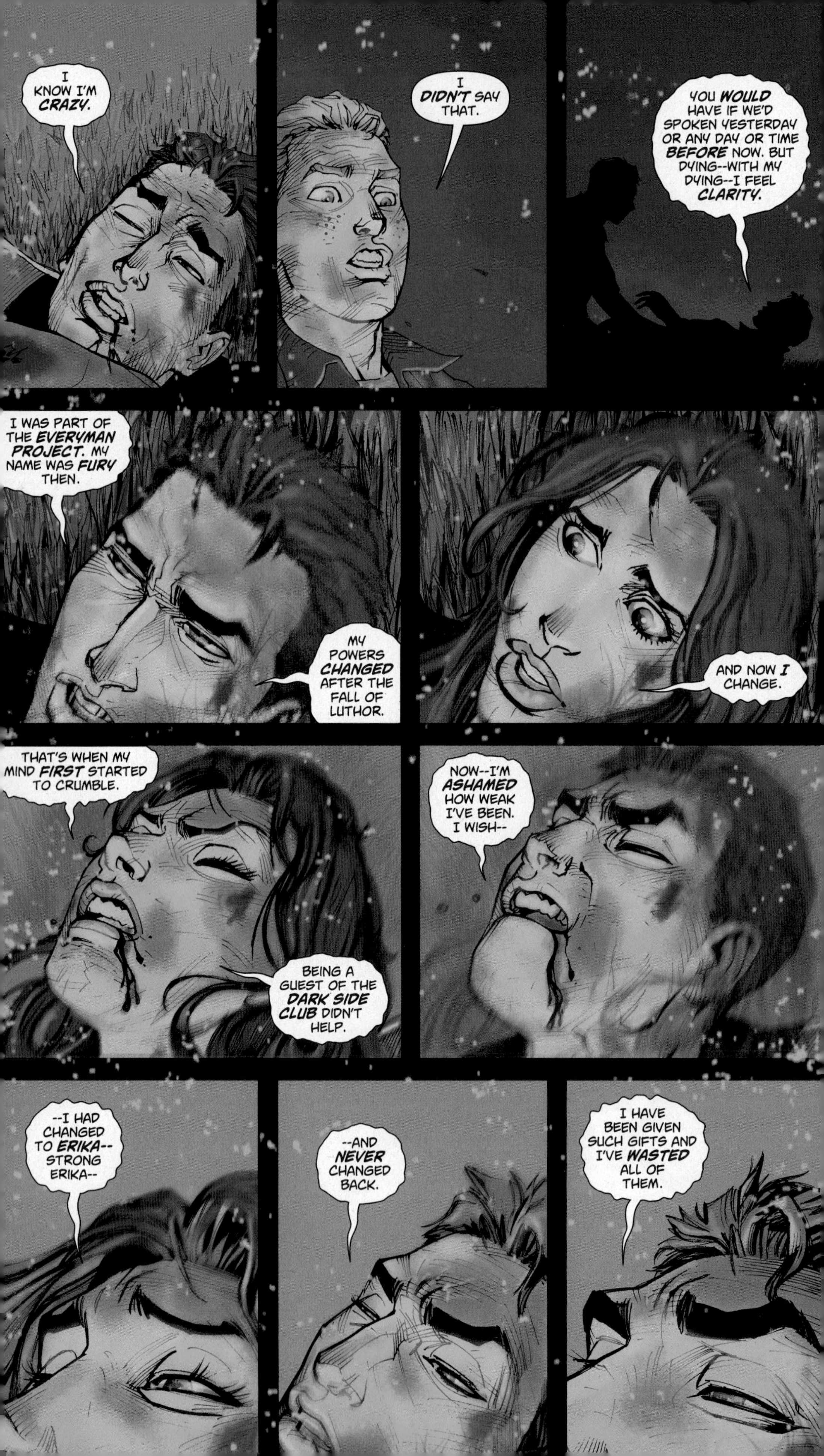
I KNOW I'M CRAZY.
I DIDN'T SAY THAT.
YOU WOULD HAVE IF WE'D SPOKEN YESTERDAY OR ANY DAY OR TIME BEFORE NOW. BUT DYING--WITH MY DYING--I FEEL CLARITY.
I WAS PART OF THE EVERYMAN PROJECT. MY NAME WAS FURY THEN.
MY POWERS CHANGED AFTER THE FALL OF LUTHOR.
AND NOW I CHANGE.
THAT'S WHEN MY MIND FIRST STARTED TO CRUMBLE.
BEING A GUEST OF THE DARK SIDE CLUB DIDN'T HELP.
NOW--I'M ASHAMED HOW WEAK I'VE BEEN. I WISH--
--I HAD CHANGED TO ERIKA-- STRONG ERIKA--
--AND NEVER CHANGED BACK.
I HAVE BEEN GIVEN SUCH GIFTS AND I'VE WASTED ALL OF THEM.

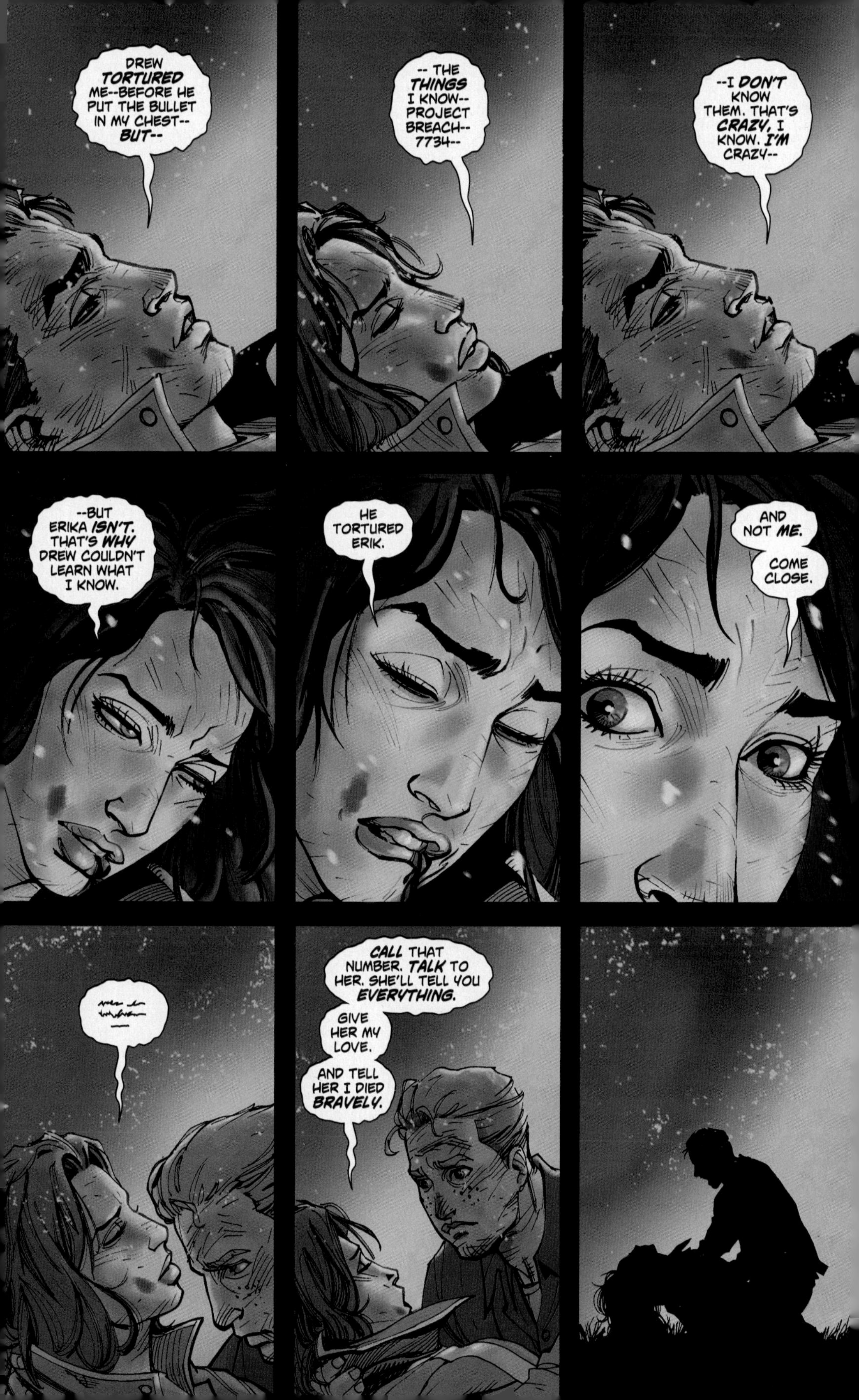
DREW TORTURED ME--BEFORE HE PUT THE BULLET IN MY CHEST-- BUT--
-- THE THINGS I KNOW-- PROJECT BREACH-- 7734--
--I DON'T KNOW THEM. THAT'S CRAZY, I KNOW. I'M CRAZY--
--BUT ERIKA ISN'T. THAT'S WHY DREW COULDN'T LEARN WHAT I KNOW.
HE TORTURED ERIK.
AND NOT ME.
COME CLOSE.
CALL THAT NUMBER. TALK TO HER. SHE'LL TELL YOU EVERYTHING.
GIVE HER MY LOVE.
AND TELL HER I DIED BRAVELY.

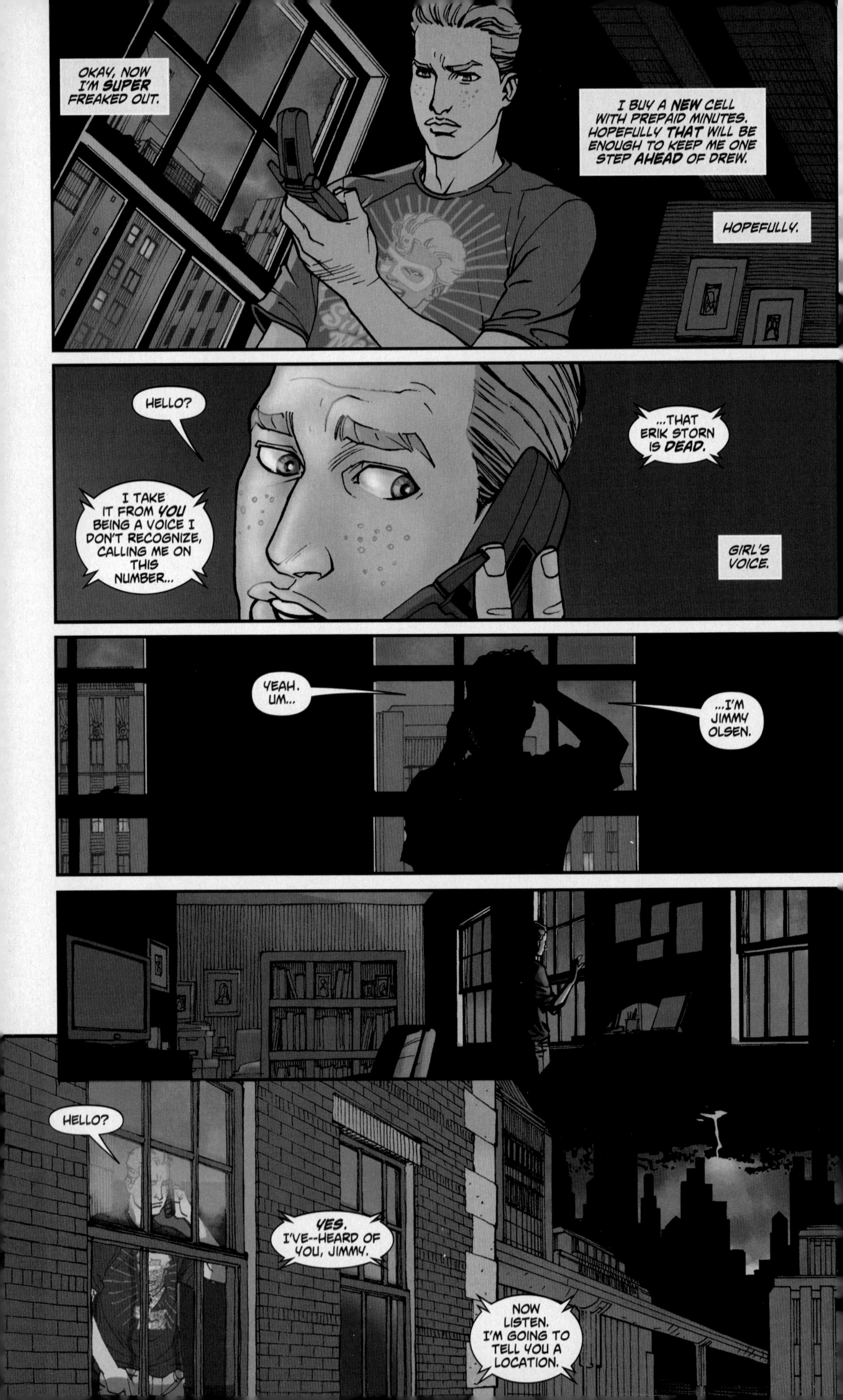
OKAY, NOW I'M SUPER FREAKED OUT.
I BUY A NEW CELL WITH PREPAID MINUTES. HOPEFULLY THAT WILL BE ENOUGH TO KEEP ME ONE STEP AHEAD OF DREW.
HOPEFULLY.
HELLO?
I TAKE IT FROM YOU BEING A VOICE I DON'T RECOGNIZE, CALLING ME ON THIS NUMBER...
...THAT ERIK STORN IS DEAD.
GIRL'S VOICE.
YEAH. UM...
...I'M JIMMY OLSEN.
HELLO?
YES. I'VE--HEARD OF YOU, JIMMY.
NOW LISTEN. I'M GOING TO TELL YOU A LOCATION.

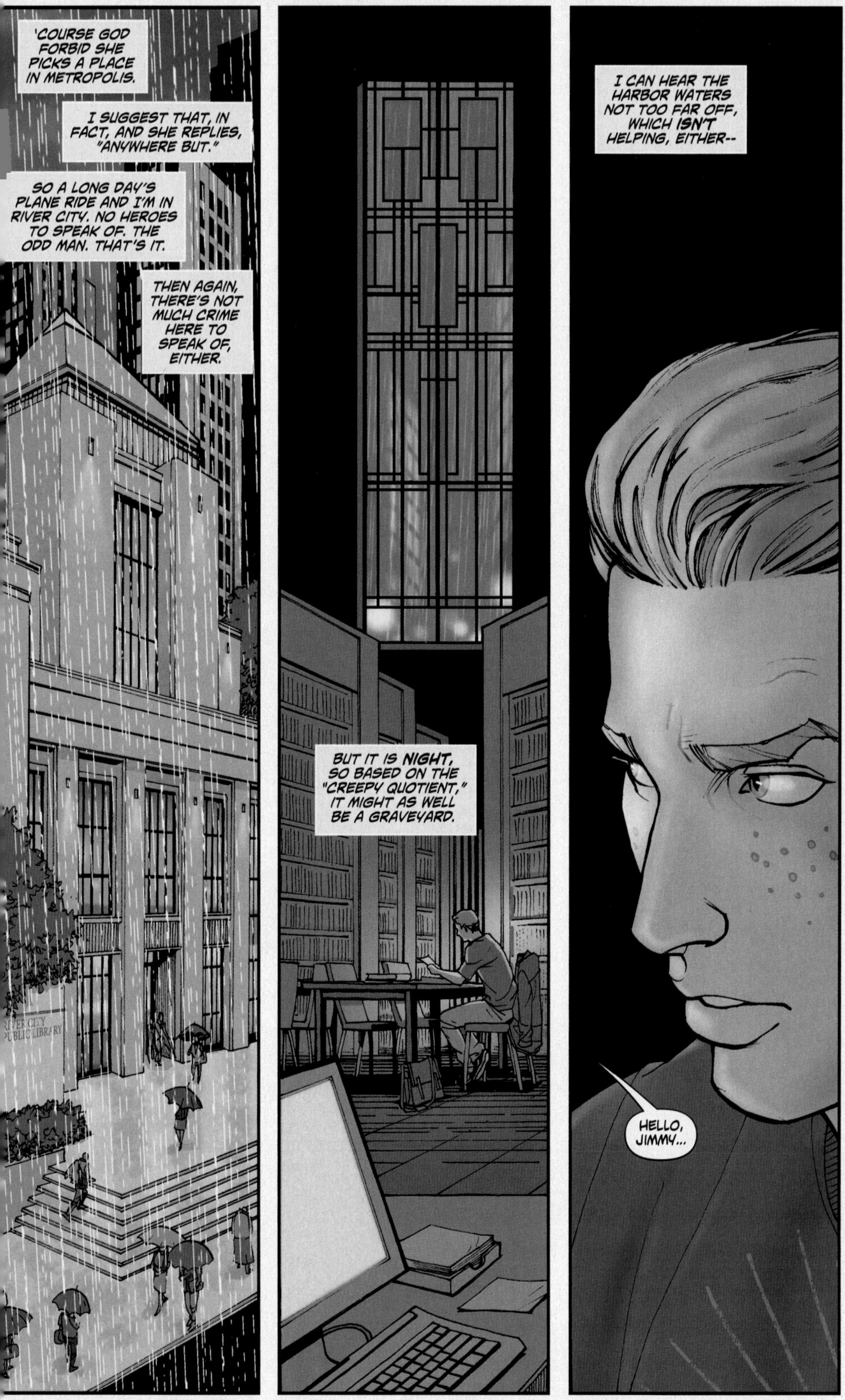
'COURSE GOD FORBID SHE PICKS A PLACE IN METROPOLIS.
I SUGGEST THAT, IN FACT, AND SHE REPLIES, "ANYWHERE BUT."
SO A LONG DAY'S PLANE RIDE AND I'M IN RIVER CITY. NO HEROES TO SPEAK OF. THE ODD MAN. THAT'S IT.
THEN AGAIN, THERE'S NOT MUCH CRIME HERE TO SPEAK OF, EITHER.
RIVER CITY PUBLIC LIBRARY
BUT IT IS NIGHT, SO BASED ON THE "CREEPY QUOTIENT," IT MIGHT AS WELL BE A GRAVEYARD.
I CAN HEAR THE HARBOR WATERS NOT TOO FAR OFF, WHICH ISN'T HELPING, EITHER--
HELLO, JIMMY...

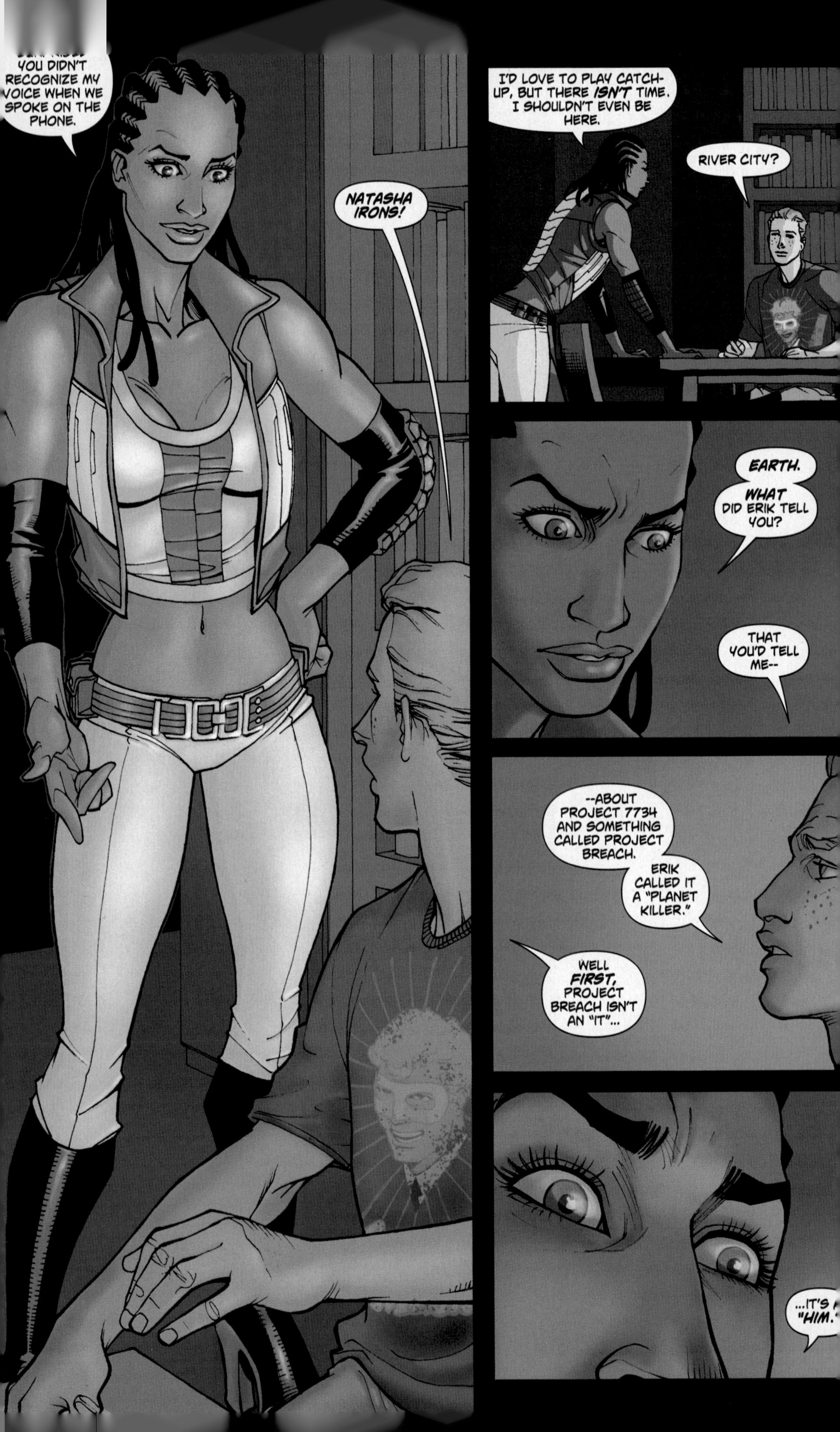

YOU DIDN'T RECOGNIZE MY VOICE WHEN WE SPOKE ON THE PHONE.
NATASHA IRONS!
I'D LOVE TO PLAY CATCH-UP, BUT THERE ISN'T TIME. I SHOULDN'T EVEN BE HERE.
RIVER CITY?
EARTH.
WHAT DID ERIK TELL YOU?
THAT YOU'D TELL ME--
--ABOUT PROJECT 7734 AND SOMETHING CALLED PROJECT BREACH.
ERIK CALLED IT A "PLANET KILLER."
WELL FIRST, PROJECT BREACH ISN'T AN "IT"...
...IT'S "HIM."

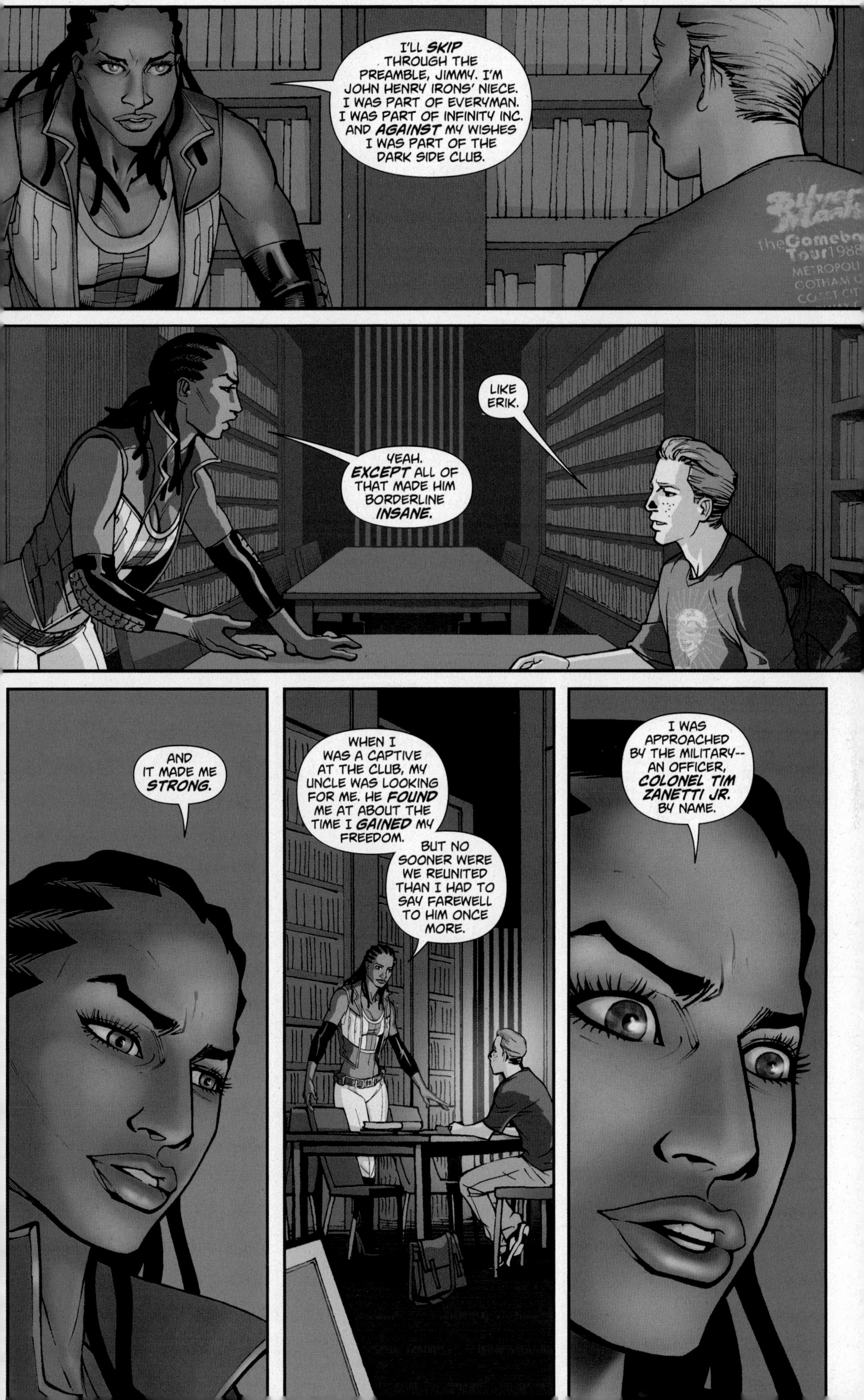
I'LL SKIP THROUGH THE PREAMBLE, JIMMY. I'M JOHN HENRY IRONS' NIECE. I WAS PART OF EVERYMAN. I WAS PART OF INFINITY INC. AND AGAINST MY WISHES I WAS PART OF THE DARK SIDE CLUB.
LIKE ERIK.
YEAH. EXCEPT ALL OF THAT MADE HIM BORDERLINE INSANE.
AND IT MADE ME STRONG.
WHEN I WAS A CAPTIVE AT THE CLUB, MY UNCLE WAS LOOKING FOR ME. HE FOUND ME AT ABOUT THE TIME I GAINED MY FREEDOM.
BUT NO SOONER WERE WE REUNITED THAN I HAD TO SAY FAREWELL TO HIM ONCE MORE.
I WAS APPROACHED BY THE MILITARY-- AN OFFICER, COLONEL TIM ZANETTI JR. BY NAME.

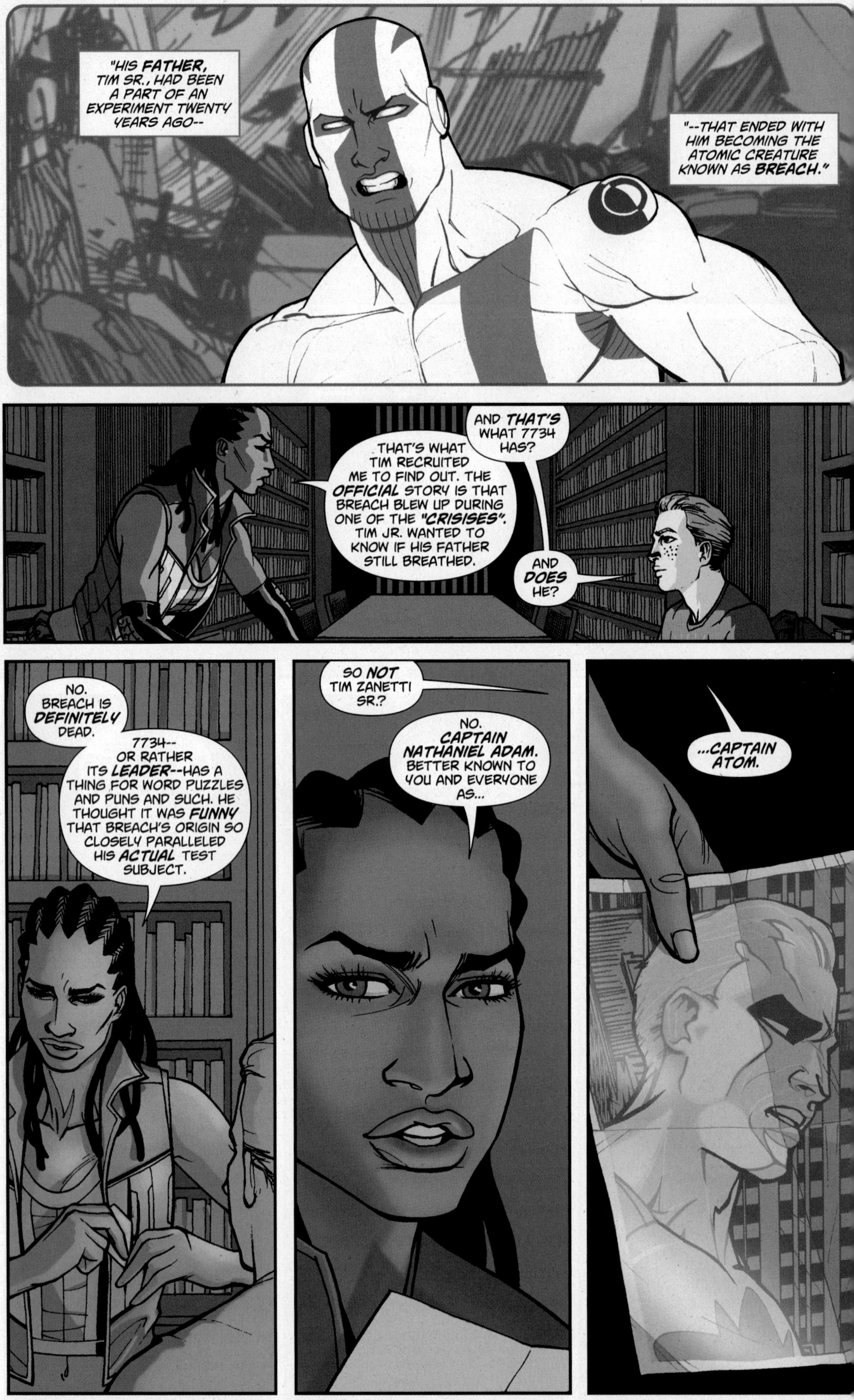
"HIS FATHER, TIM SR., HAD BEEN A PART OF AN EXPERIMENT TWENTY YEARS AGO--
"--THAT ENDED WITH HIM BECOMING THE ATOMIC CREATURE KNOWN AS BREACH."
AND THAT'S WHAT 7734 HAS?
THAT'S WHAT TIM RECRUITED ME TO FIND OUT. THE OFFICIAL STORY IS THAT BREACH BLEW UP DURING ONE OF THE "CRISISES". TIM JR. WANTED TO KNOW IF HIS FATHER STILL BREATHED.
AND DOES HE?
NO. BREACH IS DEFINITELY DEAD.
7734-- OR RATHER ITS LEADER--HAS A THING FOR WORD PUZZLES AND PUNS AND SUCH. HE THOUGHT IT WAS FUNNY THAT BREACH'S ORIGIN SO CLOSELY PARALLELED HIS ACTUAL TEST SUBJECT.
SO NOT TIM ZANETTI SR.?
NO. CAPTAIN NATHANIEL ADAM. BETTER KNOWN TO YOU AND EVERYONE AS...
...CAPTAIN ATOM.

7734 **FOUND** HIM SOMEHOW. HIS MIND WAS **WIPED**. A BLANK SLATE THEY COULD TAKE THEIR CHALK TO.

WAIT, **WAIT**, I'M NOT QUITE GETTING THIS. YEAH, I GET THAT ZANETTI RECRUITED YOU, BUT **HOW** DID YOU LEARN ALL THIS STUFF? I'VE BEEN TRYING, AND--

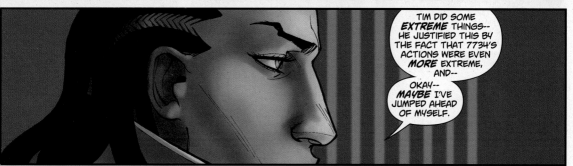

TIM DID SOME **EXTREME** THINGS-- HE JUSTIFIED THIS BY THE FACT THAT 7734'S ACTIONS WERE EVEN **MORE** EXTREME, AND--

OKAY-- **MAYBE** I'VE JUMPED AHEAD OF MYSELF.

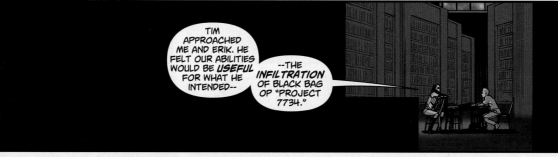

TIM APPROACHED ME AND ERIK. HE FELT OUR ABILITIES WOULD BE **USEFUL** FOR WHAT HE INTENDED--

--THE **INFILTRATION** OF BLACK BAG OP "PROJECT 7734."

TIM HAD LEARNED WHAT **YOU** MAYBE HAVE--JUST **ENOUGH** TO HOOK HIM--

--BUT **NOTHING** HE COULD PROVE.

RIGHT. HE NEEDED PEOPLE ON THE **INSIDE**. LIKE I SAID, HE APPROACHED US. HE WAS **PERSUASIVE**. WE AGREED.

THEN TIM BEGAN TO SEE ERIK **WASN'T** STABLE ENOUGH. HE DIDN'T TRUST **LUCIA** TO REPLACE HIM, SO THAT LEFT JUST **ME**.

HE GOT ME A **RANK** IN THE ARMY. GOD KNOWS **HOW** HE DID IT.

TO YOU I'M NATASHA IRONS. TO THE ARMY I'M **SPECIALIST JENNY BLAKE**. I'M A COLD-HEARTED THING WHO'S SPENT **MOST** OF HER ADULT LIFE ON ONE COVERT OP OR ANOTHER.

SO OF COURSE 7734 SNAPPED ME UP.

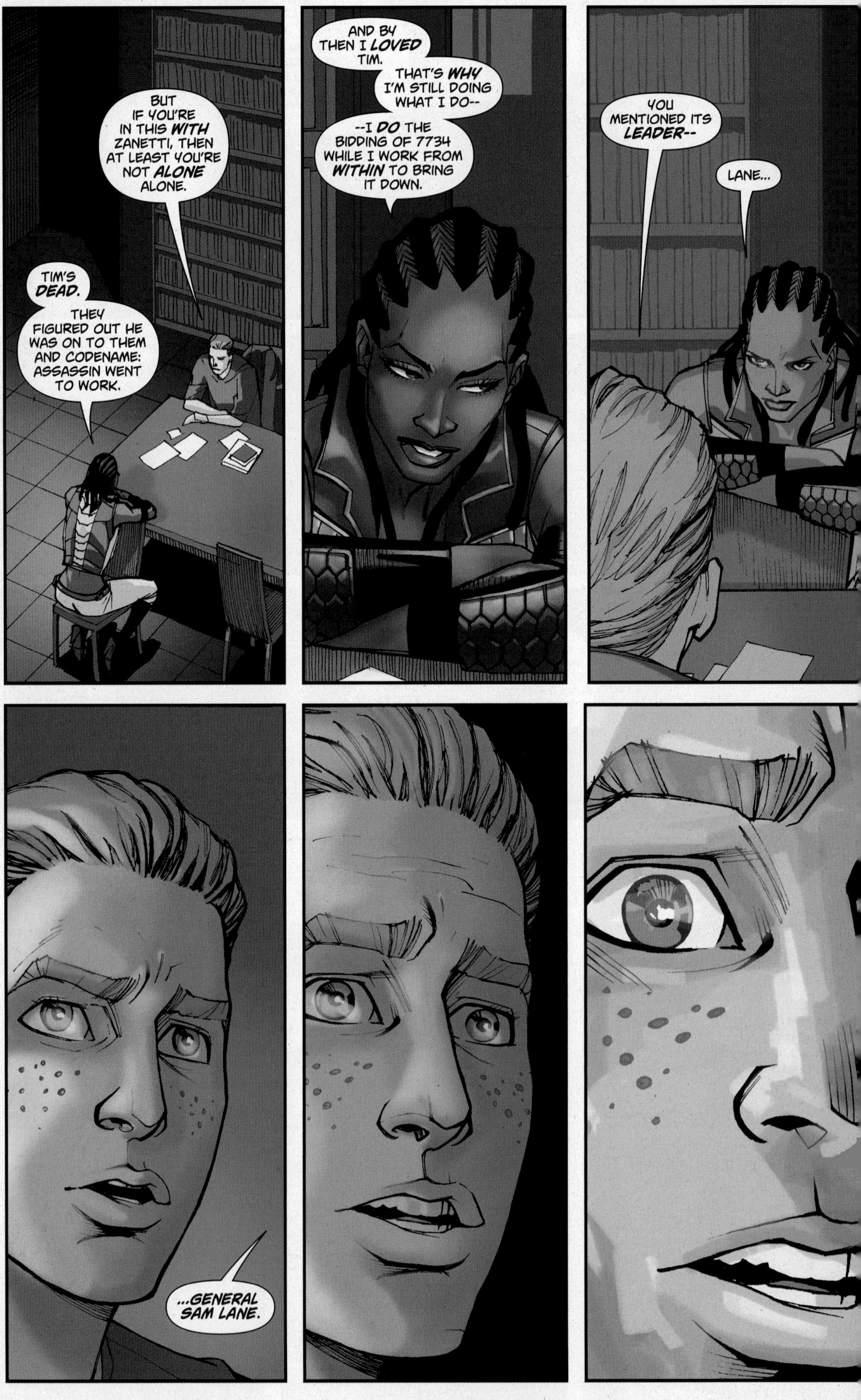

BUT IF YOU'RE IN THIS WITH ZANETTI, THEN AT LEAST YOU'RE NOT ALONE ALONE.
TIM'S DEAD.
THEY FIGURED OUT HE WAS ON TO THEM AND CODENAME: ASSASSIN WENT TO WORK.
AND BY THEN I LOVED TIM.
THAT'S WHY I'M STILL DOING WHAT I DO--
--I DO THE BIDDING OF 7734 WHILE I WORK FROM WITHIN TO BRING IT DOWN.
YOU MENTIONED ITS LEADER--
LANE...
...GENERAL SAM LANE.

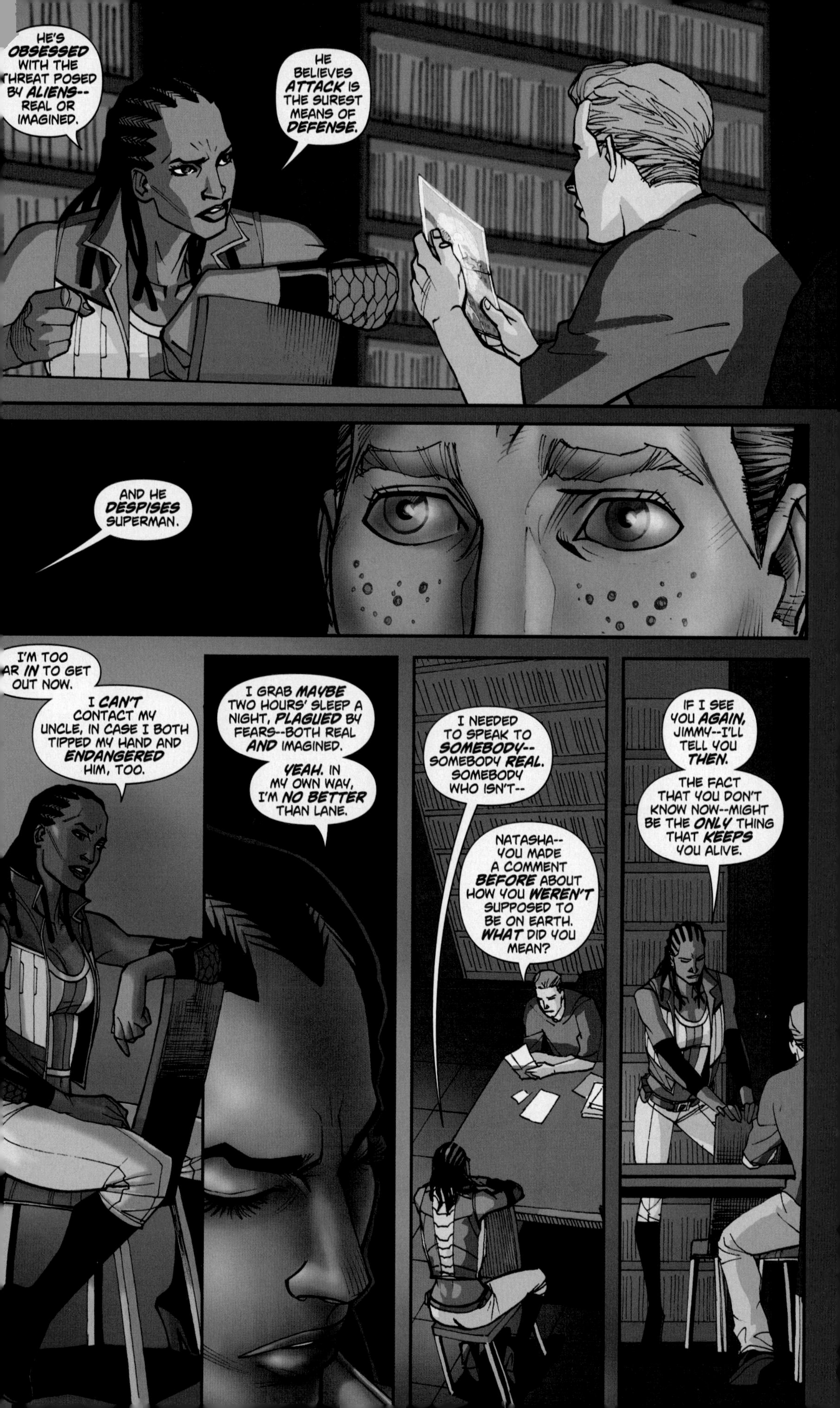

HE'S OBSESSED WITH THE THREAT POSED BY ALIENS-- REAL OR IMAGINED.
HE BELIEVES ATTACK IS THE SUREST MEANS OF DEFENSE.
AND HE DESPISES SUPERMAN.
I'M TOO FAR IN TO GET OUT NOW.
I CAN'T CONTACT MY UNCLE, IN CASE I BOTH TIPPED MY HAND AND ENDANGERED HIM, TOO.
I GRAB MAYBE TWO HOURS' SLEEP A NIGHT, PLAGUED BY FEARS--BOTH REAL AND IMAGINED.
YEAH. IN MY OWN WAY, I'M NO BETTER THAN LANE.
I NEEDED TO SPEAK TO SOMEBODY-- SOMEBODY REAL. SOMEBODY WHO ISN'T--
NATASHA-- YOU MADE A COMMENT BEFORE ABOUT HOW YOU WEREN'T SUPPOSED TO BE ON EARTH. WHAT DID YOU MEAN?
IF I SEE YOU AGAIN, JIMMY--I'LL TELL YOU THEN.
THE FACT THAT YOU DON'T KNOW NOW--MIGHT BE THE ONLY THING THAT KEEPS YOU ALIVE.

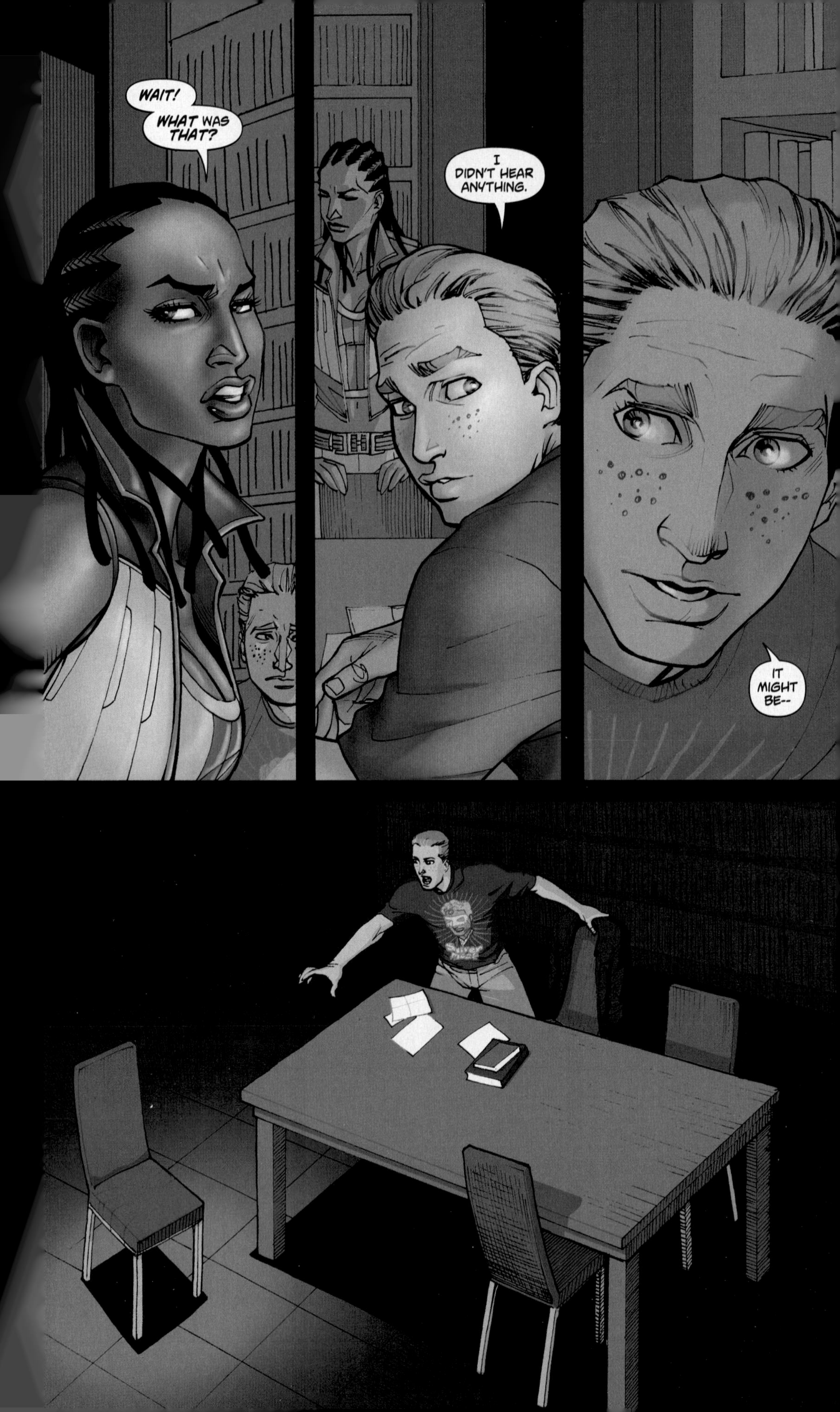
WAIT!
WHAT WAS THAT?
I DIDN'T HEAR ANYTHING.
IT MIGHT BE--

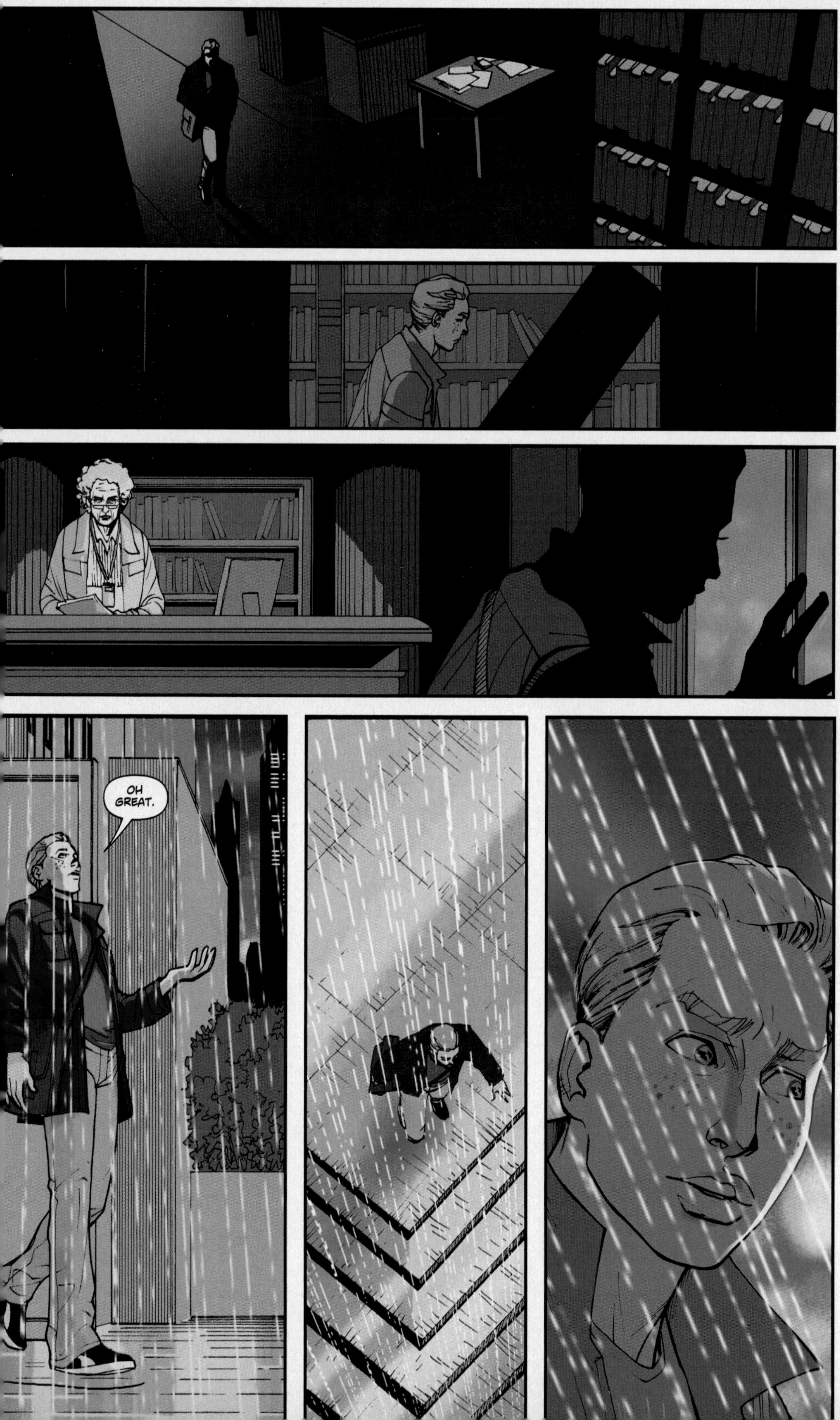
OH GREAT.

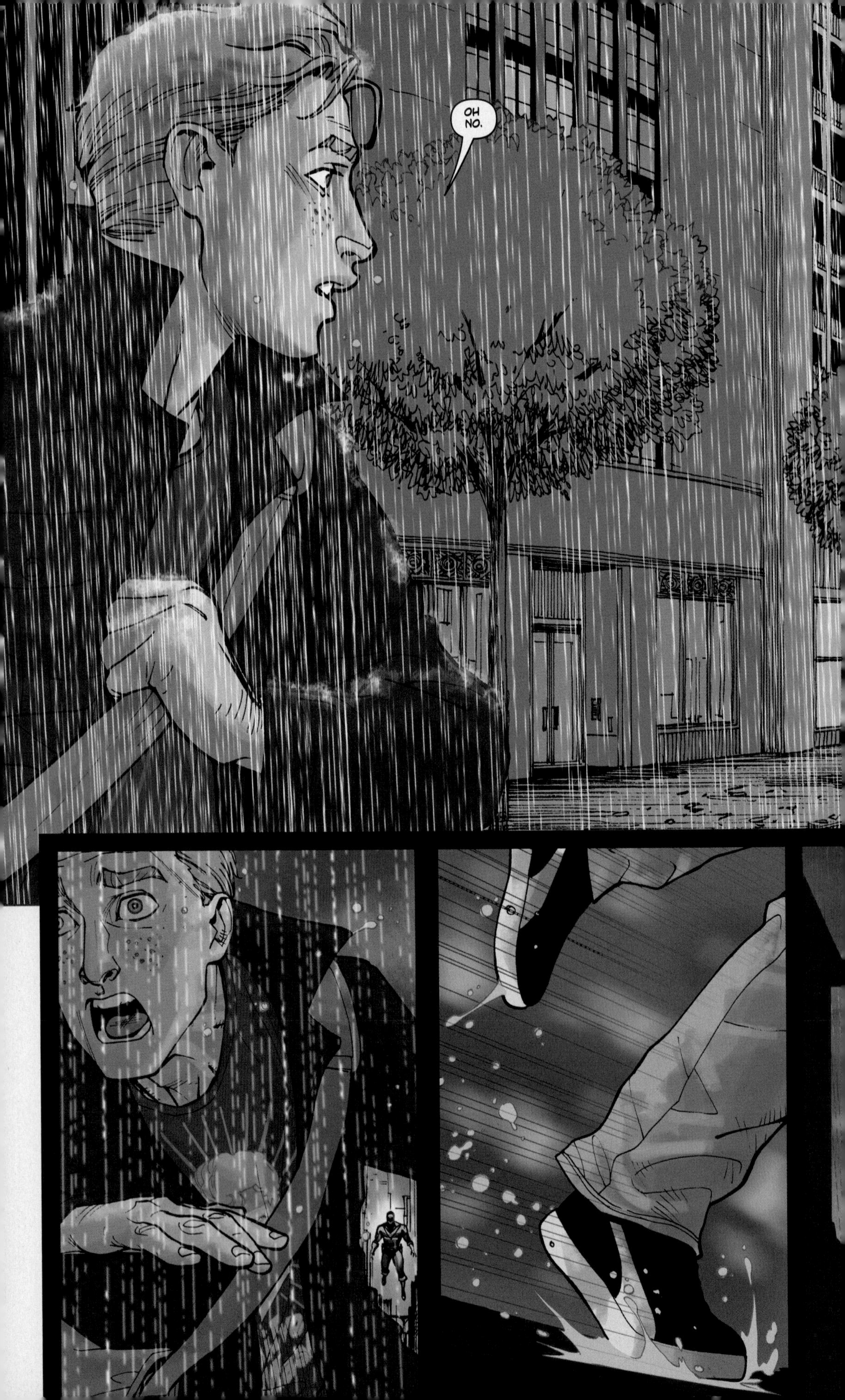
OH NO.

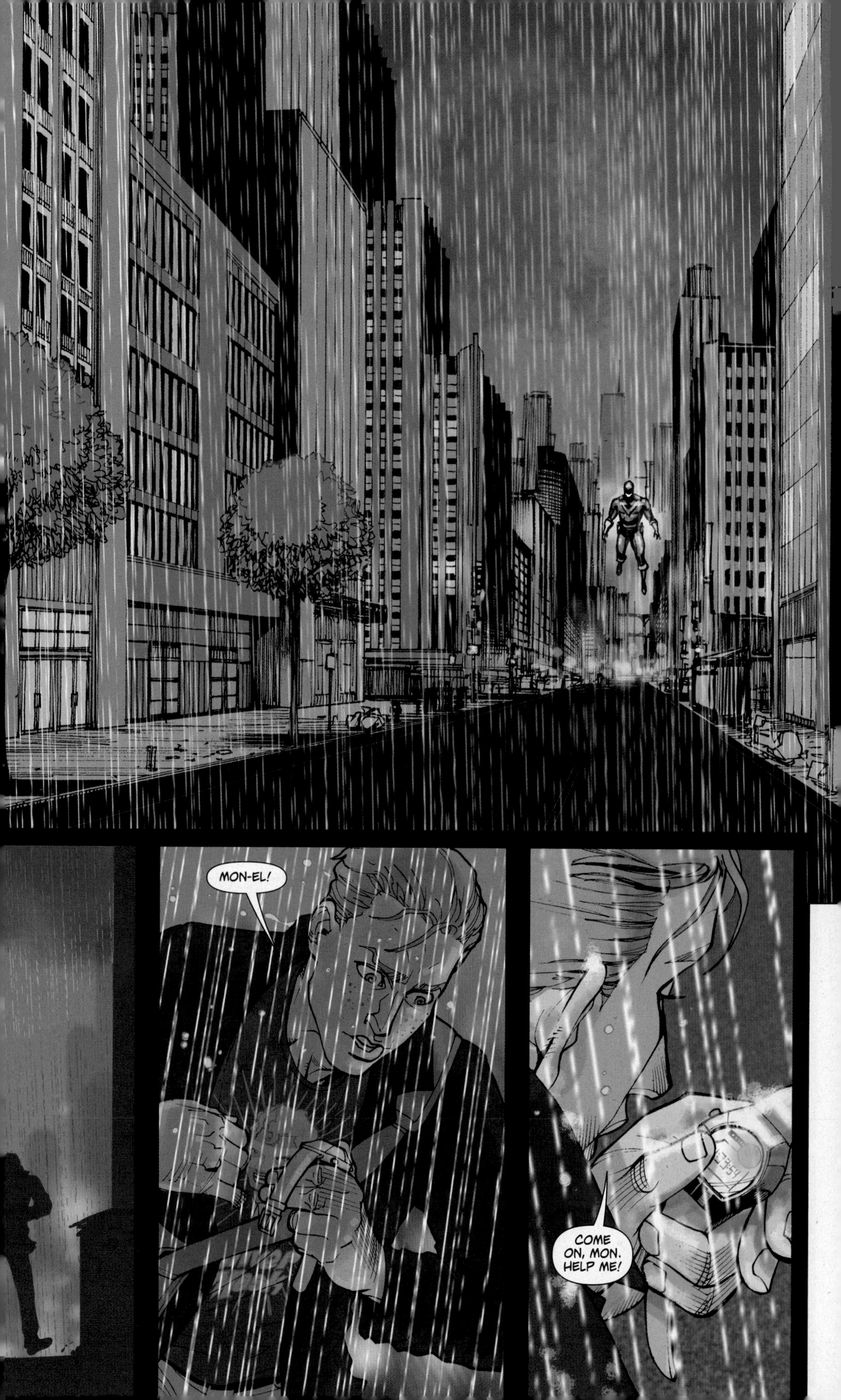
MON-EL!
COME ON, MON. HELP ME!

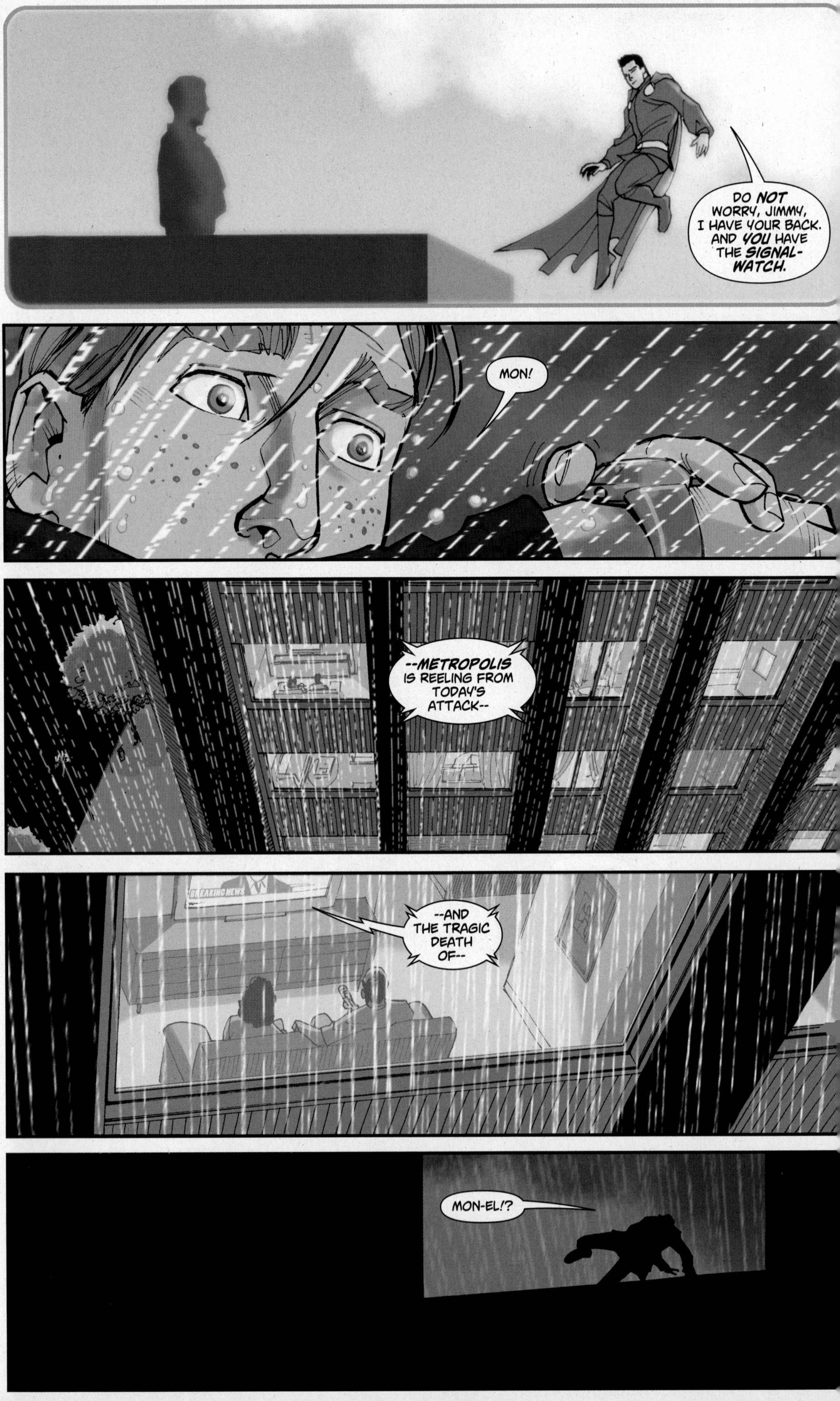

DO NOT WORRY, JIMMY, I HAVE YOUR BACK. AND YOU HAVE THE SIGNAL-WATCH.
MON!
--METROPOLIS IS REELING FROM TODAY'S ATTACK--
BREAKING NEWS
--AND THE TRAGIC DEATH OF--
MON-EL!?

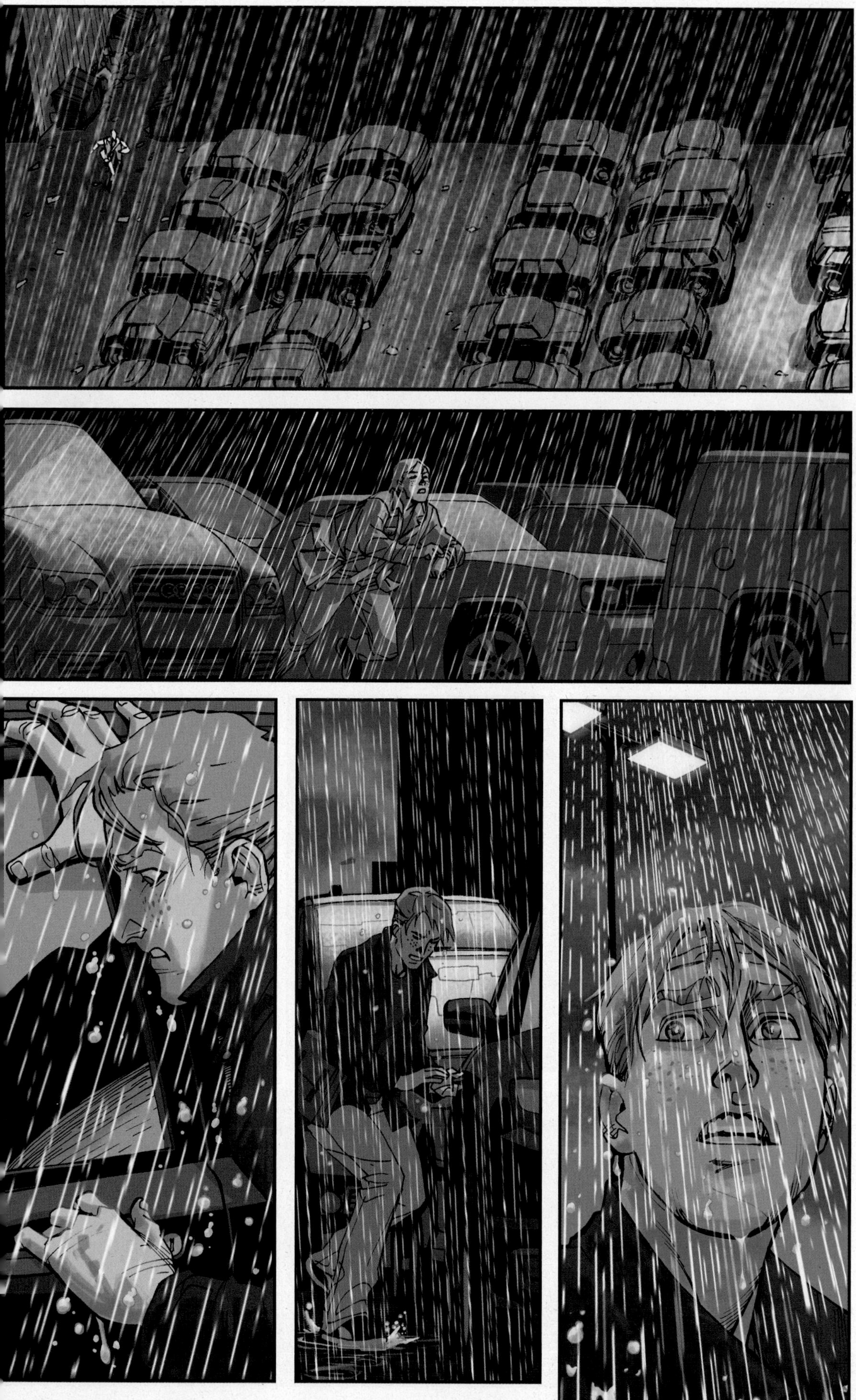

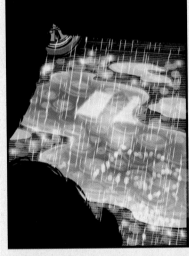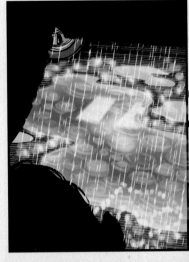

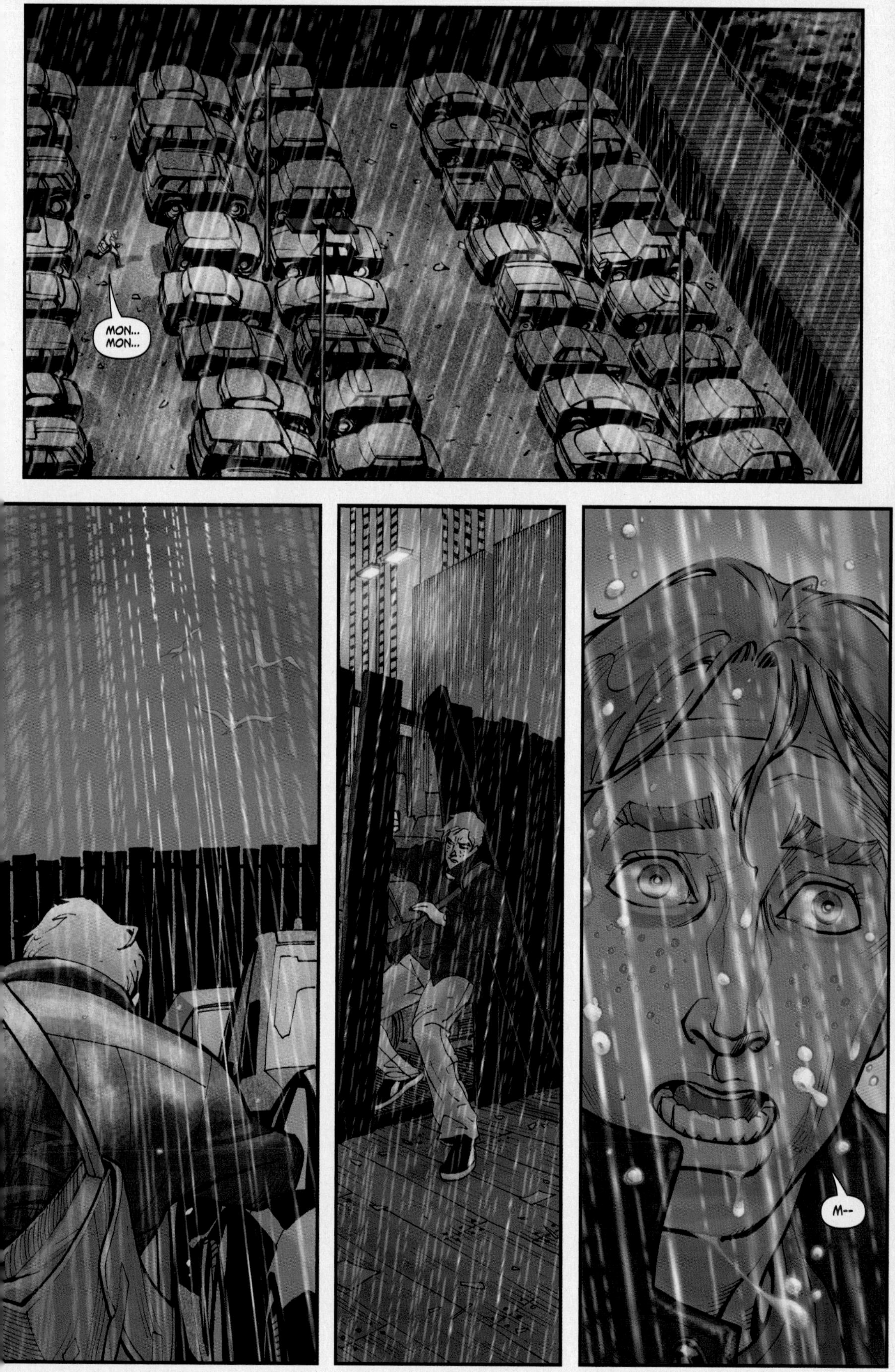
MON...
MON...
M--

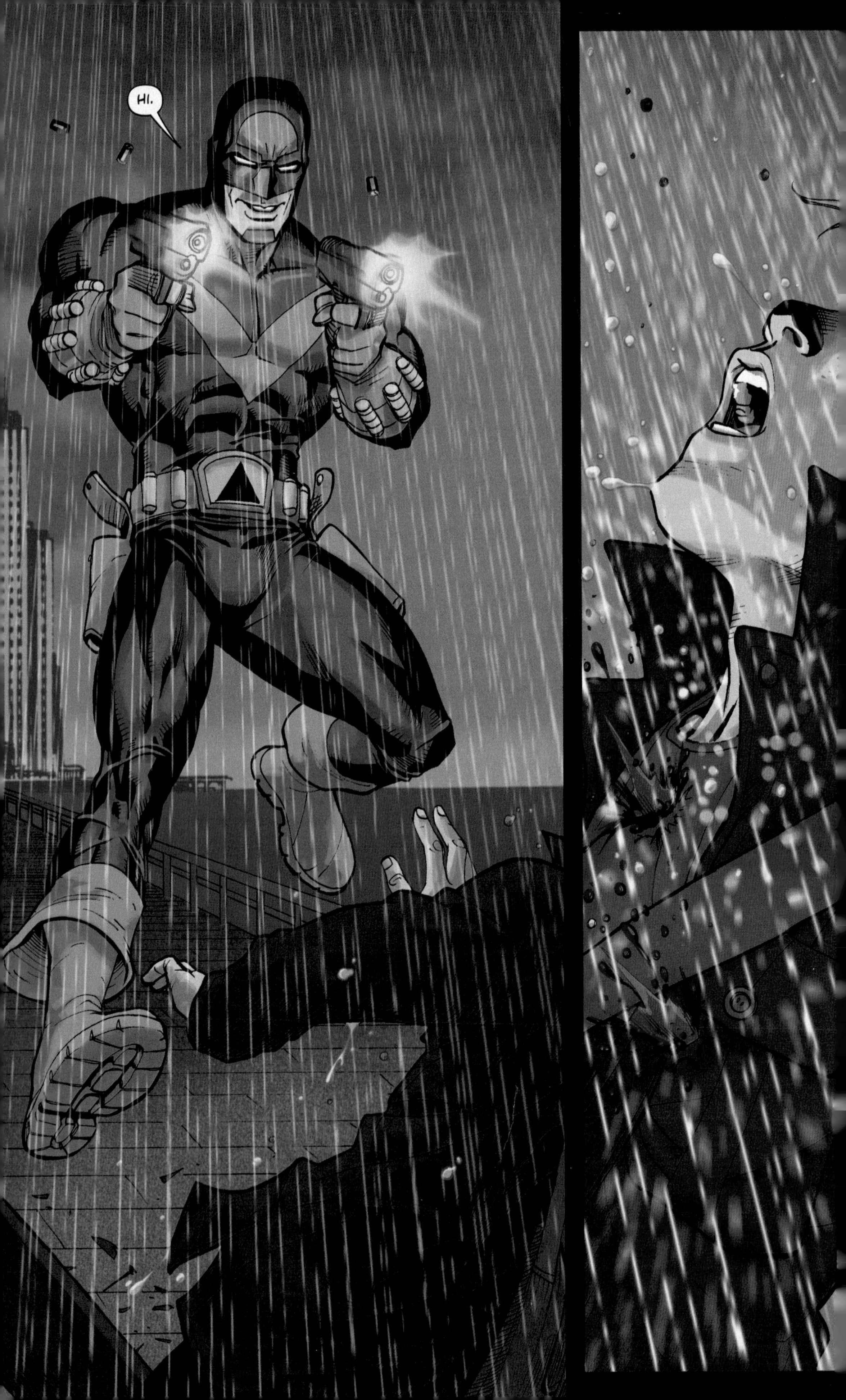
HI.

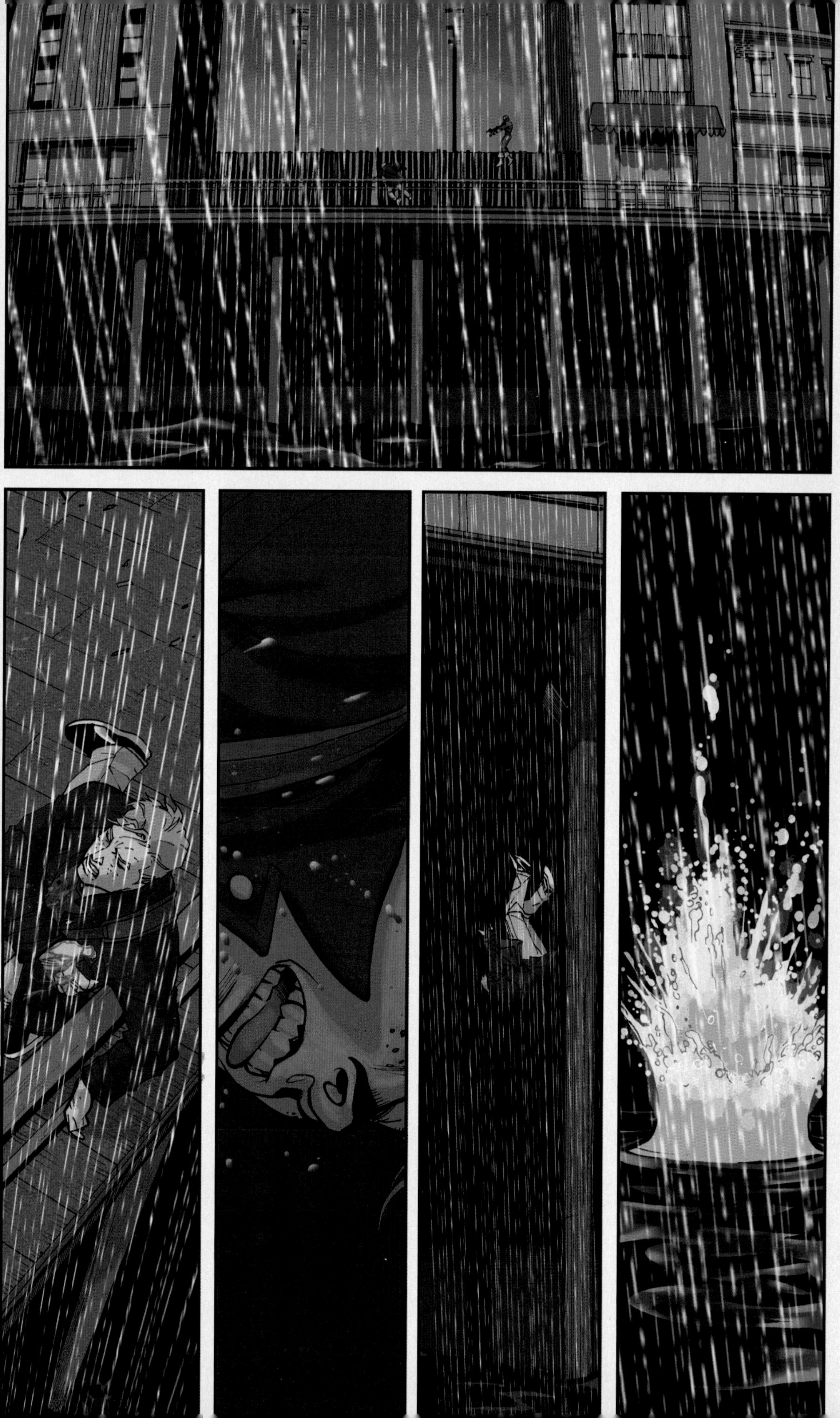

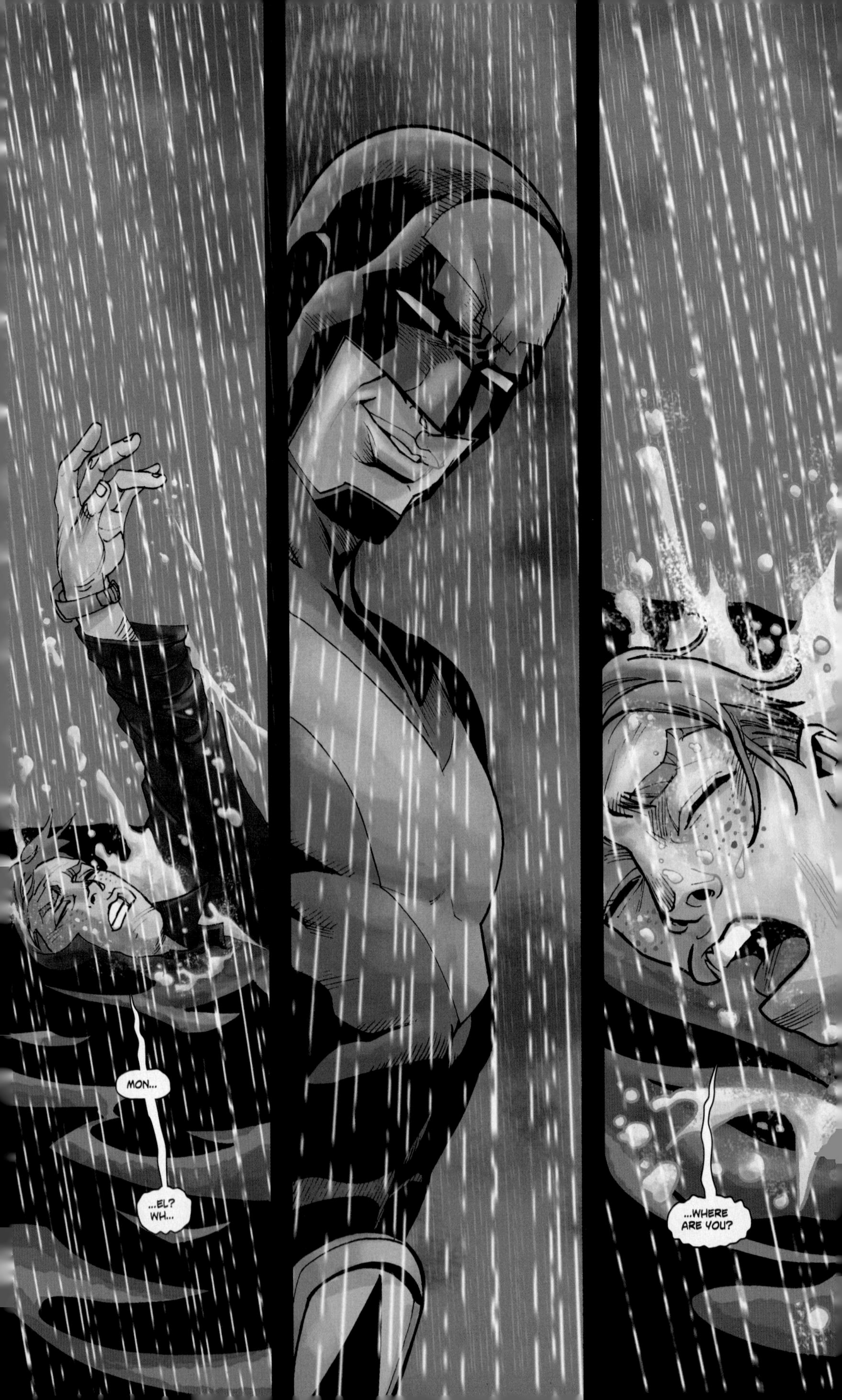

MON...
...EL?
WH...
...WHERE
ARE YOU?

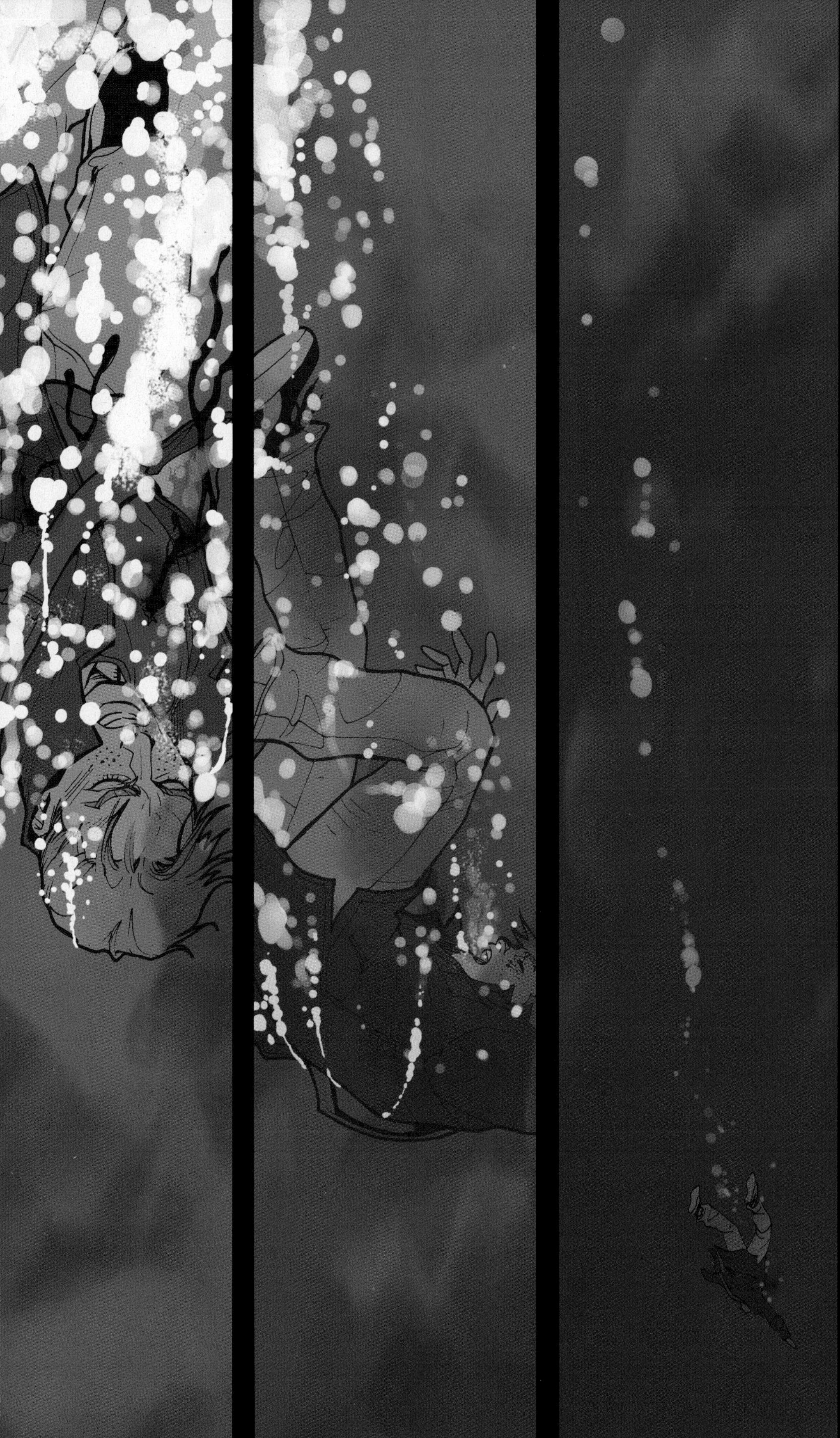

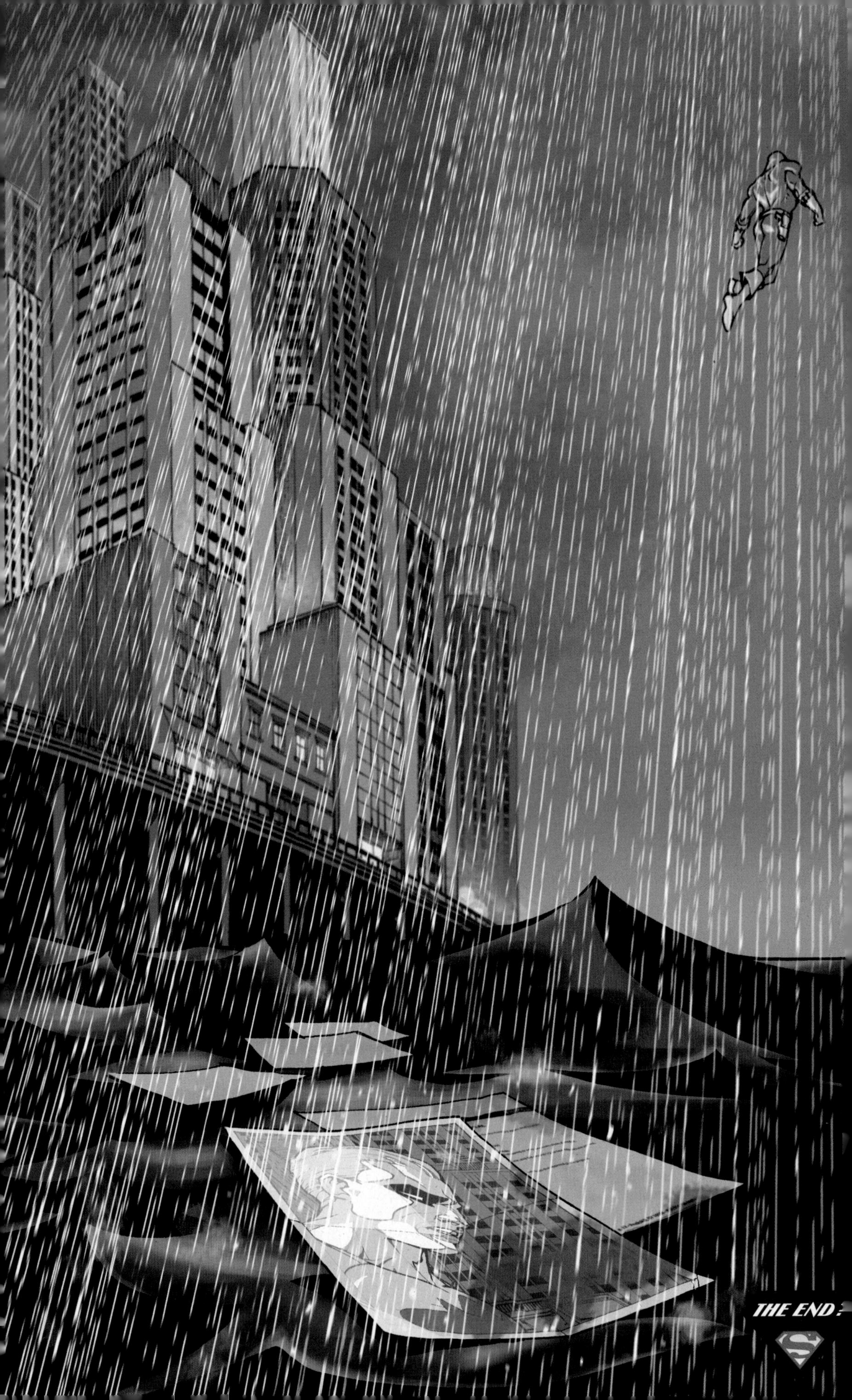
THE END

<SUPERMAN: WORLD OF NEW KRYPTON 6 VARIANT>
BY **EDDY BARROWS** & **RUY JOSÉ** WITH **ROD REIS**

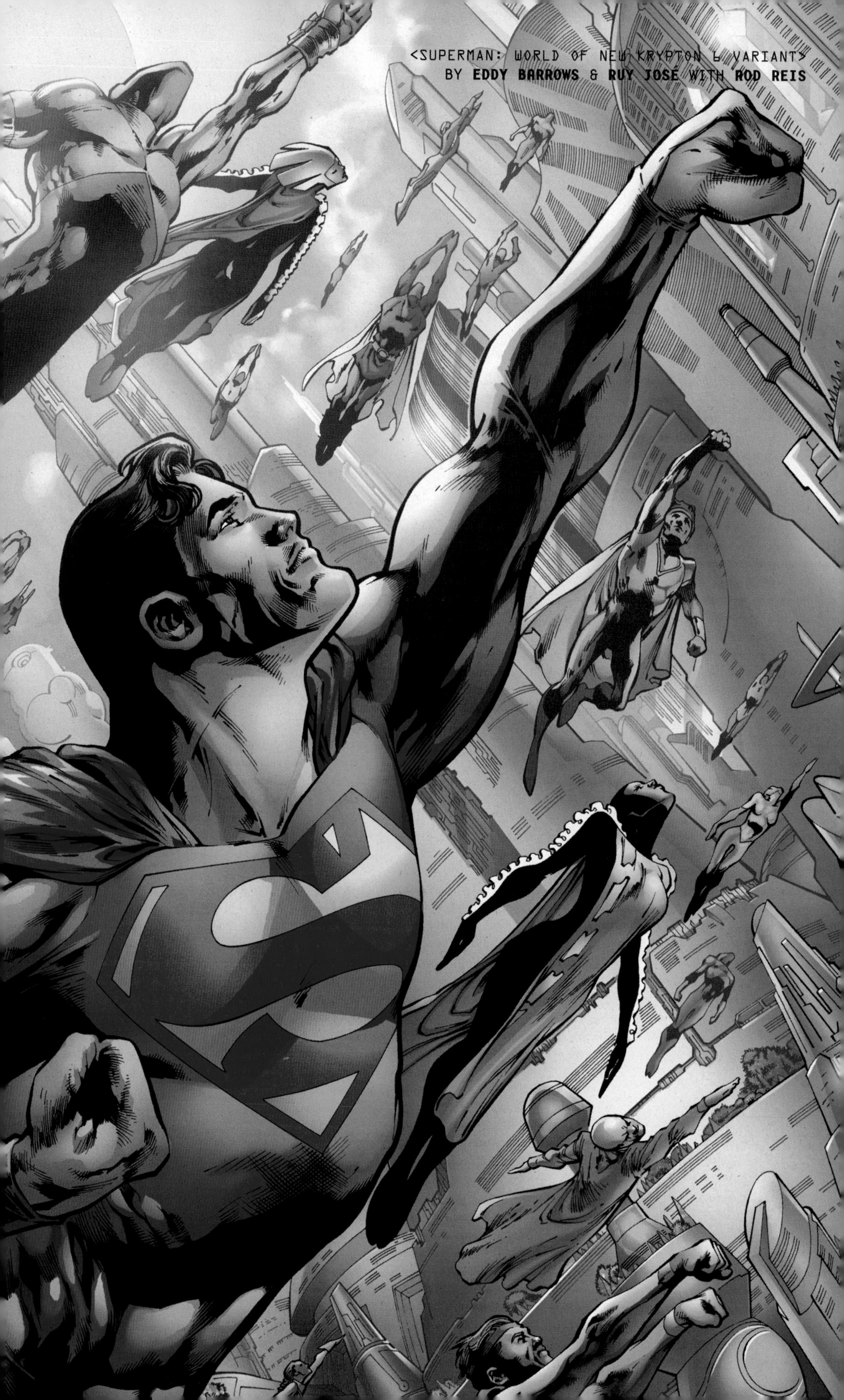

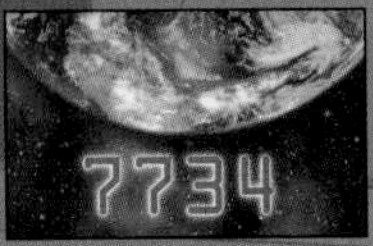
7734

PROJECT 7734

BASE OF OPERATIONS: 7734 Bunker, location unknown

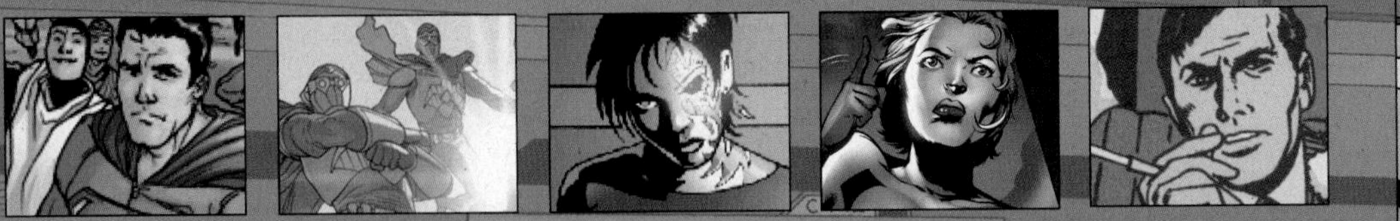

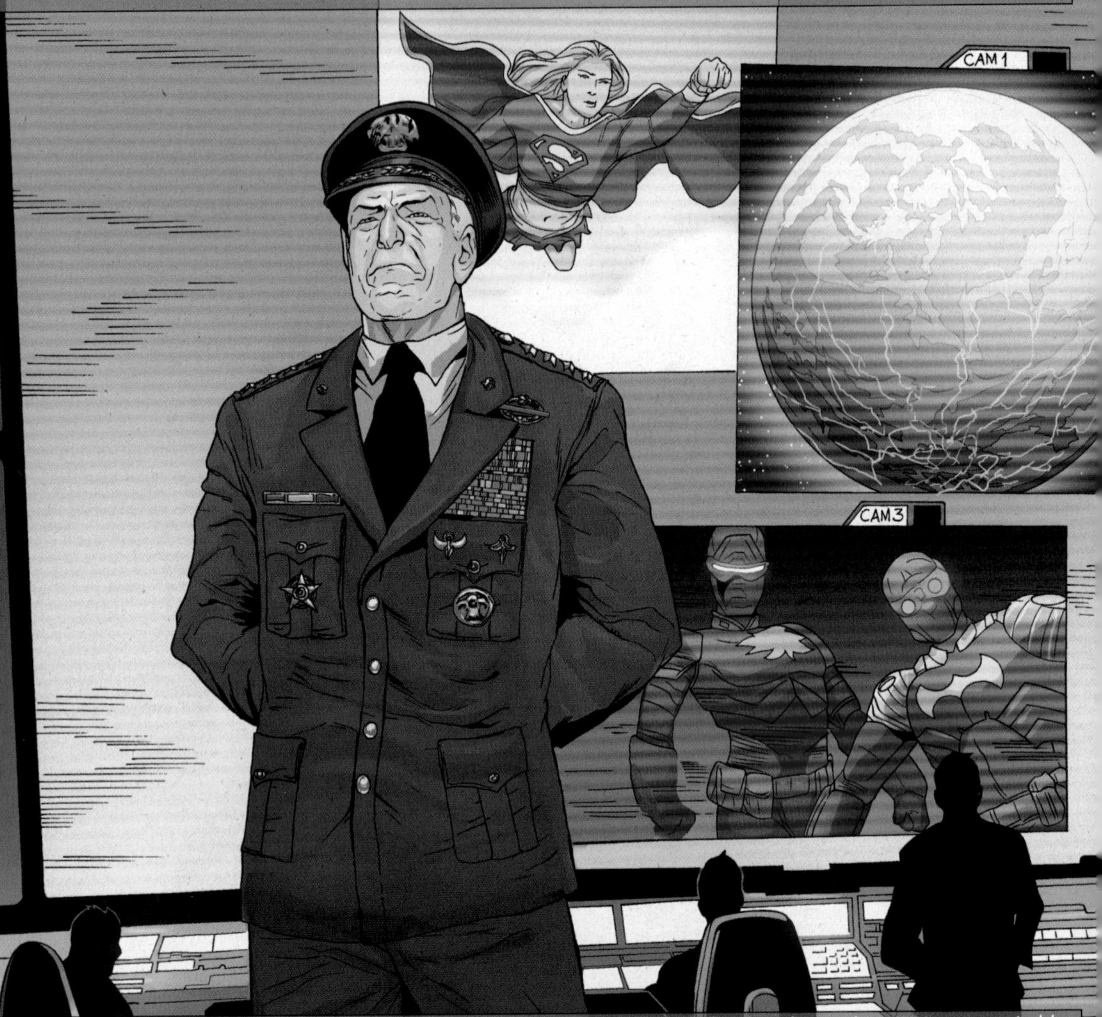
CAM 1
CAM 3

Created under the umbrella of safeguarding the planet against the threat of alien invasion, Project 7734 was created by General Sam Lane. Lane altered its focus to prepare the Earth to battle one thing: Kryptonians. More specifically, the Kryptonian called Superman.

The location of the bunker it operates from is unknown, but its cameras are seemingly everywhere, tracking everyone General Lane wants to keep his eyes on.

GENERAL SAM LANE

BASE OF OPERATIONS: 7734 Headquarters and the world stage.

POWERS/ABILITIES: Lane is a genius-level strategist able to outplan and outthink almost anyone. As a combat-trained soldier, he remains a capable hand-to-hand combatant and a skilled marksman.

HISTORY: Hard-bitten, "take-no-prisoners" U.S. Army General Sam Lane died a hero's death defending Earth from the alien energy being known as Imperiex. His death, however, was faked, allowing Lane the freedom to set up black bag op Project 7734, based on his overriding distrust of aliens and Earth's need to prepare for any and all attacks from them.

Lane's focus, though, was **SUPERMAN**, whom he saw as a ticking bomb for America and the world. His distrust of the Man of Steel has grown to an intense level of hatred. The arrival of the citizens of Kandor on Earth and their relocation to New Krypton on the other side of Earth's sun has done nothing to curb that hatred.

Lane has secured an almost unlimited amount of funding that has allowed 7734 to acquire every form of weapon that it might need to combat the "Kryptonian Menace." These include metahumans, Kryptonite, magic and countless forms of high-tech weaponry. Lane has also managed to get both **SQUAD K** and the Human Defense Corps under his control, as well as ally himself with the mysterious **MIRABAI**.

Lane's strategy for the destruction of Superman and the Kryptonian race has slowly been unfolding. He has masterminded the death of Supergirl's father, Zor-El, as well as the infiltration within Kryptonian society of his daughter **LUCY** posing as Superwoman. And with the cooperation of **MORGAN EDGE**, he is building society's distrust of New Krypton. What his plans are for Mon-El, Nightwing and Flamebird have yet to be revealed, but based on his prior actions, it can be assumed they won't be good.

Text by JAMES ROBINSON, art by RENATO GUEDES & JOSE WILSON MAGALHAES, color by DAVID CURIEL

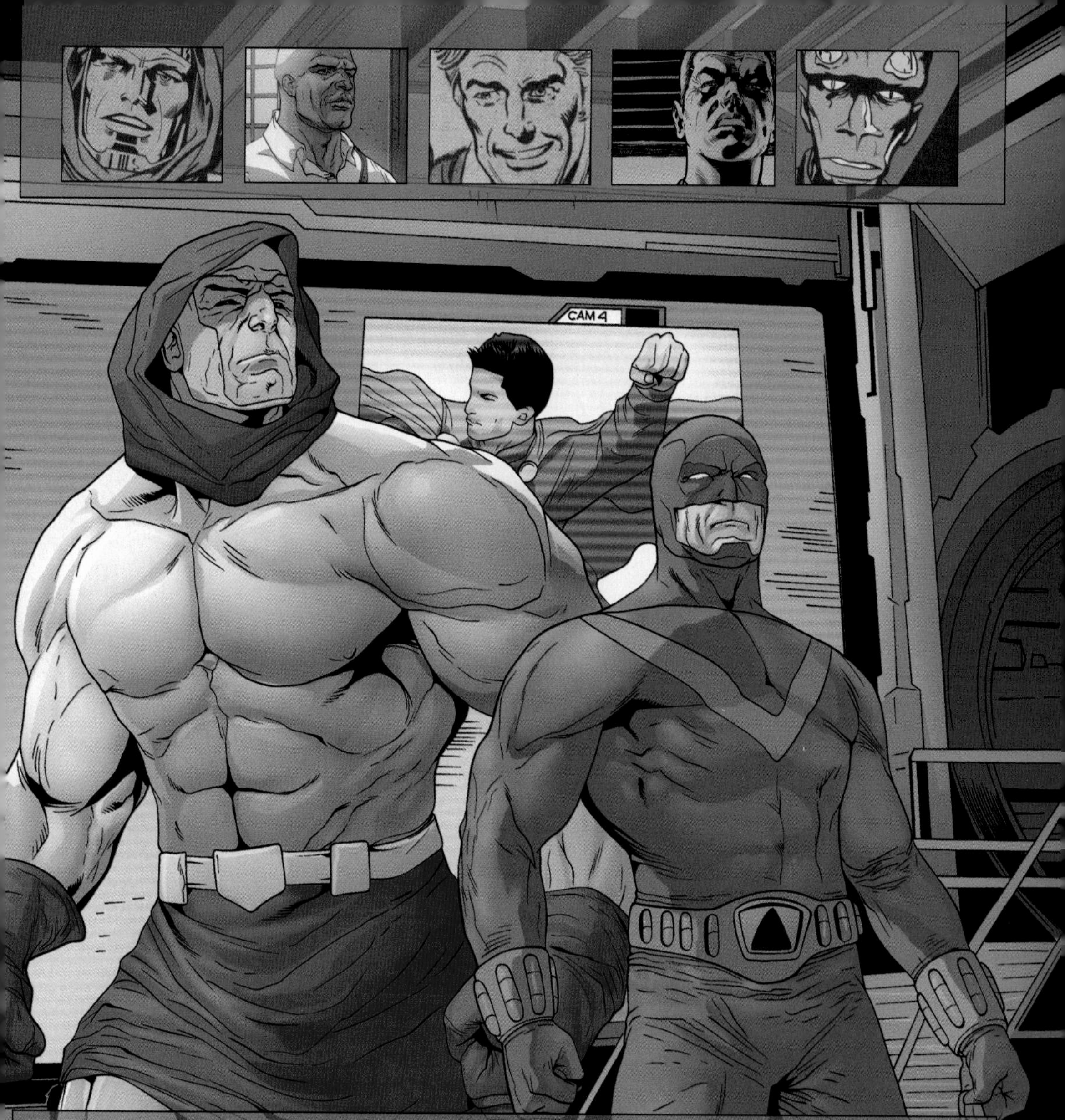
CAM 4

ATLAS
ALTER EGO: Tom Curtis
BASE OF OPERATIONS: 7734 Headquarters and wherever in the world General Lane wants someone hurt.

POWERS/ABILITIES: Atlas has superhuman strength, agility, and invulnerability sufficient to combat Superman.

HISTORY: A champion and **KING** in an ancient mythological era, mighty Atlas was snatched from the past by General Lane using Time Pool technology.

At first openly hostile to Lane, Atlas has made a wary truce with the general. He does Lane's bidding but has an agenda of his own that he has yet to reveal. On orders from Lane, Atlas attacked Superman as cover for 7734 to test its arsenal of magic on the Man of Steel. Superman ultimately defeated him with the help of Krypto. Since then, at the behest of Lane, he won the trust of **JOHN HENRY IRONS** only to betray the hero, for reasons still shrouded in mystery.

CODENAME: ASSASSIN
ALTER EGO: Jonathan Drew
BASE OF OPERATIONS: 7734 Headquarters and wherever in the world General Lane wants someone dead.

POWERS/ABILITIES: Drew has the power of telepathy, which allows him to sense emotions, read minds and project visions into the minds of others. He is telekinetic, allowing him to fly, generate force fields, and lift heavy objects with mental force alone. He is also a skilled marksman and superb hand-to-hand combatant.

HISTORY: Antioke University student **JONATHAN DREW** participated in an extrasensory perception experiment conducted by his professor, **DOCTOR ANDREW STONE**. During the experiment, Drew's mind was linked to a device that accidentally exploded. As a result he developed mental powers, which he used to punish the murderers of his sister.

Drew was recruited by the military for use in covert operations. For a brief time, he was head of security for Project Cadmus but was reassigned after he murdered the original Guardian. At some point he was recruited to General Lane's Project 7734 and now serves as Lane's staunchest ally and supporter. In the course of following Lane's orders, Drew has murdered Stone and the alien **DUBBILEX**, among others. He was unsuccessful in killing Jimmy Olsen but awaits the order from Lane so he can try again.

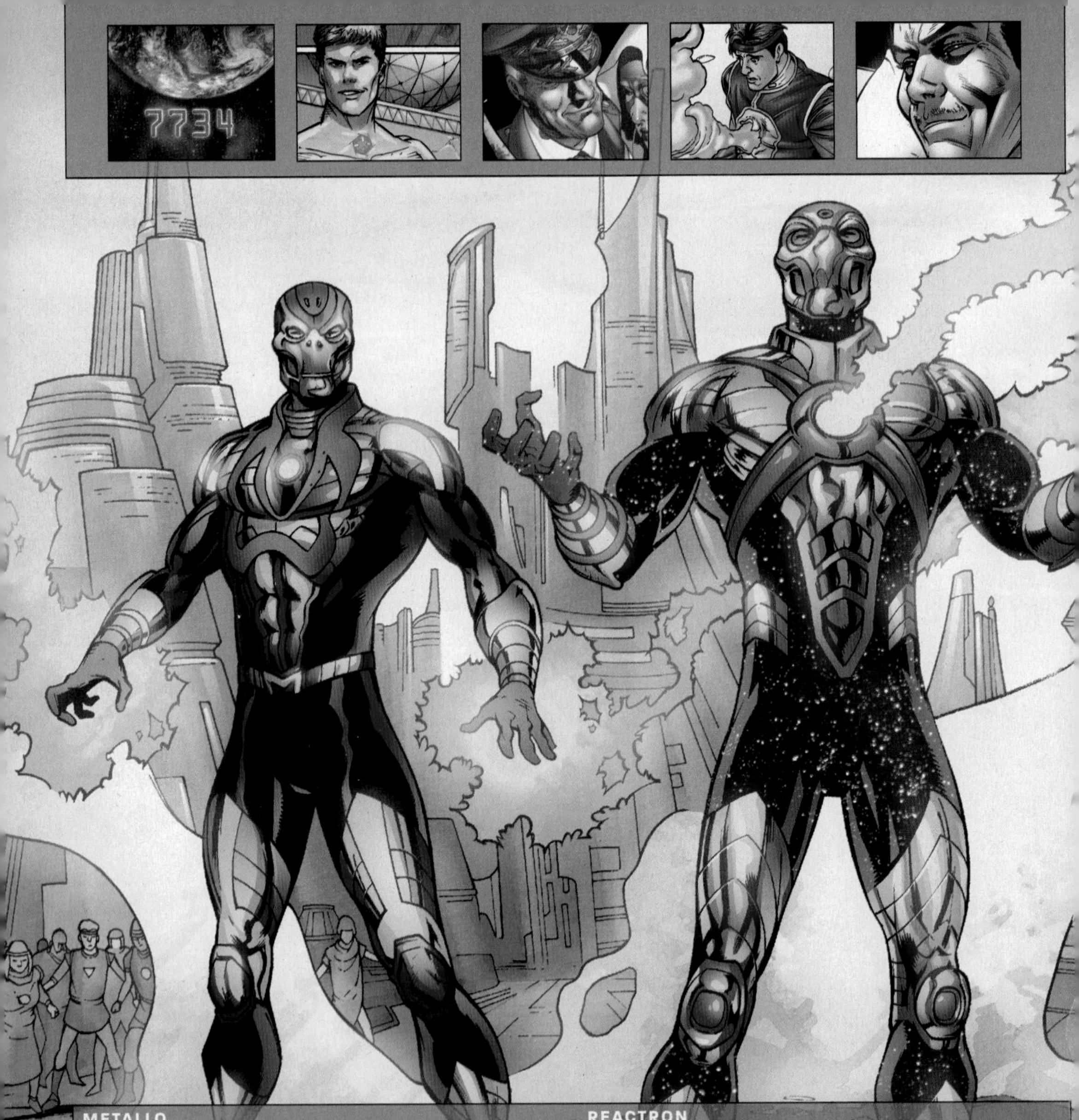
7734

Text by STERLING GATES, art by FERNANDO DAGNINO & RAÚL FERNANDEZ, color by PETE PANTAZIS

METALLO

ALTER EGO: John Corben

BASE OF OPERATIONS: Project 7734 Bunker (location unknown); Metropolis

POWERS/ABILITIES: Metallo possesses a super hard skeleton laced with metallo, the alloy from which he draws his codename. Within his chest is a piece of Green Kryptonite, giving him the ability to harm, and eventually kill, Kryptonians.

HISTORY: JOHN CORBEN was [REDACTED BY THE U.S. ARMY - REDACTED BY THE U.S. ARMY - REDACTED BY THE U.S. ARMY - REDACTED BY THE U.S. ARMY - REDACTED BY THE U.S. ARMY] a test subject for [REDACTED BY THE U.S. ARMY - REDACTED BY THE U.S. ARMY] Kryptonite heart and a metallic alloy lacing his chest cavity. Naming himself Metallo after the type of metal in his body, Corben [REDACTED BY THE U.S. ARMY - REDACTED BY THE U.S. ARMY] and a long history with Lois Lane.

Corben was stunned when the Green Kryptonite in his chest was able to take down the Man of Steel, but was eventually stopped by Superman. The once [REDACTED BY THE U.S. ARMY] was now a full-fledged supervillain.

Recently, Metallo has been recruited into Project: 7734 by **GENERAL LANE**. He and Reactron were part of an elite team that infiltrated Kandor after its enlargement. They murdered several Kryptonians, including the Kryptonian leader **ZOR-EL**, before being evacuated from the city by Superwoman. Now a man wanted by the Kryptonian government, Metallo is smart enough to lie low before showing his face again.

REACTRON

ALTER EGO: Major Benjamin Krull

BASE OF OPERATIONS: Project 7734 Bunker (location unknown); Metropolis

POWERS/ABILITIES: Reactron has a piece of Gold Kryptonite embedded in his chest, giving him the ability to neutralize a Kryptonian's powers for approximately fifteen seconds. He's also able to fire blasts of energy from his hands.

HISTORY: BENJAMIN KRULL was a loser who didn't know what to do with his life until he joined the U.S. Army. One night, while guarding an experimental [REDACTED BY THE U.S. ARMY], Krull was injured. Knowing he was going to die, Dr. [REDACTED BY THE U.S. ARMY], the man in charge of Project [REDACTED BY THE U.S. ARMY], decided Krull needed a new uniform, one that they hoped would prolong his life: the StarSuit.

Soon after his initial defeat at the hands of Supergirl, Krull was approached by General Lane with an offer to join Project 7734. Krull accepted, and he was fitted for a new suit — one with a piece of Gold Kryptonite in the middle.

Reactron was part of an elite team that infiltrated Kandor when it appeared on Earth, and was directly responsible for the death of the Kryptonian leader Zor-El. It is unknown what the ramifications will be once a Kryptonian finally gets hold of him. Fortunately for him, the piece of Gold Kryptonite in his chest will make it a fair fight.